COPYRIGHT

Motivate Your Writing

Using Motivational Psychology to
Energize Your Writing Life

Stephen P. Kelner Jr., PhD

To David C. McClelland, who got me started
and
to Toni L. P. Kelner, who got me to finish
and
to the many writers, artists, and other creatives in my life who
motivated me to update this book

INTRODUCTION TO THE SECOND EDITION

The first edition of this book came out in 2005, after an extended effort that proves the value of sustaining long-term motivation.

The origins of this book came about when helping my wife, Toni L.P. Kelner, AKA Leigh Perry, who is now an award-winning author of numerous novels and stories in a variety of genres, but at first was a struggling writer like any other. I helped her finish her first book (and second, and third, and 17th...), and somewhere around the middle of the third book she turned to me and said "you should tell *other* people about this. It could help a lot of people."

Me being me, I then spent about seven years doing the research for this book: first, by asking for help from the many writers we know, assessing their implicit motive patterns, and interviewing them on their processes; second, by reading every applicable quotation by an author I could get my hands on; third, by going to writers' conferences where I facilitated panels, interviewed writers, and presented content for others to explore; and, finally, writing it all down and showing it around. Most of the writing was done in chunks, which isn't a bad thing for nonfiction books generally, but is especially helpful for someone who had (and has) an extremely engaging career occupying time, and who tends to work in bursts anyway.

When I had a more or less complete manuscript, it then took me another year or two to speak to agents, none of whom took me on at that time, despite definite interest. I eventually sold the manuscript directly to a small publisher; an academic press, which I think found this book aimed at a popular audience a bit bemusing. For example, I had not captured the primary source of every single one of the several hundred quotations scattered throughout the manuscript, much to their dismay. (We reached a compromise.)

In those days, blogs were new, so of course I started one on LiveJournal, which I eventually moved to Facebook, and no doubt will move to the next technology that becomes generally useful and available when necessary. Through interactions on my blog I learned a great deal that I wished I had put into the book, but I at least had it there, and shared my learnings at the conferences and writers' groups at which I appeared.

So why go to the trouble of writing it up now?

In part, because my publisher never got this book into electronic form. In 2005 that was still rare; in 2020 it is necessary.

Mostly, however, because the writing *business* has changed dramatically in the past fifteen years, and the critical mass of change demands an update.

As a scientist and expert in capability assessment, I could not help but notice that the nature of publishing has changed, even if writing as such has not, but it opens the door to a wider range of approaches to writing and publishing.

While this book was and is aimed at anyone who wants to write, the toughest test as I saw it was to enable people to publish at book length, so all the initial group I assessed wrote and published at that length. While I was well aware that short stories are in some ways just as difficult (some people only ever write novels, in fact), I was also aiming to help people sustain themselves over the longest period of time, and that meant looking at book-length works. Anything that works at that length should work at shorter lengths as well. Case in point: I published a short story in 2016 that I began writing in 1999…

But I digress. While I still think it is useful to look at that length as the extreme case, it also narrowed the findings.

At that point, almost any path to publication took significant time on the part of the writer and the publisher. Now, people "publish" in a variety of forms: the classic book with publishers as we have seen for much of the last century, but also online magazines, serials on blogs that interact with the audience, short posts, long articles, online books, interactive novels, print-on-demand, etc. While I think all the content of this book is useful to virtually any writer, I've also been exploring some other channels and how it affects the motivation of writers today.

I've thus taken the opportunity to make some revisions based on my findings, and to add some sections requested by readers that I simply overlooked the first time around, or which were not possible back in those ancient days of 2005.

As a consequence, I've added over ten percent more content of this edition and revised about another 20%. I hope you find it useful.

Any comments can be sent to me via my Facebook page, www.facebook.com/motivateyourwriting.

ACKNOWLEDGMENTS

A gawdawful lot people helped make this book possible. Though thanking everyone is difficult and well-nigh impossible to accomplish properly, I can but try.

First, I must thank my many contributors who gave generously of their time, their thoughts, and their motives to this project: Sarah Smith (with a special thank you for past criticism rendered), Susan Oleksiw (a big editorial thank you), Marilyn Campbell, Carol Soret Cope, Phil Craig, Tony Fennelly, James Neal Harvey, Alexander Jablakow, Ellen Kushner, Margaret Press, Delia Sherman, David Alexander Smith, Patricia Sprinkle, Elizabeth Daniels Squire, Les Standiford, Kelly Tate...Go on out there and buy their books. You'll find them (and a few of their myriad titles) described throughout this book. Indirectly, I thank Writer's Digest for their numerous articles quoting writers and how they do things, and Jon Winokur for his excellent little tome Writers on Writing.

Next, I must thank Professor David C. McClelland, my late mentor, who introduced me to the wonders of motivational psychology and guided me to a Ph.D while never for a moment defining my direction for me. I took on a monstrous dissertation, and he let me, and I am the better for it. I refer to Nietzsche here...and also directed me toward my first career as well as encouraging me in my second and third.

My friends have offered support, readings, and occasional smart remarks: special thanks to Mike Luce, Dan Schaeffer, Libby Shaw.

No acknowledgment would be complete without mentioning my family, who supported me directly and indirectly: my siblings Bill, D'Arcy, Kathe, and Tamsin, my father who taught me to enjoy craftsmanship, and my mother who taught me to read before I was two and who instilled in me a genuine love of the printed and written word. I have never suffered from "the watcher" to any significant degree, and I have her to thank for that.

Last and always, I must thank my wife Toni L. P. Kelner: my best friend, favorite companion, lover, writer, critic, wit and raconteur. She was the one who told me I had to write this book. Fair's fair. I helped her write hers.

Addendum for the second edition:

I must also thank my enormously creative children, Maggie and Valerie, who caused me to think about the needs of other creatives, such as visual artists and musicians. I've benefited from watching their growth as artists and people above and beyond the obvious pleasures of being a parent to such delightful human beings.

INTRODUCTION: MOTIVATION AND WRITING--SO WHAT?

"I can't understand why a person will take a year to write a novel when he can easily buy one for a few dollars."

—Fred Allen

"I am convinced that all writers are optimists whether they concede the point or not... How otherwise could any human being sit down to a pile of blank sheets and decide to write, say two hundred thousand words on a given theme?"

—Thomas Costain

"I write because I like to write."

—Paddy Chayefsky

How often have you thought you could write a book, if you could only make yourself do it? There are many stories to tell in this world, and with enough work you can tell them.

And yet, you may have a fine prose style, command of the language, and interesting stories but simply cannot begin writing. Or worse, if you do get started, you cannot finish. How do the professionals manage the mysterious writing process?

"A writer writes," said Harlan Ellison, who should know: he won awards for speculative fiction, fantasy, mysteries, essays, and screenplays. He held that there is no "secret" to writing, no mystery. He wrote stories sitting in storefronts to demystify and demythologize the process of writing. He wrote daily in various genres, and won many awards for it. He is also far from the first person to make that statement; Epictetus said, "If you wish to be a writer, write" around the year 110.

Isaac Asimov said he never set time aside to write without interruption, because he never had a choice; when he began to write seriously, he was working in his family's candy store. His family needed him to work, so he worked and wrote wherever he was. He wrote in crowded rooms and at the counter of the store, simply ignoring distractions. He had no privacy, so he wrote without privacy, and despite constant interruption. Almost five hundred books later, he showed no sign of stopping: "The one absolute requirement for me to write...is to be awake." He wrote the last installment of his autobiography in longhand on his deathbed.

So what of the rest of us, those who would like to write just one book, or story, or whatever? Those guys who can write in a store window or with constant interruption—these people have got to be obsessive, right? They're the kind of people who wouldn't stop if they could. They are different, right? Abnormally gifted?

Yes and no, in that order. They are obsessed in a sense, but they do not differ dramatically from anyone else. At least, not where the ability to keep writing is concerned. Apart from practice, training, and checks from editors, the only difference between these people and you: they feel *motivated to write*. Interruptions don't stop them, because their drive to write charges them up to retain their single focus, and they do not get distracted from the work at hand.

Being motivated means that on a deep emotional level, you want something, enjoy doing it, and get frustrated if kept away from it. When you want to do something that strongly, you do it! What's more, you find time to do it.

If you have enough interest in writing to read this, I would guess you have at least as much interest in reading. (If not, go right out and get a good book. There's lots of them out there.) If you have a real page-turner in your hand, how do you react when you have to stop reading? Violently? Do you think of the book all day, return to it anywhere you can, and stay up late to finish it? That is a simple case of motivation in action: the emotional drive to continue. You can apply it to writing as well as to reading, and indeed to anything in life.

You can find a lot of material on motivation these days, from "subliminal tapes" to webinars to full-blown courses to sober tomes, most of it put together by earnest people who think they have the **ONE SURE WAY TO SUCCESS**.[1] This is not such a book. I will state with great sureness (though less earnestness, I hope) that there are *many* ways to success in writing. This book will help define your personal pattern of motives, show you how your writing relates to it, identify potential obstacles and sources of assistance, and, finally, enable you to adjust your writing to fit that pattern. In other words, to identify what turns you on, and explore how to use it. That allows your natural motivation to support your writing. The source of this knowledge is not my personal experience or a pet theory, but the field of motivational psychology. This particular brand of psychology dates back to the 1930s, so it isn't a new idea. Research has continued steadily since that time, so we now have quite a body of knowledge.

I'm also tapping research done over the decades on creativity, the writing process, goal setting, obstacles, and other issues that can help or hinder your ability to write.

This scientific research on motivation has been applied to management, salesmanship, entrepreneurship, teaching, leadership, and other jobs quite successfully. This book discusses the scientific research from the writer's perspective, and offers some practical suggestions for determining how you can apply these decades of research to write your book (or short story, or essay, or whatever).

And just in case the idea of psycho-babble gives you the pip, let me reassure you. The research is no good if you can't understand it, so we'll take a look at some real people facing the problems of professional writing. I'll describe how real life writers write based on actual examples, and I'll also use an awful lot of quotations. Some have written or spoken about their craft in the past; some were interviewed and studied directly by me. They're good writers, and I'll rely on them to make some of my points for me.

But before we get going, I have three caveats:

Caveat # 1: There is no easy approach (but you can do it).

Some people start with advantages; writing comes easier for some than others. No matter what your natural gifts are, you must expend effort—perhaps an extensive effort. While I firmly believe that virtually anyone can write at some length if they really want to and that most people can even enjoy writing, the effort required may be more than you want to spend. This is not a "you can become a writer overnight" book. I don't believe you can become a writer overnight. On the other hand, don't expect boot camp or sweating blood in this book, either. (Though Red Smith said: "There's nothing to writing. All you do is sit down at a typewriter and open a vein.") Finally, don't expect to read a chapter of this book and write 20,000 words (60 printed pages) a day. Though if you do, please let me know so I can quote you on the cover of the third edition.

Caveat #2: Motivated writing does not equal good or salable writing.

Having motivation will enable you to write, but not necessarily to write competently. I make no judgments nor guarantees regarding your writing ability. I can only offer this: the more you practice, the better you will get—eventually.

Fantasist Ray Bradbury thought you should write a million words, and then throw them out, because the first million are for practice. You might want to consider that a worst-case scenario. Please note that Bradbury also <u>sold</u> a good deal of his first million words. He wasn't being a snob; he based his statement on his own first million words, most of which he thought were pretty bad. He isn't alone in this thinking. He also knew that good writing and salable writing do not always overlap. There are good books that do not sell, and books that sell but are not good. The intent here is to get you to a point where you can get better and get sold, neither of which are possible if you don't write at all!

As bestseller Richard Bach put it: "A professional writer is an amateur who didn't quit." Lots of people write books on how to write well; I won't bother to share my opinions on the subject. Ask the experts. This book is about writing —motivating yourself to write, and finding ways to keep yourself writing.

You may also feel that writing the book is more important than selling it. There are online groups that share their fan writing with each other, either because they can't sell work set in someone else's universe (though Star Trek has spawned quite the collection of "professional fan fiction," and most published authors start by imitating another writer), or it is work that appeals only to a very small audience. One writer I spoke with wrote very explicit fanfiction, with a very specific focus, which she shared with the seven people in her circle of online friends who had the same tastes. But she was happy with that. If that's what you want, more power to you.

Caveat #3: You must find your best way to write.

In the course of researching scores, possibly hundreds of professional writers, I never found two who wrote exactly the same way. Different people write at different times, in different spaces, on different themes, with different tools. That's fine. We're going to focus on helping you identify what works for you. That means what other people do need not be right for you, no matter what they say.

As far as I am concerned, Rudyard Kipling nailed this one long ago, in his poem "In the Neolithic Age:"

> *"There are nine and sixty ways of constructing*
> *tribal lays,*
> *And every single one of them is right!"*

So let's get on with finding yours!

SECTION I: MOTIVATION-- WHY PEOPLE DO WHAT THEY DO

"'If you knew you would be poor as a church mouse all your life—if you knew you'd never have a line published—would you still go on writing —*would* you?' 'Of course I would,' said Emily disdainfully. 'Why, I *have* to write—I can't help it by times—I've just <u>got</u> to.'"

—Lucy Maud Montgomery

"Any writer is inevitably going to work with his own anxieties and desires. If the book is any good, it has got to have in it the fire of a personal unconscious mind."

—Iris Murdoch

CHAPTER 1: WHAT IS MOTIVATION

We are going to use a particular definition of "motivation" in this book, and it differs from the one in the dictionary. When we talk about "motives" here, we describe a very specific concept, developed through psychological research on tens of thousands of healthy, productive people. As a working definition, try this on for size:

> A motive is a recurrent concern for a general goal of which one may not be consciously aware; this concern drives, directs, orients, and energizes behavior, and can be seen in fantasy.

> —McClelland, 1984

Let's turn this into more common English. A motive sits in the back of your head (metaphorically, not literally —let's not get into psychobiology here) and influences you. It isn't as specific as "I want to make money" or "motive to get published." It is something more general, such as "enjoyment in doing better" or "emotion around being liked."

People show an infinite range of behavior, so it may sound ludicrous when I say that only three motives can explain about eighty to eighty-five percent of human behavior overall. Nevertheless, it is true that for most people, a few basic drives explain most of their thinking and actions. That doesn't mean that people are simple, or psychology would be a lot easier to study. What it means is that a few general drives influence a wide range of possible behaviors. Furthermore, your actual behaviors and actions are not just based on these unconscious motives. They come out of what you value, what you have been taught, what you can do well, many other characteristics of you as a person, and what is going on outside you.

For example, you may have a strong need to impress people. (This is known as the *influence motive*, and will be discussed in more detail later.) Some can satisfy this need by public speaking—as a politician, or as an actor. But if you stutter, you are unlikely to want the opportunity to stutter in front of an audience. In fact, you may be highly motivated <u>not</u> to do so, since you might have a negative impact on an audience if you tripped over a word. Making a bad impression arouses strong emotion in you—fear, anger, whatever. This emotion pushes you away from public speaking. Instead, you may take up writing, hoping to impress people with your written words.

On the other hand, you may decide that you will not let stuttering get in the way of impressing an audience, because you value public speaking ability. Then your emotions (strongly wanting to be able to influence others through speaking) push you towards working to overcome this obstacle. Actor Samuel L. Jackson did exactly this. He still stutters on occasion. He says, "I have my days. I have *G* days, I have *P* days, I have *B* days, I have *S* days, and I'm still stuttering." But as someone who loved acting (influencing) from an early age, and also because he was bullied, he found ways to master it – sometimes by switching the word, sometimes by using his favorite obscenity, which he says mysteriously breaks the pattern – and one reason he did it was for "revenge." That's an impact!

Influence motive drives the key actions in both of these cases, but in different directions. That's why we say that motives predict behaviors—and not the other way around. Many behaviors can flow from the same motives.

In fact, motives may not predict consistent behaviors in the same person, let alone across people. Researchers have found that motives predict *patterns* of behavior, not specific decisions. That is why we talk about the general "concern for impact," which can be fulfilled by public speaking *and/or* wearing dramatic colors *and/or* coaching people *and/or* driving flashy cars *and/or* creative writing, etc. All these things involve having an impact on people, in different ways. The exact behaviors you prefer come out of the unique person you are. So don't worry that psychologists can read your mind. They can't even read their own.

"...a recurrent concern..."

A motive is a *recurrent* concern because it does not go away. When your mind drifts, you are likely to fall into a pattern that is consistent with your motives. In other words, you think about what you like thinking about. (Think about it.) This does not apply at every moment of every day, but frequently enough to be an ongoing trend for you. When you make a choice from equally important options, you are more likely to pick one you enjoy – that is, that aligns with your motives. When you enter a new situation, you are likely to see it in terms of your motives: where can I find enjoyment? Or what looks exciting here? In other words, when all else is equal, you go with your gut: what feels right.

If I examined all your decisions over a year, I would probably find them tilting toward your strongest motive, because you would tend to go with that when you have a chance. For example, imagine yourself at the office, where most people have a range of tasks they like and dislike. You can spend time crunching numbers, or you can go around and talk to people. You may wind up doing both every day, but which one do you do first? Which one do you stretch out, and which one do you postpone? The pattern of these things over time is a good indicator of your motives.

"...not be consciously aware..."

Because the motives are deeply buried, you may not consciously know yours; you just know that some things feel more enjoyable than others. Motives are essentially emotional in nature, and (we psychologists think) come from older parts of the brain than your frontal lobes.[1] You probably would not put together the pattern of your motives from many individual enjoyable actions without concentrated and lengthy thought and self-analysis.

No, I'm not recommending years of expensive therapy. (Unless you feel you need it, of course.) For our purposes, it is possible to identify at least some of your own motives, especially your strongest, with a little hard work and objectivity, using a few tried-and-true techniques. These techniques derive from another part of the definition above: motives can be seen in fantasy. But, you may ask, why should we care? Because motives influence your behavior.

"...drives, directs, orients, and energizes behavior..."

People do what they want to do. That is the reason to look at motives. A motive is where you find excitement, energy, and enjoyment. Therefore a motive will tend to *drive* behavior, to get to your motivated goal. It tends to *direct* your choices; if all else is equal, you do what you like. It *orients* a person toward possibilities; that is, you are more alert to signals that relate to something you like. Finally, it *energizes* you to go after something that emotionally satisfies you.

Motivated behavior is energized behavior: the kind of thing you leap toward rather than shy away from. Sustainable behavior, the kind of thing you want to do over and over again for years to come, comes primarily from the motives. Pushing your motive button activates a source of renewable energy you can tap again and again.

"...can be seen in fantasy."

Motivated subjects are enjoyable to think about, so people's thoughts tend to drift that way. Daydreams, cherished dreams, and passing whims are likely to come out of your motives. The method used most to tease out motives relies on this fact. You can try it out for yourself using materials included later.

Since the actions that satisfy motives feel so enjoyable, they feel rewarding in and of themselves. Why do people work for hours, days, or weeks building a backyard deck or acting in local theater, or fishing, or painting, or writing? Not because someone pays them (well, not *just* because somebody pays them, in some cases) but because they enjoy it. If you enjoy it, you are more likely to do it.

That is the key to this book. First, to understand your

own pattern of motives and what they mean; then to find ways to make the process of writing rewarding to you based on that information; then finally to set up your environment and yourself to enable writing that feels rewarding. Other people suggest building regular habits, to try to train yourself into writing. That practice can help, but I suggest you focus on building enjoyment directly into the process of writing. Again, if the process becomes inherently rewarding, you will be more likely to do it. Indeed, you may make time to do it. Writers have sometimes referred to their vocation as an addiction—for good reason. Tennessee Williams said, "When I stop [working], the rest of the day is posthumous. I'm only really alive when I'm working." If writing is that rewarding all by itself, with no external reinforcement, what can stop you?

One more story of a highly motivated writer: Jane Austen, renowned for her lengthy and subtle novels of manners, was an extremely busy member of a Victorian household. She was never alone, and virtually never without work to do—even assuming that people at the times encouraged women to write professionally, which they certainly did not. She set a blank book on a sideboard, and every time she walked by, she wrote a few words. A phrase, perhaps a sentence, and no more. Every one of her books was written that way, a few words at a time.

> **Remember:** If you are like most people, you <u>don't</u> have to be that motivated to write. Furthermore, you can motivate yourself despite obstacles.

One caution, however; I am not talking about magically inserting motivation that does not exist, I am talking about tapping that which you already have—and you certainly do have motives. It's part of the human animal.

The issue is not to insert, but to arouse, motivation. Everyone already has motivation, to different degrees, and in different forms. That's my objection to "motivational speakers," or, for that matter, managers who think they can put motivation into people. That's not the way it works. Using what already exists does work.

A word on this subject from writer, performer, and always comedian George Carlin: "What's all this stuff about motivation? I say, if you need motivation, you probably need more than motivation. You probably need chemical intervention or brain surgery. Actually, if you ask me, this country could do with a little *less* motivation. The people who are causing all the trouble seem highly motivated to me."

Just assume that you have the motivation—all you need is to aim it properly.

Extrinsic Motivation

"Sir, no man but a blockhead ever wrote except for money."

—Samuel Johnson

"There <u>are</u> no retired writers. There are writers who have stopped selling ... but they have not stopped writing."

—William A. P. White ("Anthony Boucher")

Motivation can be divided into two basic types: *intrinsic* motivation, the kind mostly discussed in this book, which includes both values and motives, and *extrinsic* motivation, the kind mostly discussed in this section. Extrinsic motivation comes from outside you; the most obvious kind is money. "Once I get paid for it," thinks the hopeful writer, "I will write all day long."

In fact, extrinsic motivation does not enable sustained effort. With rare exceptions, outside motivators end—and when they do, the motivation disappears too. The prop is gone. You can ruin perfectly good motivation that way. So take this as a warning now: you *cannot* depend solely upon external rewards to motivate your writing. (Of course, new writers often don't have a choice in the matter!)

In one experiment comparing these two kinds of motivation, psychological researchers Edward Deci and Richard Ryan took people and asked them to work out puzzles, but did not mention monetary rewards. They found that if you rewarded people monetarily afterwards for something they thought they were doing only for fun (i.e., out of intrinsic, unconscious motives), they would lose interest in the task or even reject the money! The characteristics of the task had changed. As gonzo journalist Hunter S. Thompson once said, "I've always considered writing the most hateful kind of work. Old whores don't do much giggling." His next sentence is telling: "Nothing is fun when you *have to do it*—over & over, again & again—or else you'll be evicted, and that gets old." (Emphasis his.) However, he made this statement in the middle of an essay describing a writing project he *did* enjoy (which became *Fear and Loathing in Las Vegas*), which he wrote on the side while covering a "very heavy" journalistic assignment that could have gotten him killed. The daily work was difficult, but the optional work was fun. But note that both were forms of writing! One he hated, and procrastinated on; the other he loved, and he would work on it spontaneously at night, despite heavy demands in his daily life.

> **Remember**: Don't rely on motivation outside yourself. You cannot depend solely on external rewards to motivate your writing.

Don't get me wrong. I do not recommend that you reject monetary recompense—quite the contrary! How else can you keep time available for writing instead of "honest work?" Instead, I recommend that you master the art of engaging your intrinsic motivation, and try to keep that as your reason for writing, especially if you do not intend to live from the earnings of your publications right away. Money is the icing on the cake, not the cake itself. Therefore, I disagree with the learned Dr. Johnson. Speculative fiction writer Robert Heinlein (the target of William White's comment above) believed *consciously* that he wrote only to make a living, and when he made enough to get by he would stop. He found that he was wrong.

When you have the intrinsic motive well established, as did Anthony Boucher and Robert Heinlein, you will write. Selling what you write is a different issue.

As author William Wharton put it: "Don't write with sales or money in mind—it poisons the well at its source. If writing isn't a joy, don't do it. Life is short, death is long." Motivation from within goes with you wherever you go, while motivation from outside goes away from you. Of course, some people do write for survival, but not all writers, and it is not common enough for you to rely on being able to do it yourself. Science fiction writer Theodore Sturgeon had a desperate need to support himself and his family, but it did not break his writer's block. He had every extrinsic reason to keep writing, but could not do so. It is even possible that his strong extrinsic motive was stifling his intrinsic desire to write, and we'll discuss this later when we discuss writer's block.

Even for those who say they write only as a job, why then did they select writing for that job? On some level, I am willing to bet that most of them like it, or at least feel addicted to it. It doesn't pay enough to be worth forcing yourself. Stephen King has said that he would write even if they didn't pay him for it—which is not to say he doesn't expect pay for his books now, just that he loves writing too much to stop just because they aren't paying him for it. In fact, when he announced his retirement from publishing (not writing), he said in a number of interviews that he fully intended to keep writing, because what else would he do between nine in the morning and four in the afternoon? (And of course, he didn't stop publishing or writing.)

I'm going to be brutally honest here. As of this writing, the average advance for a first novel is $5,000 to $10,000.

It does not matter whether you took a year to write your novel, or a month, or ten years; you are lucky to get more than that. That amount has not changed significantly in thirty years, as far as I can tell, and some evidence suggests it has actually declined, and of course inflation means writers can no longer live on advances. Worse yet, the "midlist" of writers who can make a small or marginal – but reliable – living from writing have largely disappeared, at least in the US. Only the rich and the poor remain. The former get the lion's share of promotion, support, advertisement, and movie deals; the latter get to pay their own way to conferences, call bookstores themselves, and hope that someone, anyone, comes to their signings. Stephen King can make millions, but take a look at how many books languish on bookstore shelves.

A typical successful novelist (and you better believe King is not typical) has written numerous novels, each of which stays in print for a limited time, but which all contribute royalties for a while, and may come back into print.

E-books or print-on-demand books can stay in print forever, and this has allowed writers to make books available independently of mainstream publishers, but while they theoretically provide a higher profit margin per book, most of them have to be sold at a lower price point to get anyone to buy them at all.

In fact, few have a large enough audience, even with a lot of books in print or available online, to sustain a career on writing income alone. Most people who make a regular living from writing do not write fiction; they are journalists who write for newspapers or magazines, technical writers who receive a salary for creating reference materials, nonfiction writers who write texts, or very active self-marketers who sell stories to any market they can find, taking a single article and tinkering with it to sell the same basic content to several markets, each time with a unique twist. This is not living in luxury. The brutal truth is that you cannot rely on extrinsic reinforcement because most writers simply don't get enough of it.

The Motives

"I write in order to attain that feeling of tension relieved and function achieved which a cow enjoys on giving milk."

—H. L. Mencken

As I noted above, three basic social motives influence a large part of the behaviors we show. As with motivation itself, don't take the names too literally. Decades of psychological research and documentation have made their names official, but not necessarily the same as your own (or Mr. Webster's) definition. All are referred to as "needs," or, to avoid sounding needy, we call them "motives." Everyone has all three, but typically not all to the same degree. For educational purposes I might refer to those who are relatively strong in one or another as if it is the only motive they have, but all I'm doing is simplifying to make it clear. In other words, there are no "Achievement people" or "Influence people," there are only people with one motive relatively strong compared with their other motives.

The first (alphabetically) is the *need for Achievement* or *Achievement Motive*. People with a relatively strong or dominant Achievement motive get excitement and satisfaction out of doing better. This motive includes the desires for efficiency, improvement, improving oneself, meeting and bettering goals, and innovation, though a given person might not manifest all of the above. It sounds well suited for a writer sitting alone tapping keys, trying to meet internally set standards, but we shall see.

The second is the *need for Affiliation* or *Affiliation Motive*.

This is a concern for relationships: people with a relatively strong presence of this motive either strongly desire to be personally liked, or have concern for people in general, both positively (liking to do things for people) and negatively (cynically assuming that relationships never work out). This includes enjoyment of social situations for their own sake, wanting to belong to a group, action to improve or establish a relationship, and anxiety about the disruption of a relationship. This suits writing certain kinds of stories and perhaps to the other, nonwriting tasks a writer must sometimes undertake (such as cocktail parties and dealing with fans).

The third is the *need for Influence* or *Influence Motive*[2]. This motive is sometimes seen (especially by English-speaking people) as negative or sinister somehow, but in fact it is just a concern for influencing and having an impact on others. People with this motive particularly strong get excitement out of seeing others respond or change based on their impact or influence, whether individuals reacting or influencing larger groups or the world at large. The Influence motive can help a writer to understand how to write to an audience. Do not assume that those high in this motive are out to conquer the world—only to impress it, influence it, or make a mark on it. It has nothing to do with morality, but a lot to do with writing for others.

In fact, it's worth noting that *none* of the motives relate to morality as such; that comes from your conscious, explicit motives, which we'll discuss later. These are deep emotional drives, which can energize positive or negative behaviors depending on the person and the situation.

These three motives define different patterns of life: meeting internal standards on your own, socializing with people in a friendly manner, and leaving a mark on people or the world at large. You may have any or all of these motives to high degree, but because they don't correlate with each other and therefore can appear in any combination, most people have one that is dominant enough that your *first* or *most common* thought is likely to match it. On average, people have one relatively strong, one in the middle, and one on the low end, though a given individual can have any combination. If you understand your motives, you can play to them, so to speak.

Motives act both as a self-replenishing energy source and as an enhancement for your perceptions. As Mencken noted above, a motive can drive you both to relieve built-up emotional tension, or to attract you to meeting goals ("function achieved," as he put it). Possessing a given motive to significant degree will sensitize you to particular kinds of information, which in turn arouse energy: You look for what you like, and when you find it you get psyched. Past studies have shown that people high in Affiliation motive, for example, are better at interpreting facial expressions than others, and as a result are more alert to people's feelings about them. If you show people with high Affiliation motive photographs of pairs of people, some of whom are romantically involved and some of whom are not, they will tend to correctly identify those in a relationship.

Those high in the need for Influence are adept at identifying (and often using) hierarchies, power structures, and influence opportunities, even those that are not explicit. If you show people with high Influence motive photographs of pairs of people, some of which are boss and employee and some of which are just random pairs, the high-Influence people will be able to identify the boss-employee pairs fairly accurately.

The strongly Achievement-motivated person looks to maximize efficiency or productivity by balancing moderate risk against moderate benefit. They are adept at assessing risks, and find it natural to adjust their aim accordingly. They also try to improve their performance over time, and tend to be constantly dissatisfied with it.

CHAPTER 2: IDENTIFYING YOUR OWN MOTIVES

"The character of a man is known from his conversations."

—Meander

"It is with trifles and when he is off guard that a man best reveals his character."

—Arthur Schopenhauer

In this chapter I introduce the themes in motivated thought. In other words, what do people strong in a given motive tend to think about? You can use these themes to think about what you think about, including why you do what you do. In the appendices you will find more formal exercises to identify motives which also rely on these themes, but if you are able to see these patterns of thoughts in many situations—your daydreams, writing, preferences—you will go a long way towards awareness of your motive pattern. These sets of "imagery," as they are called, describe the exact thoughts found in people relatively strong in a given motive. The next few chapters will look at how individual motives can manifest in a given writer. Then we will spend some time delving into yours!

Motive Imagery

To use this, you need practice in the technique of content analysis, also known as thematic analysis. One of the advantages of being adept at this technique is that it applies to many part of a writer's life, or indeed anyone's life. It is possible to code for motives in movies, books, speeches, even casual conversation. With somewhat more advanced knowledge you can even measure doodles.

The specific thoughts attached to the three main motives are listed below.

The Need for Achievement

The criteria for scoring the need for achievement are to look for a concern for excellence or doing better. This can emerge in any of several ways:

- Outperforming someone else who represents a standard of excellence
- Meeting or surpassing a self-imposed standard of excellence
- Accomplishing something new, unique, or innovative
- Long-term career planning

The Need for Affiliation

The basic criteria for the need for Affiliation have to do with a *concern around relationships*. How that concern manifests, however, varies in three ways:

- Positive. Includes taking actions on another's behalf with no thought of recompense other than improving the relationship, feeling part of a greater whole (He was proud to be an American), and enjoying relationships
- Cynical. Includes stories about hypocrisy (presenting yourself as better than you are), deception in a supposedly affiliative relationship (he was cheating on his wife)
- Anxious. Includes discussions of an interpersonal relationship, flow experience, negative reaction to separation.

The Need for Influence

The criteria for scoring the need for Influence are to look for a *concern for impact or influence on others*. There are, again, several ways in which this can emerge:

- Taking strong, powerful actions

- Unsolicited help, advice, or support
- Attempts at controlling another through regulation of behavior or conditions of life, or

through seeking information that would affect others

- Attempts at influencing, persuading, or making a point with others for the purpose of convincing others to comply rather than to compromise
- Attempts at impressing another or the world at large

• A person doing something that arouses strong positive or negative emotions in others

• Concern with reputation or position, or with what others think of one's influence

Practice Scoring for Motive Imagery

Below are three stories, each of which can be scored for one motive. See if you can decide which is scored for which. Answers are on the next page.

1. The two young lovers sighed as they talked and walked together. They really enjoyed each others' company, and hated the idea of parting this evening and going to their separate homes.
2. The two young lawyers laughed as they contemplated the surprise they were going to spring on the opposition the next day. They had a plan to get to the jury in a way that would knock him right off his feet.
3. The two young inventors grinned as they studied the plans. This might actually work! They had a shot at creating the first device of

its kind, something that no one else had been able to do.

Answers:

1. Affiliation: the "lovers," "enjoying each others' company," "hated the idea of parting."
2. Influence: "the surprise they were going to spring," "the opposition," "get to the jury," "knock him right off his feet."
3. Achievement: "inventors," "creating," "the first device of its kind," "something that no one else had been able to do."

In the next section are depictions of writers with a single primary motive. You may see yourself in these depictions; you may have seen yourself already. You may also be inaccurate. Remember that these motives are unconscious, whereas your professed self-image is largely consciously created and strongly affected by the expectations of the world around you. Elsewhere in this book, you will find a method by which you can determine your own motives with a fair degree of accuracy. It will not be quite as precise as using formal motive assessment methods, but you can "reality check" your motives based on your actions and likes as well.

As you read the next chapter, try to assess how much each type resembles you. Do not be alarmed if more than one seems to fit; you may just be high on more than one motive. Combinations of motives will be discussed later, and after that, what my research has found to be the typical motive profile of writers who have published long-form works (e.g., novels, books), as well how this may vary for other writers. It helps to know what is available before focusing on one.

Please note again: Motives are *not* conscious. If you want to assess yourself accurately—a challenging job indeed without assistance—you have to distinguish between what you think is important and what you enjoy regardless of need. When you find yourself doing something you know you don't need to do and you don't know why, you may well be following a motive. (And yes, before you ask, Murray identified the need for sex as one of his list of motives. Don't look for it here.)

One caveat: I assembled the descriptions below from knowledge of how people of a given motive *might* write, remembering that you can try different approaches. It might help you think about your own motives. While I will show the patterns I found in a number of published writers, read this section first, so you will feel comfortable with how a motive looks when expressed in a given set of behaviors. Ultimately, the plan is to use your motives, whatever they happen to be.

Here's what you can expect to see in the following sections on the three most important motives:

1. A detailed description of the motive in question
2. The characteristics of effective feedback for someone with that motive
3. Concrete suggestions to help those with this motive write more
4. Dealing with writer's block from the perspective of that motive

Note:

Frequently below I will refer to the word "feedback."

Once limited to engineering and electronics, this word has entered the common domain as a description of performance information returned (fed back) to a person. Motives being energizing cycles, as it were, you can think of feedback as adding energy to the loop. To engage your motives, one way is to feed the motive's specific desires —frequently.

CHAPTER 3: THE ACHIEVEMENT-MOTIVATED WRITER

"As a rule reading fiction is as hard to me as trying to hit a target by hurling feathers at it. I need resistance to cerebrate!"

—William James

"If I could I would always work in silence and obscurity, and let my efforts be known by their results."

—Emily Brontë

"The writer must always find expression for something which has never yet been expressed, must master a new set of phenomena which has never yet been mastered."

—Edmund Wilson

The Achievement-motivated work alone happily. They reach for standards that may be known only to them, which must be met and exceeded. They enjoy coming up with new ways to do things, and may spend some time considering the most efficient process to get the job done.

These people also need frequent feedback, to keep track of their progress toward their goal. Unfortunately, the nature of the writing business means that outside feedback is often not forthcoming. Even very successful writers may not be able to thrive on feedback that arrives weeks or months after the story was written. An occasional check is not sufficient as feedback for daily writing.

What is appropriate feedback? That varies from person to person, but in general this kind of person will want frequent responses, closely linked to the process that is being assessed. The person with a high need for Achievement wants to reach a goal, but also wants to know how well he or she is doing on the way. Feedback—preferably positive and negative in balance—provides a way to measure the progress toward a goal. If the feedback becomes more negativistic, then you must work a little harder; if the feedback leans toward the positive, then there is satisfaction from knowing that you are beating your goal.

However, unrelentingly positive feedback arouses distrust in the Achievement-oriented, or deprives them of the sense of challenge. They are not engaged by easy tasks. Likewise, if the feedback is unrelentingly negative, the challenge may appear too great, discouraging the effort. The Achievement-motivated person thrives on the balance point: the moderate risk, the good chance of payoff that nonetheless takes some work.

William James' quote above refers to that sense of challenge—"resistance" in his word—needed to "cerebrate." It is interesting to note, in the light of James' quotation, that the Achievement-motivated person frequently reads nonfiction, such as how-to books, or mysteries rather than other forms of fiction. That challenge must come one way or another—and the degree of challenge is not stable, either. Robert A. Heinlein wrote that he had to produce more and more words to get "that warm feeling" that writing provided him—eventually as high as 250,000 words, which is nearly four short novels' worth. As he mastered longer and longer novels, he had to work harder to make the writing process difficult enough to be interesting to him.

Some Achievement-motivated people reading this may have helpful spouses or friends around to give frequent, useful and detailed feedback on the content or progress of their writing. Others have readers (the commoner sort in my experience) who have a vocabulary composed entirely of "good," "I dunno," and "I don't understand it."

For our purposes, I assume that you belong to those surrounded by the latter group, and therefore need some helpful feedback, and that you are not yet at the point in your writing career where an editor or agent can help you instead. If you are high in the need for Achievement, you will need some kind of feedback on your performance or progress that will encourage you from day to day. When I say "performance," I don't mean quality, necessarily, but perhaps just quantity—are you performing? I'm not assuming you are bad! But you <u>do</u> need performance-related feedback, whether it is around the amount you have produced, the pages you have edited, or the research you have done.

So your challenge is to provide that for yourself.

Characteristics of Achievement Feedback

There are several important characteristics that define useful feedback for the Achievement-motivated person. Not just any feedback will do. Your feedback mechanism must be:

1. Specific and consistent
2. Measurable
3. Applicable

Specific

Useful feedback must be quite specific in nature. A general note is not really feedback: "I worked on writing today." How? Did you jot notes? Write an outline? Write prose? Unwind on the typewriter for a while? Make journal notes? Edit? Some activities are more useful than others as a measure of accomplishment. For solid feedback, you need to specify at least one type of measurement.

Don't limit yourself to only one if more than one are helpful to you, but don't try to keep track of everything, either. That can get in your way if you spend more time accounting than writing. I would recommend that you select a consistent measure, and if you find you have easy breakpoints in your writing process (e.g., notes, outline, first draft, editing) then set a different specific measure for each interval. It is silly to count "words added" if you are editing down a manuscript and removing lots of prose, because you will be getting negative results (though you can count words subtracted!), but it could be very helpful in the first draft, where generation is more important than refinement. As long as your measures are internally consistent, you will find it feels more reliable as a measure of your accomplishment. You know when you are fooling yourself: don't give yourself the opportunity. Make your goals clear.

Measurable

This relates closely to the first point of being specific, but is independent of it: You can be very specific without having a reliable measurement. "Number of paragraphs added," for example, is very specific, but varies too widely for it to be of much use to people. The paragraphs of narration or of nonfictional exposition tend to be longer and paragraphs of dialogue can be very short indeed. ("Oh?" "Yes.") Words, full lines, or full written pages are somewhat more reliable indicators.

Whatever you choose needs to be a reasonably clear, cleanly delineated ruler. A good ruler has reliable units of measure, which do not vary too far. If the divisions of your yardstick varied from half an inch to three inches apart, competent carpentry would be impossible. Make the measurement of your craft a little more precise.

Applicable

David Frost: How do you work? Do you get up early every day and write music?

Jimi Hendrix: I try to *get up* every day.

Time spent sitting at the typewriter is a very consistent, reliable, and specific measure which is not terribly useful —if you don't do anything there. Getting up early and writing music was not the way Jimi Hendrix wrote music. When keeping track of your progress, your accounting should directly assess your writing or something directly related to it. It is not enough to focus on something around the writing.

An acquaintance of mine told me once that he was keeping track of the cups of coffee and cigarettes he had consumed while sitting in diners making notes for his book. After several years this person had yet to finish a chapter. You see, you can drink coffee and smoke without writing (and this person often did), so the association with writing produced simply lacked strength.

If you only drank coffee while writing (and drank at a steady pace), the "coffee ruler" might work better. Directly linking one addiction with another could get you into trouble, however; Freud found himself dependent on his cigars to think, even knowing he had developed cancer, and he had previously relied on cocaine to gain mental stimulation. Ideally, your writing productivity should not rely upon an external stimulus with negative consequences for your health. Despite the myths and legends, alcohol consumption is not obligatory to be a great writer, and is much more likely to harm your writing in the long term (see below).

The lesson here is that you must measure your writing, or the feedback you get will not be helpful to you.

Concrete Suggestions

1. If you have a word processor with a word counting feature, use it every time you write. That way you can track (and you should keep track) of your progress as measured by word count. If you are a "Beethovenian" writer, who edits and rewrites a great deal as you write,

don't worry—just be aware that your goal may
be more modest in the short term but more
daring in the long-term, assuming you don't
edit later drafts as much. When you begin
redlining a manuscript, count the number of
lines of red or the approximate number of edits
made or even pages marked up.

2. "Mozartian" writers, who generate highly
readable first drafts fluently and who write at a
fairly constant, steady speed, can time their
writing. Rex Stout tracked the number of hours
a day he spent writing so thoroughly that his
biographer identified exactly how many he
spent on each short story, novella, or novel.
Stout would plot in his head, and then move to
the typewriter when he had his story ready, so
marking time worked well for him. (I'll discuss
Mozartian and Beethovenian creators in more
detail below.)

3. People who compose at the keyboard can keep
track of their pages, or a rough count of words,
since word counts are more consistent for
typewritten pages. Handwriters could use pages
again, or an estimated word count, or even lines
of script. Whatever you use, make it consistent,
reliable, and really measurable. Even inches of
text work fine, as long as you use a ruler to
maintain accuracy. If you are a napkin-
scribbler, either transfer to a regular sheet for
counting or figure out a way to count napkins
with some reliability. You could distinguish by
size, for example, since that is fairly
standardized; and then count large, medium,
and small napkins filled with prose or at least

verbal content. As you transfer to regular sizes of paper, you can count those too. This may sound silly, but I know writers who write most of their early ideas on check stubs, sticky notes, and receipts. If it works for you, use it.

4. If you have uninterrupted periods of time to spend writing solidly, you can count those.

5. Get a person to give you feedback. The new writer may find this tricky, since poor feedback can be worse than none at all. The Achievement-oriented person craves feedback that will provide guidance as to the accuracy of movement toward the goal. A simple "that's good," or "I liked it," is not sufficient. Writers with an agent and/or an editor have a professional available to give feedback that may not be ideal but is at least well-informed, though this is not the kind of feedback you can get daily or even weekly. Whomever you may choose, make sure they have genuine interest in the work, and will be both honest and balanced in their feedback. Some studies suggest that the most motivating "kiss to kick" ratio should be about three to four to one over time: that is, three positive comments per each negative. Be aware that if there is a particular issue that merits detailed discussion, this ratio isn't important. Go ahead and talk about it rather than trying to force it into this balance.

6. If you do things methodically (as many Achievement-motivated people do), you can count things like "outline-points-turned-into-prose" or scene cards turned into actual scenes. Mystery writer Kelly Tate not only did that, but

kept two piles of scene cards: to be written, and written. Moving cards from one pile to the other was "gratifying" to her. Eliminating the pile (which could be four inches thick) was very satisfying indeed. I note also that the generation of scene cards enabled her to track herself in the early stages of her writing.

7. Do a combination. For jot notes, count pages; for outlines, count major or minor categories or both. If you want to get really sneaky, determine how many pages of outline translate into how many pages of prose for you, and multiply pages of outline by that amount. While updating this book, I knew I wouldn't be generating the same amount of original text as I did originally (since I was mostly editing and revising), so I tracked date, total word count (including incremental increase and cumulative increase to see how much more I was adding), and what page I had reached, since my first pass was from beginning to end.

Dealing with Writer's Block and Achievement Motive

What happens when you stall? For the Achievement-motivated writer, there are ways to get the juices going. If you already have a fair amount of prose, just read it over and edit. I guarantee that the Achievement-motivated writer will change <u>something</u>. Every change you make is a small step of improvement—that much closer to perfection.

I should warn you now, however—people high in this motive are rarely satisfied. The constant quest for improvement can drive you to rewrite over and over again. In a construct as complex as a book, there is no end to this kind of activity. You must exercise willpower and stop long enough to direct yourself to a different goal. As Paul Valery said: "A poem is never finished, only abandoned." (Or, as W. Arthur Rydee wrote: A masterpiece requires two people—one to create it, and one to stand behind him with a club to hit him when it is finished.) As Washington Irving put it about his own books:

> "I scarcely look with full satisfaction upon any; for they do not seem what they might have been. I often wish that I could have twenty years more, to take them down from the shelf one by one, and write them over."

Achievement-motivated people are always aiming at goals; as long as you have an *interesting* one in front of you all the time, you should be fine. Never let yourself get into a position of waiting for a response that could take months. That is obviously not useful feedback. I can suggest a number of strategies to cope with this, but the simplest is to start a new goal: begin your next book, start sending query letters to agents (assuming you don't have one) and publishers, start considering the marketing and map out places you would like to send copies. There are many possibilities around the external process of delivering your work to readers; it does not hurt to keep them in mind between writing bouts.

Some people may get so involved in the creative process alone that they never get to the point of actually selling their books. I again quote from Heinlein, whose Fourth and Fifth Laws of Writing proclaim: "You must put your work on the market" and "you must keep the work on the market until it is sold."

See, for example, the graphics below. Where have you

put your goals? Remember that they have very different results. How do you keep yourself going?

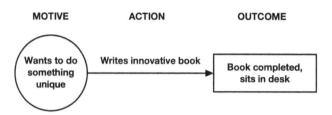

Graphic 1: A Way to Write an Unpublished Book

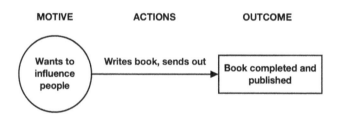

Graphic 2: A Way to Publish a Book

The alert reader will note that the first graphic aligns well with the Achievement motive, whereas the second aligns well with the Influence motive. This is true, and is one reason we see certain motives more frequently in writers published at book length. However, it is entirely possible to set a goal so that the *process* is satisfying to a motive that is different from the *outcome*. For example, I knew a human resource professional for a major petro-chemical firm who was extremely high in the Achievement motive to the exclusion of all else. This is not typical: having an impact on others energizes most HR people. But he made other people's development goals into his own: he got Achievement-motivated satisfaction when *someone else* got better. Tricky, and not something everyone can do, but worth keeping in mind!

Another way to break writer's block is to send copies to "reviewers:" Family, friends, anyone who will read it. Even if they do nothing but find typos, they have contributed, and you will get some kind of feedback. While it is better to get information that improves the book in some noteworthy way, it is not absolutely essential in all cases. Simply getting content returned to you can be enough, in the sense that every "no" is that much closer to a "yes," as many sales people put it.

CHAPTER 4: THE AFFILIATION-MOTIVATED WRITER

"When I was a ten-year-old book worm and used to kiss the dustjacket pictures of authors as if they were icons, it used to amaze me that these remote people could provoke me to love."

—Erica Jong

"When I write, I aim in my mind not toward New York but toward a vague spot a little east of Kansas. I think of the books on library shelves, without their jackets, years old, and a countryish teen-aged boy finding them, and having them speak to him. The reviews, the stacks in Brentano's, are just hurdles to get over, to place the book on that shelf."

—John Updike

"We romantic writers are there to make people feel and not think."

—Barbara Cartland

These folks may have trouble shutting themselves into a room when there are people to see. To focus, these people need to consider how many others they can respond to through their book, or how much pleasure it will give those people, or even how warmly they will be liked (assuming they write books that make them appear likable).

Research has identified several types of affiliation; all are concerned with relationships, but in different ways. Some people worry about whether others like them, and work hard to become liked. They sometimes fail, because their anxiety to be liked leads them to overdo it. These people fear rejection, and avoid conflict because conflict is painful. This makes it difficult for a writer to face rejection or deal with an editor who might criticize him or her, so these people must set up structures to carry them through the tough parts. One such structure may be a support system of people who give unconditional and unrestrained support to continue writing, regardless of setbacks.

A well-designed writers' workshop can provide that support. These groups form to help each other continue writing, and to give feedback as to their progress. (There is a section on what makes for a good workshop later.) Many have associated rules or a charter, such as requiring that all members participate equally, in order to prevent abuse of the system by those who are unwilling to help critique—or by those who are unwilling to share their work but enjoy criticizing others. One group I know starts their first critique of any work by *solely* positive feedback. In other words, after the person reads their work in the first session, everyone else provides a cheering session, citing only positive things, in order to get past the uncertainty that plagues many people at an early stage of their work. This makes a lot of sense: Some people try to write, conclude that their writing is bad, and then quit before really getting started. Their assessment may be absolutely correct at that time, but who said they cannot improve? In the first sessions of this particular group, members may only say, "I like this," and "I want to see more." This lays the groundwork of confidence for moving on.

Note that not all workshops need this rule; after I assessed members' motive patterns, finding that virtually all of them had significant levels of Affiliation motive, I advised them to think of ways to manage the anxiety associated with feedback, and this was their solution. According to members of the group – two of whom are award-winning fantasy authors – this *increased* their productivity as a group.

The workshop—when done properly—fits the Affiliation-oriented writer beautifully. By contrast, the primarily Achievement-oriented person may think at first that workshops are wonderful for the feedback opportunities, but in the long run putting up with the other people can frustrate the Achievement-motivated. All they want to do is go home and work alone, where they control the results. (Although they may find it satisfying to mark goals in terms of reading other people's work, that isn't our task here.) The primarily Influence-motivated person may like the idea of having an impact on all those people, but get absorbed into the enjoyment of direct impact (e.g., coaching others, convincing others of a point) instead of thinking about writing for an indirect or at least postponed impact of their own. The affiliative person, however, might well love this opportunity to work as part of a group all helping each other – as long as they continue to belong to the group writing.

A supportive writing group can provide the uncritical

friendliness some of these people crave (regardless of the actual assessment of the written material) and give them the security to feel comfortable writing. These folks will take the criticism happily as long as they feel the critics like them personally —regardless of the reaction to the text. This may sound contradictory, but they are more worried about their relationships than the content of the writing; a friend providing even negative feedback can feel positive in intent, and for the anxiously affiliative, this makes a huge difference. This may mean that they will not finish their writing task quickly, however; they do not think in terms of goals like "finishing a book." Indeed, they may feel reluctant to finish a book associated strongly with positive, personal reinforcement.

The second type of affiliative person – the trusting, group-oriented - does not worry about people liking them; they simply enjoy doing things for people, especially to benefit other people. This sort can do things that help others without considering (or worrying about) the eventual outcome of a relationship. For these people, satisfaction comes from a feeling of linkage to others, even in terms of just giving a benevolent action. Depending on the type of book you write, this can fit well with writing, with a final endpoint of giving someone pleasure or helping them somehow. Self-help and inspirational books sometimes fall into this category. I've seen people substitute this type of Affiliation motive for Influence motive, in fact, even in leadership roles.

The third type of affiliative person rejects the possibility of benevolent, mutually satisfying interaction. They are cynical, and they may well write of rejection, deceit, and hypocrisy. However, they value others like themselves, especially the witty. The Oscar Wildes, Dorothy Parkers, and James Thurbers of this world may exemplify this.

These people can masterfully dissect the foibles of others, and can be enormously entertaining, if a trifle unkind.

As is evident from my examples, I suspect that these people make fine satirists, commenting on the sad state of the world. Their motive in writing can be to make this sad state visible to others. In this they relate to Influence-motivated individuals as well, though it is not disinterested; those with this cynical Affiliation crave relationships as much as anyone else. If they put up public lists of their goal accomplishments as feedback, rather than the number of words, they may prefer to post the number of "air strikes" against the target: keeping track of good lines that truly skewer the opponent. This somewhat nasty criterion can support satirical writing, journalism (especially the "new journalism" of Tom Wolfe, Hunter S. Thompson and the like), and even scientific writing. There is a great satisfaction (for these people) in puncturing an inaccurate theory in public.

In any case, you should be alert to your feelings here. Delia Sherman, a fine fantasy writer, found she had a significant amount of Affiliation Motive, and chose to join a writer's group that reinforced her; she found it helped her produce by satisfying this motive and (presumably) removing it as a concern.

Characteristics of Affiliative Feedback

1. Friendly
2. Uncritical
3. Warm

<u>Friendly</u>
Affiliative feedback is essentially friendly in nature—

you should feel happy with it, feeling it is on your side. That does not mean it cannot be constructive criticism or even include negative assessments, but it does mean that it is delivered in a way that makes it clear it was for you, because you are a friend.

Uncritical

I do not mean by this that you should have no sense of improvement—but the baseline should be "I am good!" or even "I am a good person!" The Achievement person values balanced negative and positive feedback, to assess the moderate risk that hovers between them. The Affiliation-motivated person wants reassurance as to personal value. "Attaboys/girls" or cheerleading are good, reinforcing choices for these people, who would really prefer being with somebody else or a group than sitting in a room alone.

Warm

Emotion matters a lot to the affiliative person. If they feel warm, secure, and loved, they can produce far better than if they are insecure and lonely. Loneliness distracts many—for the affiliative it may cripple their functioning. The comfortable affiliative writer can feel warm by thinking of the reading audience; early in a career I suspect it takes a more immediate presence. On the other hand, research has shown that affiliative people tend to write more letters to friends and loved ones, too. How many people do you know who take pride in their list of Facebook friends, or use the Internet to track down their friends from grade school or high school? Affiliation motive leads people to reach out to friends and family to connect.

Concrete Suggestions

1. Have someone in the room. This person need
    not be distracting, but should be a presence
    who can reassure you on demand. This will
    probably matter more in early days; you will be
    able to get by without immediate affiliative
    feedback as your self-confidence grows. I have
    heard of writing workshops that actually do
    "writing camps" where they sit in a room
    together and write. "It keeps you honest," say
    participants. I think it keeps you happy as well.
2. Talk about it with people. The writer's
    workshop can come in handy here, but not to
    impress people, as the Influence-motivated
    person would desire. Instead, this should give
    you an opportunity to get reassurance that *you
    can write.*
3. Find appropriate targets for your work. If you
    are aiming at a particular audience, take a
    sample from that audience (assuming one is
    available), and ask them to read it regularly and
    comment on it. Hopefully most of the
    comments will be positive.
4. Write for a specific, real person. You need not
    actually send it to that person (though it helps),
    but write it with the same focus as a letter.
    Some books have actually been written that
    way. Tolkien, for example, wrote many stories
    in letters home to his children. This allows you
    think of the audience as real people you care
    for. The drawback of this is that you may write
    for their taste and not yours, but you can always

rewrite—and some people find that more fun than writing new material.

5. You simply may not have this as an option, but I list it for the sake of completeness: if you have an audience demanding your work, an audience composed of intimates, the drive to write may well be enhanced. Charles L. Dodgson was just another Oxford mathematician until a trio of young girls demanded that he tell them stories, and then asked him to write them down. Thus was born Lewis Carroll—and Alice in Wonderland.

Dealing with Writer's Block

In some ways, these people are similar to those with a high need for Influence (see the next section) in that they require another person to provide effective feedback. However, they require approval of *themselves as people* rather than a reaction to the book or an impact on the world at large. An influence-motivated person might feel pleasure if someone has a violently negative reaction—because they want a strong impact, regardless of direction. Not so the affiliative. They want to be considered good people, or to do something positive for another. To break writer's block may require hand-holding, or an enthusiastic person saying "Oooh! When can I read it?"

CHAPTER 5: THE INFLUENCE-MOTIVATED WRITER

"If we had to say what writing is, we would define it essentially as an act of courage."

—Cynthia Ozick

"You don't understand the humiliation of it—to be tricked out of the single assumption that makes our existence viable—that somebody is *watching*..."

—Tom Stoppard

"There is nothing more dreadful to an author than neglect, compared with which reproach, hatred and opposition are names of happiness."

—Samuel Johnson

Ah, the glory of having a book before the world! This writer may dream of going on talk shows, appearing on convention panels, or somehow changing people's lives. A chief peril for this person is looking forward to having written a book rather than actually writing—which is, after all, a solitary occupation, Harlan Ellison's window-writing notwithstanding—or to short-cut the process and just influence people directly, one at a time or in groups, instead of taking the time to writing a book first.

Your challenge: meet this need, and feel that you make an impact. The impact can even be on yourself. A primarily Influence-oriented person can get a charge out of writing an emotionally arousing scene—after all, how do you know it arouses people unless it arouses you? Thoughts about powerful scenes—scenes that hit home and hit hard—come naturally to someone with this motive well represented. Unfortunately, most works require linking content between powerful scenes, which may not hold the interest the same way.

How to feel that you have made an impact? Well, ideally, you should have an actual person available. This reader will give you a sense of having had an impact on a human being. This impact need not take place every session—unlike the primarily Achievement-motivated person, the feedback can remain less constant or immediate—but it must be a reaction. Given enough practice and confidence, you <u>may</u> not need a local or immediately accessible audience to provide feedback, but I know many bestselling writers who still rely on "beta readers" to provide feedback on their books.

> "I write the big scenes first, that is, the scenes that carry the meaning of the book, the emotional experience."
>
> —Joyce Cary

I have already alluded to some possibilities for

impressing yourself: rereading sections, for example. If, in the middle of another part of your writing work you come up with a powerful idea, just jot it down. The temptation will be to hold off on your filler writing and get on with the hot scene. Save it instead, to motivate you to return to the keyboard. Set yourself the goal of accomplishing your current task in order to reward yourself with more exciting writing later. In the same way that some people complete jigsaw puzzles by going for a particular color or the edges, you can go after certain kinds of scenes to propel yourself.

You can also display your work in various ways. Like the Achievement person, you can count lines, words, or pages—but don't just write it down someplace hidden. Take a piece of paper and write it in HUGE characters. Post it on your wall—someplace reasonably public. Tell someone. Remember, the Influence-motivated person thrives on reactions. Putting the number up in public forces you to change it, or people will notice. In this way, you use the pressure of external people's impressions to drive your feelings—even if no one says a thing. If they do comment that your number has changed frequently (use different colors on successive signs for more contrast), then you have earned attention that will give you positive reinforcement. During NaNoWriMo (National November Writing Month), I often see people posting their daily progress on social media, for even broader impact.

Here I should put in a word for politeness. Nothing irritates people more than writers who prattle at length about their "work-in-progress," particularly those who quote their favorite lines in public places. ("I prefer dead writers because you don't run into them at parties." —Fran Lebowitz) Such behavior will create an impact, all right, but not the one you might prefer. But there is nothing wrong with having a mysterious six-inch-tall number posted on your wall in a prominent position. If they ask you about it...well, that's <u>their</u> problem now.

While the Achievement-dominated person gets motivation by the internal knowledge of visible progress, the mostly Influence-motivated person gets energy from knowing that someone knows about that visible progress; sometimes oneself is enough.

To the primarily Influence-motivated person that number on the wall might also be a threat—if someone comes by after a week and your number remains the same, they will wonder why, and you are going to have to tell them. Removing the number (to avoid that question) will have an impact, too. So you have, in effect, committed yourself to going on because you cannot bear to have someone know you have stopped. You must save face. It's worth noting that research shows that a public declaration of a goal increases the likelihood of completing the goal, and this may be one reason why.

If you feel strong fear about being "caught out" not changing that number, then I strongly recommend that you do not use this particular method. Fear does not provide a terribly good motivation for extended periods of writing. Enjoyment works much better here.

If you are writing a "useful" or "important" work, keep thinking how many people you could affect, and how. Politicians with this motive tend to come from grass-roots movements, because they would rather know they have gotten one dollar from a million people than a million dollars from one person. They count the people they have influenced, no matter how little, not the dollar efficiency of fundraising. (Achievement-motivated politicians, by contrast, often get indicted for fundraising irregularities, since they find it easier to get their funds from a few rich people. Hey, it got Nixon.)

Make a list, if you like: How many people could read this book and gain from it? If you are writing a scientific work, how many colleagues do you have who might read it? Don't worry about whether they will—that comes after you finish the book.

In the course of writing this book I offered to make a presentation on the topic at hand for a mystery writers' conference. This kept me focused on what people would think of both me and this book. It also guided the organization of my writing, and in my mental rehearsals of my presentation I determined which sentences flowed well, and which did not. I have spoken to writers' groups, conferences, and whatnot on numerous occasions, which kept my interest fresh, if only because I could continue to test the interest of my audience. Large chunks of this book came about specifically because I was asked to speak on some aspect of writing, and I ultimately turned that speech into a chapter or section.

Characteristics of Influence Feedback

1. Dramatic
2. Arouses strong emotion
3. Impact

Dramatic

> "Good writing is supposed to evoke sensation in the reader—not the fact that it's raining, but the feel of being rained upon."

—E. L. Doctorow

You are concerned with making a strong impression, or influencing people. Dramatic forms of feedback may influence you. For example: Use bright colors on a progress form, or write a brief report that you mail to yourself, or announce it loudly somehow—even if only to yourself. If the latter, find a room with good acoustics, and belt it out. Enjoy the resonance.

Arouses strong emotion

"I write because I hate. A lot. Hard."

—William Gass

The primarily Influence-oriented person tends to arouse emotions strongly in others, either positively or negatively. Emotion indicates significant influence on a person, so people with a lot of this motive crave emotional impact. Arouse strong emotion in yourself, and you have given yourself a powerful form of feedback. Being dramatic can help; so can playing certain kinds of music that arouse you the right way. (Be careful—don't play Beethoven's Fifth Symphony if you are planning a quiet, professional document. They might clash.) If you need to stop occasionally and scroll through the entire document, or riffle pages, or howl at the moon—do it!

Impact

"Give me a museum and I'll fill it."

—Pablo Picasso

Do something you will remember. Memorize the latest number, or write it on your palm, or post it in a really noticeable place—your door, for instance. That way you cannot miss it. If you get into the habit of seeing something in a particular place, then move it around or hang it at an angle. Surprise yourself. Pique your interest. People tend to get used to things—otherwise they would go bananas just keeping up with the world around them every day. You need to fight this tendency in order to trigger yourself.

Concrete Suggestions

1. Post progress dramatically. Colored writing will help—especially in red or some other contrasting color.
2. Make a stack of your latest manuscript and place it someplace visible. (Use a copy or keep it someplace very safe as well as visible.)
3. If you are a Mozartian writer who writes from beginning to end without editing, post the last page you have written with a large, red page number marked on the page. Again, make sure it is visible. Your refrigerator door is a fine place, as long as the page stands out.
4. Announce your achievement to someone who will respond strongly—significant other, mother, friend, social media connections—whomever will shout hooray sincerely. Faked or lukewarm responses won't do it. You might have to be sparing with this one, to avoid the "Boy Who Cried Wolf" syndrome. You may want to set a

solid goal to be met before announcing, to ensure a meaningfully dramatic statement. "I finished a sentence!" is not very impressive unless you write *very very slowly*. "I finished twenty pages!" or "2,000 words!" or "25% done!" is more significant and meaningful. Be aware that the primarily Influence-motivated person tends to set unrealistic goals. If you choose not to announce until your book is half-finished, you may lose steam. Give yourself a moderate set of "rah-rah points." If you aren't sure what that might be, ask yourself how often you need reinforcement before flagging—or ask an Achievement-oriented person. They usually set moderately risky goals on their own, spontaneously.

5. Have short-term and major-announcement points—little cheers and big cheers, as it were. If you write each night, you have no reason not to take pleasure in your accomplishment each night, but don't get out of hand until you have justified your pleasure.

Dealing with Writer's Block

What happens when you stall? For the Influence-motivated writer, as for the Achievement-motivated writer, the reason may be because the process of writing is no longer associated with the motive. In other words, it isn't fun. For a person high in the need for influence, this could take several forms. First, the writer may not have a feeling of having impact. At such times an audience becomes critical in order to have a sense of a reaction from another. Don't be afraid to ask friends and family to read your work; all they can say is "no." If they do say no, you don't want them reading your work at that point anyway. Even if the person you want to read your stuff lives far away, go ahead and send them a package (with their permission, of course), or e-mail them your work. You'll have to do that eventually to sell your book, after all, assuming you want to do that.

Another reason for writer's block may be because you have waited too long between writing sessions, and the work has gone cold. If you have enough material, read it from beginning to end, and see what reaction it provokes. Where appropriate, try writing again, just to get words on paper. If your work is quite long—novel length, say— spend a couple of days reading. Keep your continuity, and start thinking how to make a better impact again.

I described a prophylactic for the Influence-based writer's block above—don't write the powerful scenes out of order. Save them up for the slow times. It may be easier to get psyched up for an exciting scene.

If all else fails, write something completely different. Keep the association of writing and excitement.

Here's an example of Influence Motive influencing writing: Sarah Smith, describing her book *The Moon Rock of Stars*:

> "I thought I was losing my mind because I was on chapter 16 of 20 and I realized I was doing it wrong. I had to lose two characters. I couldn't figure out where it was going. I had no sense of being in control. I said 'this is a good book to write for a second book. It kills you to lose control. You can write a book like the previous book you wrote.' It was easy—except for things like plot and character!... This book—it really felt perverse. It felt like I was destroying myself—which in a sense I was. I

wanted to get out of the sense that I had to write in this way and I had to succeed in this way to do what I was doing."

In this case Sarah Smith describes the sense of losing power through losing control of the work. For her, the loss of direction was disturbing; especially since the book she was writing was beyond the way she had learned to write at that time, so that writing it felt like a loss of identity. Losing power <u>and</u> identity is too much. As she put it, the book "felt perverse...I was destroying myself." Where another person (say an Achievement-motivated person) might have said, "I was doing it wrongly," or "I wasn't up to the challenge," Smith felt she was "destroying" herself, a clearly Influence-related image. Fortunately, she recognized what was happening well enough that she could take appropriate action.

First, she identified that this <u>was</u> beyond her abilities *at the moment*. She did not attribute her failure to complete inability or stupidity (see the Attributional Style section later in the book for more on this); she said, "this is a good book to write for a second book." She knew she was stretching herself, and realized that her task was to write something very different. It took her several months to write a twelve-page chapter, but she knew it was the right way to go. She already knew something that many newer writers do not: not every part of a book goes the same way, and not every writing effort works the same way. She had enough objectivity to realize that this would take a different kind of approach, rather than letting the helplessness and lack of ability steer her away from it entirely.

CHAPTER 6: THE WRITER WITH MULTIPLE MOTIVES

"Everyone has the obligation to ponder well his own specific traits of character. He must also regulate them adequately and not wonder whether someone else's traits might suit him better. The more definitely his own a man's character is, the better it fits him."

—Marcus Tullius Cicero

I once asked David McClelland, one of the great guiding minds behind the field of motivational psychology, how he would describe a person who had all three motives relatively strongly. He said: "Confused."

The multiple-motive personality will enjoy a wide range of things, and may shift from one choice to another based on which motive happens to have the upper hand. Since these motives are unconscious, it is much harder to resolve contradictory desires than it would be if you were just told to make a choice—all you know is that you cannot decide, because everything sounds fun. You may be highly motivated in general (adding them all up), but unless you have a focus, you will bounce like a ping-pong ball instead of aiming and using all that motivational energy.

John F. Kennedy was high in all three, and he was seen as dynamic, active, and bursting with energy despite being largely crippled by his back problems. The energy of your personality can project well beyond the limitations of your physique. When working together, multiple motives can give you a great deal of drive—you may have the possibility to shift gears when one motive is on the decline, or adjust to a different situation that demands different thought patterns. Furthermore, it enlarges your sensory sensitivity to include a richer array of images. The flip side of that gift is that it also makes you more susceptible to distraction.

It should be possible to balance or interweave your motives effectively, but you may have to apply main force or external frameworks to do so. It helps to be aware—knowledge is power!—and then you can adjust your reward system to take all motives into account.

Below, I will describe the commonest combinations briefly, keeping in mind that in practice no one is that simple. I will talk about how it looks overall to have two or three motives high, the strengths of that combination, and potential dangers.

Achievement and Affiliation: The "Team Achievement Profile"

People possessing this combination of motives high are often great for participating in teams: they want to get things done well (Achievement), and they care about the people around them in personal terms (Affiliation), and the combination becomes "helping everyone do well."

When part of a team effort, this can become a virtuous cycle of motivation (assuming you have relatively positive Affiliation motive, rather than the Cynical or Anxious subtypes!): you want to do well, but that means you have to help the team; you want the team members to be happy, but that means they have to do well.

Obviously, a writer's workshop can be a powerful tool for people with this profile.

However, as with single motives, there are negative "hot buttons" as well keeping in mind two danger spots from these motives: first, that Affiliation makes people sensitive on a personal wavelength; remember the workshop that gave everyone pure positive feedback for the first reading, because you might need something similar. Second, the negative side of Achievement is that it is <u>not</u> about working with people, so when frustrated by someone else, the reaction is either to take over the task or to withdraw to work alone.

A group that lacks good rules could lead to people feeling personally hurt or frustrated or both. For example, <u>all</u> feedback should be given as optional: the writer controls the work. No one has the right to take over someone else's writing or other creative work. I've seen this done, where someone thought they were "improving" it, and all they did was infuriate the other person.

<u>Affiliation and Influence: The "Missionary Profile"</u>

People with both these motives high think about helping the world: caring about people (Affiliation) and having an impact (Influence) combined.

They tend to want to affect things for everybody's

good. People with Influence motive tend to want to run things, but those with Affiliation may worry about whether people are okay with that. Since both motives are about being aware of others, it doubles the sensitivity to what other people are thinking and feeling, which can get in the way of taking or giving feedback. It is possible for someone with this profile to want to help others but be uncomfortable with receiving help themselves. They may start a writing group, for example, but position themselves as the facilitator, which can be great for the group, but potentially bad for them if they lead rather than participate.

Similarly, both motives push people to want to be with others and engage with them, albeit in different ways. People with this profile may find it doubly difficult to closet themselves away to write! They probably enjoy conferences and gatherings tremendously.

Achievement and Influence: The "Agentic Profile"

People with both these motives high push doubly hard to get things done: getting results and goals met (Achievement) and influencing others as well as themselves to get there (Influence).

Both of these are "agency" motives, taking action, as opposed to the "communion-based" motive of Affiliation, where someone can just enjoy being present and part of the group. This double-agency may help someone propel themselves in their writing, because they not only want to influence through their writing, but they gravitate towards measurement, improvement, and results.

In a writer's group, this person is likely to be impatient, wanting to nudge people to work, while the more affiliative people want to socialize. As long as they can restrain their desire to influence in person, they can probably drive on with their writing alone, as long as they don't get lost in the details they want to improve with their Achievement motive.

All three high: The "Confused Profile"

The real issue for having all three high is that, even more than with these other profiles, you become highly distractible, because *everything* becomes interesting. Some people are more adroit than others at what I think of as "gear-shifting" – being able to move from using one motive to the next at will, instead of being jerked around by their own emotions and interests. There are also those who have more "brake" for their motivational engine, and we'll discuss Activity Inhibition later, because having these brakes can keep people from derailing themselves.

The good gear-shifter (or good self-manager), can move more freely from one task to another, and bring good energy to all of them: spend some time researching an issue (Achievement), calling a friend and chatting while getting advice (Affiliation), and crafting a message to write about that issue (Influence). The challenge is managing oneself from minute to minute, or setting up a structure outside yourself to help you manage.

Managing multiple motives

The important thing is to retain focus. If you can find ways of linking in more than one motive, your chances to keep your focus go up enormously. The job of writer has opportunities for all three motives, but the degree depends on you. J. D. Salinger, who rejects any kind of publicity or even the presentation of his image to the public, is unlikely to have a strongly externally-focused Influence motive, since he works hard to suppress a viable reward for it.

On the other hand, he could equally well comprehend the temptation for the writer to get so involved with the social life of being a famous writer—talk shows, parties, interviews, politics, and so on—that he ceases to actually *write*. (Remember, do not judge a person's motives solely by their behaviors; that way lies madness). Truman Capote leaned in this direction, and wrote far too few books for a person of his talent. If Capote had isolated himself occasionally, he might have done more writing.

Science fiction and mystery authors have an option not available to many other authors: they can attend conventions. There is a science fiction convention (and usually more than one) on virtually any given weekend in the United States, and all of them delight in having a writer available to bring in more fans. However, some writers just go from convention to convention enjoying the socialization—the affiliation, or the direct influence—so much that they never write again.

Conventions can be valuable in many ways: they provide access to fellow practitioners of the craft to learn from them, they are places to get new ideas (satisfying Achievement motive), they provide a source of positive, friendly reinforcement (appealing to Affiliation motive), and they give opportunities to create a reputation and make an impact on readers, writers, and publishers (Influence motive). But if you have more than one motive pumping, make sure it is the right one for the purpose of *writing and selling your work*.

Motives are emotional, as noted above; you may find it hard to avoid doing something very satisfying in order to do something important. If you go into a situation with many choices, you need to sit down and *think* about what you need *before* you go. Otherwise you may run on "gut instinct," which (contrary to popular belief) is not your best guide.

Now that you can see how differently motivated people may write, let's take a deeper look at *your* motives, using a simple method: finding out what you do for fun.

CHAPTER 7: DISCOVERING MOTIVES USING REALITY TESTING

"There is never a better measure of what a person is than what he does when he is absolutely free to choose."

—William M. Bulger

"The real character of a man is found out by his amusements."

—Sir Joshua Reynolds

Motive-Related Behaviors

Since motives predict behaviors, you might expect that you can read someone by what they do. However, motives predict *patterns of* behaviors and the *reasons for* behaviors more than they do specific actions.

You cannot judge a person by a given workday, for example, because too much of work is governed by the needs of the moment, not personal enjoyment. Also, as I have noted before, there can be many motives driving the same behavior.

For example: Salespeople often learn good people skills. But salespeople, especially in shorter-cycle sales, are often best *driven* by Achievement motive. A paradox? Not really. These people learn influencing behaviors to get to their truly enjoyable goal—the challenge of making a sale or beating a quota. The means are not the end where motives and behaviors are concerned.

Similarly, you cannot stereotype motivated behavior. I have frequently worked with people who complained about tyrannical behavior on the part of a manager, and early on attribute it to Influence—they must be power-mad, a dictator. Upon investigation, these people often have no intent to crush their employees—what they do is focus completely on the goal, even if people are in the way, or they zero in on such a high level of excellence that it is impossible to carry out without their direct interference and coercion. This is Achievement motive in action, not Influence. Indeed, Influence-motivated people are more likely to be aware of how other people are reacting, assuming they have the basic empathy or emotional intelligence to see it.

So what is the point of this section? Well, now that I have terrified you on the subject of judging motives by behaviors, I am going to tell you how to do just that, as a prequel to judging yourself, but also as a way to think about character design.

First, try to find out what people *enjoy* doing, rather than what they have to do. How do they spend their free time, if any? What do they read for fun? We are looking for spontaneous action, not controlled by thinking—for then values get in the way. Keep in mind that people who enjoy their job are getting *some* motive satisfaction there, so the rest of the time may relate to other motives, and not present a fully balanced understanding of a motive profile. I once assessed a manager who was highest on Affiliation motive, but who was able to separate his work and home lives so thoroughly that people did not perceive him as affiliative at work, because that was almost completely devoted to his family at home.

Second, try to identify *why* people like doing something. The *why*, if stated in emotional terms, will give a better clue to motivation than the *what*.

See the Identifying Your Motives Worksheet attached here for a checklist of items that can be reasonably believed to associate with one motive. I do list a few that belong in more than one category, but I try to define them. You can use this on yourself, and add up the numbers at the bottom, and get at least a very rough read of motives.

Identifying Your Motives Worksheet

by Stephen P. Kelner, Jr.

Instructions

The following sections have a variety of activities, which relate to one or more motives if done for enjoyment. Go down the list and check whichever ones you enjoy. If you want to add extra strength, you can put more than one check. At the end is a key to add up which support which motives.

#	Hobbies			
1.	Handicraft	☐		
2.	Working on cars	☐		
3.	Being with family		☐	
4.	Being with friends		☐	
5.	Running committees			☐
6.	Performance (act, sing, dance)			☐
7.	Writing (!)			☐
8.	Correspondence with family or friends, social media connection		☐	
9.	Cooking for self	☐		
10.	Cooking for others			☐

#	Hot buttons			
1.	Testing myself against targets, goals	☐		
2.	Meeting new potential friends		☐	
3.	A friend needs help		☐	
4.	Getting my point across to people			☐
5.	Politics			☐

#	Telephone Use			
1.	Efficient, brisk, short (avoiding contact)	☐		
2.	Calling to get specific questions answered	☐		
3.	Friendly, calling to say hello, hard to get off phone		☐	
4.	Calling to connect with people		☐	
5.	Being called more than calling, distributing information			☐
6.	Calling to gather general information			☐
7.	Don't like calling, would rather email, v-mail, fax so I don't have to get into a conversation	☐		
8.	Dislike calling because it feels cold and impersonal		☐	
9.	Dislike calling because I can't see people's faces			☐
10.	Dislike calling myself because there are ways to connect with more people at once			☐

#	Books Read for Fun			
1.	Learning techniques, skills	☐		
2.	How-to, Do-it-yourself	☐		
3.	Mysteries (puzzles, "cozies," amateur sleuths)	☐		
4.	Mysteries (hard-boiled, private eyes)			☐
5.	Mysteries (historical)			☐
6.	Romances		☐	
7.	Stories with well-developed relationships		☐	
8.	Biographies of leaders			☐
9.	Psychology			☐
10.	Theology			☐
11.	History			☐
12.	Stories with sexual content			☐
13.	Stories with violent content			☐
14.	Spy stories, thrillers			☐
15.	Science fiction ("hard")	☐		
16.	Science fiction ("soft," "sociological")			☐
17.	Science fiction (military)			☐
18.	Fantasy (epics)			☐
19.	Urban fantasy			☐

#	My Greatest Satisfaction Comes from:			
1.	Creating something new	☐		
2.	Creating something of the highest quality, even if no one else sees it	☐		
3.	Being with friends		☐	
4.	Being with family		☐	
5.	Having an impact on people			☐

#	What Makes Me Sorrowful?			
1.	Lost opportunities for unique action	☐		
2.	Lost relationships		☐	
3.	Lost visibility			☐

#	Sports			
1.	Golf (against handicap)	☐		
2.	Golf (with friends)		☐	
3.	Golf (competitive or with betting)			☐
4.	Bowling (against scores)	☐		
5.	Bowling (with friends or league)		☐	
6.	Bowling (competitive)			☐
7.	Beach volleyball		☐	
8.	Basketball			☐
9.	Baseball			☐
10.	Softball		☐	
11.	Football			☐
12.	Track and field	☐		
13.	Shot-put	☐		
14.	High jump, long jump	☐		
15.	Professional or amateur competition (beating a record)	☐		
16.	Professional or amateur competition (beating others, a nemesis)			☐
17.	Soccer (football)			☐
18.	Rugby			☐
19.	Water Polo			☐
20.	Equestrian			☐
21.	Hiking	☐		
22.	Kayaking			☐
23.	Computer games (adventure)			☐
24.	Computer games (cards, puzzles)	☐		
25.	Computer games (team, MMO)		☐	

The table scoring is relatively simple: when looking at the three columns with checkboxes, the first column is Achievement, the second is Affiliation, and the third is Influence. You can tally them up and get a rough sense of your motives, keeping in mind that they are not equally matched.[1]

This must be used with *great* caution. To illustrate the ways in which many motives can predict the same behavior, take three people playing golf together. One may be playing to improve his handicap (Achievement motive), another may be playing because they are friends of his and he enjoys the company (Affiliation motive), and the third may be playing because this is an opportunity to influence them for later use (Influence motive). All of them are playing golf (the same behavior), but for different reasons. That is why we do not use behaviors to *predict* motives, but only to help validate them.

Now that you can see how differently motivated people may write, let's take a look at a range of actual published writers I have studied, and what their motives tend to be.

SECTION II

MOTIVATION--WHY PUBLISHED WRITERS DO WHAT THEY DO

"Art is a form of catharsis."

—Dorothy Parker

CHAPTER 8: MOTIVES, READERS, AND WRITERS

"The man who does not read good books has no advantage over the man who cannot read them."

— Mark Twain (1835-1910)

Motives and Reading Matter

Motives relate to many actions, preferences, and thoughts—including what you choose to read for fun. In brief, primarily Achievement-motivated people like to read nonfiction to learn something ("how-to" books), or mentally challenging stories (Agatha Christie, locked-room mysteries). Affiliative people like reading stories with well-developed characters (Jane Austen) or romantic stories (Barbara Cartland or other romances). Finally, Influence-motivated people are interested in what makes people tick (they read psychology, biographies of leaders like Lincoln or Churchill) or in reading about impact or influence on others (hard-boiled mysteries like Raymond Chandler, stories with aggression or political maneuvering like political thrillers).

Did you notice that that previous paragraph explains the constant battle between the "hard-boiled" (Private Eye) and "tea cozy" (Miss Marple) mystery? Forget all those arguments about which is more realistic, which is better written, whatever. The *real* difference lies not on the intellectual level, but on the emotional. The typical PI deals with conflict, politics, direct aggression, alcohol, and manipulation—the negative side of the Influence motive. Well, you don't expect Mother Theresa to show up in a dark and gritty detective novel, do you? Though it could make for a really interesting story...

By contrast, the classic Agatha Christie novel emphasizes not the deeper feelings and interactions of characters, but an intricate puzzle that you can work out as precisely as a chess problem. Often obscure facts play a key role as well, either as the "gimmick" where everything hinges on knowing that pennies were made from steel in 1943, or by opening up another world to the reader, as Tony Hillerman does with the Navajo. As mystery writer Aaron Elkins once said, you don't waste your time with mysteries, because you learn something. This characterizes Achievement motive thinking very well: improving your knowledge and challenging yourself.

This simplifies the motives to the point of idiocy, of course; a good cozy novel requires more emotional depth than a crossword puzzle, and a good hard-boiled novel needs more intellectual depth than Rock'em Sock'em Robots. But at one conference where I pointed this out a woman came up to me and thanked me for explaining why she hated most mysteries. To her, characters just messed up the mystery. She adored Agatha Christie, but most modern cozies depend upon complex characterization, or, God forbid, romantic relationships! Her comment immediately reminded me of Dorothy L. Sayers' dedication to *Busman's Honeymoon*:

> "It has been said, by myself and others, that a love-interest is only an intrusion upon a detective story. But to the characters involved, the detective-interest might well seem an irritating intrusion upon their love-story."

Sayers' broad and enduring popularity might well come from her understanding of this fact, for her books touch upon all three motives: the intricate puzzle (the railway tables in *Five Red Herrings*), the affiliative relationship (as above), and power and class relationships (*Gaudy Night, Whose Body?*). She has, literally, something for everybody. I could use her novels as an impromptu motivational test: which do you like the most? If you prefer *Five Red Herrings* to *Busman's Honeymoon,* I think I know why...

Likewise, you can analyze more recent examples of mystery fiction and see that more than one motive seem to emerge even inside the classic divisions. Most modern cozies as well as Sara Paretsky's private eye V. I. Warshawski have an affiliative "hook" through family or friends in addition to the puzzle aspect—and don't forget that the amateur usually competes with the official detective, which can be Achievement (beat the standard) or Influence (beat the person—sometimes literally) or both, depending on how it is handled. "Urban Fantasy" writers, many of whom are putting mysteries in a universe with more uncanny paranormal creatures, often blend politics, puzzles, and relationships all at once, and this combination certainly contributes to the popularity of writers like Charlaine Harris.

People are complex, and the writer who forgets that is less likely to be successful.

In that case, what motive should the writer have? Originally, I thought the motives of writers should reflect the motives of their readers—Achievement-motivated writers would tend to write mysteries, Affiliation-motivated writers would enjoy scripting romances, Influence-motivated writers would create thrillers. If they bore any motive in common, it would probably be the Achievement motive, since people with this motive as their strongest like to work alone, set goals, and get things done—all useful things for a writer. Make sense? I thought so.

Fortunately, science marches on despite the limitations of its practitioners: my hypothesis was dead wrong—at least for *published* writers. Please note that there are several provisos on these findings – but my initial hypothesis was definitely wrong!

The Research Population

Initially, I recruited 25 published writers who kindly filled out formal motivation assessments and participated in interviews on their writing process. I also facilitated a number of panels where all participants took the formal assessment and we talked about the results and their processes on the panel – and in some cases argued about them.

Since my initial data gathering, I've had the opportunity to interview and assess a number of other writers, and I kept getting consistently striking results.

I selected published writers because my purpose was to help others to become published writers. In my experience, most would-be writers do not want to collect dirty paper by their desks; they want to have a real book in their hands, or have other people reading what they write. I share that feeling; after all, I wrote a book on this subject!

The writers crossed various genres; primarily mystery, science fiction, and fantasy, with nonfiction such as true crime and textbooks, and some oddballs here and there. They range from relatively new (one book) to highly experienced award-winners with six-figure contracts, but all of them were published at book-length by mainstream publishing companies.

When not writing, they include academics, technical professionals, journalists, advertisers, financial advisors, and physicists. They cover a lot of ground, but in retrospect, I cannot be surprised by what I found.

Changes

Since that time, the field has undergone a number of major revolutions. When the first edition of this book came out in 2005, e-books were rare. The Kindle did not come out until two years later, in November 2007. Now hundreds of millions of e-books are sold every year.

The advent of Print-on-Demand (POD) books means that people can self-publish their books on an as-needed basis (instead of keeping books in their basement), with the Internet as their bookstore.

Devices such as the "espresso machine" even allow you to print and bind books on the spot.

And the Internet has also become a haven for online publishing – magazines, books, blogs, articles, etc. I started a blog when the first edition came out, but now there are a host of platforms.

One reason to update this book is precisely because the choices for the way people "publish" their work have grown significantly, which changes the constraints on writers. In other words the job of "published writer" is not necessarily what it was in 2005.

Having said that, there is something to be said for assessing what it takes to do what may be the *toughest* form of publication: writing a book of 70,000 words or more, acquiring an agent, selling it to a publisher, waiting for it to come out in bookstores, because there are many still publishing that way, and many who want to do so. For those who don't, in effect it will be easier, and there are more options. Indeed it will shift some of the motivational patterns found. We'll start with the initial study, made up of book-length writers published through mainstream methods, but as we progress we will dig into the different ways to write and publish as well.[1] After all, this isn't just about printed books versus e-books, either: it's about novels versus technical books versus short stories versus essays, etc., etc. Rest assured we'll try to tackle them all!

The Research Findings

Remember the three motives? The normal approach is to display the findings in profile, after comparing it to a research database of 80,000 people from around the world. In this way, we see not just the raw number; we see roughly how it compares with all the people out there. In other words, if a person's motive is at 75th percentile, it means that that person has a higher raw score than 75 per cent of that huge group—better than 60,000, in fact.

You may see the results in the graph below.

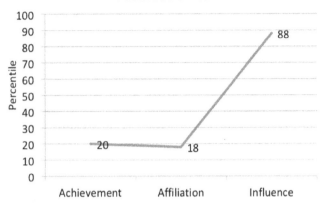

What does this mean? It means that the desire to influence drives published writers far more (on average) than the other two. These people get their jollies out of knowing others respond to them. Should this surprise us?

Remember I said "published" writers. Why get published? To put your words before others, of course. Philip R. Craig, author of a mystery series set in Martha's Vineyard, laughed when I told him his motive pattern (almost precisely the same as the graph above), because he felt strongly that it is inappropriate to manifest your will over others—yet he is a mystery writer who wrote a novel focusing on the negative aspects of politics and being in a fishbowl, and was a university professor as well. He still *sees* the influence issues, but he warns against them as being about negative power. Sarah Smith, author of *A Citizen of the Country*, would rather die than tell someone they have to write their book a certain way, but she spends untold hours helping and guiding others both as part of a writing workshop and by critiquing and coaching individuals on her own. The behaviors of seeing power relationships and coaching others relate to the Influence motive.

The Achievement-motivated person can find happiness working alone and in isolation, as long as he or she gets feedback on progress toward goals, and can constantly beat goals over time. The Affiliative person gets satisfaction from being with people and relating to them on a social or personal level. Only the Influence-motivated person gets enjoyment from seeing others respond to something they initiated because of the response itself. When a book appears on the shelves, people see it. When people read books, their thoughts change, and the author made that change happen. These writers need to know that somebody is there, and they have reacted.

Many writers are known as wits and raconteurs, going beyond their gifts for written language. With the desire to influence backing them up, some like to be in the limelight; and if they are too shy, too introverted, or too slow to speak well in public they may well hide so that no one knows what they look like, and rely on their writing to speak for them.

One may easily mistake extraversion for Influence motive. The extravert is often Influence-motivated, but the reverse is decidedly not true. J. D. Salinger may be fanatically protective of his privacy precisely because he understands what publicity means. An Achievement-motivated person might not care, or notice, or even understand what it means to be in front of others until it is too late.

Hence these writers. Impress thousands (even millions) even though you may be awkward, shy, or unattractive. Be impressive by proxy! Influence the world! Get people to think what you want them to think!

By now, you may be anxiously examining yourself or writers you know and love, looking for signs of incipient megalomania. Dear Lord, you might think, little did I know of these monsters in our midst. And they seem so nice and retiring.

Take heart. Motives are where you find emotional satisfaction, but the thought does not equal the deed. As T. S. Eliot would put it, between the idea and the reality falls the Shadow. Who knows what evil lurks in the hearts of men? The Shadow—or more prosaically, the values.

Both Hitler and Mother Theresa have demonstrated strong Influence motives; the latter just managed to use her desire to influence in a rather more socialized manner, thanks to her conscious values. The uninhibited person with a high need for Influence may appear to be an egomaniac manipulating others for personal gain. The inhibited, or socialized, Influence motive works for the betterment of a group—using influence to help everyone get along, for example.

Conscious values leap to the fore, saving writers from becoming raving maniacs. Your values shape the way in which your motives emerge into behavior. For example: thirty years ago, American society generally did not accept the idea of women at the executive level of business. But you could be president of the Parent-Teacher Association, and no one would blink an eye. Both are leadership positions, both are appealing to those with the Influence motive. One had society's approval, one did not. Values made the difference.

Unlike a person's motives, which stay relatively stable in adulthood, values can change rapidly in a person or in a society. Today female CEOs, while not as common as they should be, are at least more frequent. Likewise, while the most basic way to satisfy the Influence motive may be to hit something, how many people do that on a daily basis?

As people grow into adulthood, they learn to channel

the raw emotional energy of their motives into appropriate channels. The key to this is restraint. Even going back to Freud, who thought that the primary purpose of society was to force the instincts into a socialized path, to serve society better. Why do we see "immediate gratification" as a dirty phrase? Perhaps because adulthood means the ability to postpone satisfaction to the appropriate time and place, or in the appropriate manner. We call those who cannot do this immature, and for good reason. We might not survive as a species—certainly not as a civilization—if we merely responded to our basic animal needs at whim.

We can measure the tendency to restrain motivational energy with an odd little measure derived from the same exercise (the Picture Story Exercise, or PSE) we use to track motives; it is called Activity Inhibition or AI. This is a simple count of the number of times that the word "not" or "n't" appears in stories written to specific ambiguous pictures over roughly a half-hour period (I know this sounds cryptic, but it works. It will make more sense later). A typical Picture-Story Exercise averages about 450 words long. In an American population, the average adult has around 1.75 "nots," plus or minus 0.25. That means having two or more means you are significantly above average, and thus capable of more restraint or socialized influence. Interestingly, the British need four or more to be considered socialized, which must say something about the respective cultures. In European countries speaking Romance languages (Spanish, French, Italian), having *any* "nots" indicates AI. AI will give you an idea of how much you naturally tend to inhibit or control your motives. This can be useful to you in many ways, and can be applied to any motive.

As a matter of course, I measured the AI of the writers in my database. The average is eighteen. Eighteen! *Nine times* the level of the typical well-socialized person in the USA. More than four times that of a socialized Brit! I had never seen such numbers in my life, and, I knew, neither had anyone else in the field of motivational psychology. What did it mean?[2] I suspect that the very act of putting thoughts to paper (instead of simply acting on them or speaking them) requires a high level of inhibition of motives. It is just plain harder to take a thought and write it down, let alone do so regularly and then edit it.

David McClelland captured it for me quite neatly. His answer amused me: "When a typical person gets mad at you, he hits you. When a mystery writer gets mad at you, he takes a year to write a novel killing you off." How much more socialized can you get? My wife, Toni L. P. Kelner, bumped off her ex-boyfriend in her novel *Country Comes to Town*, a mere fourteen years after she started dating me and eight after she married me. Now that's a mature expression of influence!

But What About Me?

You may now wonder: what about me? What if I lack the Influence motive? Am I doomed to fail as a writer?

Of course not. It just isn't as much fun, or you have to get your fun out of different parts of the process, or you may need to write things that are satisfying to your motives. The issue is that if you get fun out of the process of writing and not the idea of being published, then you might collect a stack of unpublished books. If that's okay with you, then more power to you – and carry on! But I want to be specific here; most people want someone else to read their work, including some people I know who used to claim they didn't need to be published. Some of them were just afraid to admit it, or thought they weren't good enough.

But let's focus on those with motives that may not be as aligned with the task at hand, regardless of what it is.

How do you deal with a lack of motivation? One way is to provide yourself a structure. That is, setting up circumstances that will <u>force</u> you to write—or send out notes, or edit, or whatever part of the process you lack motivation to do. Schedule it in your book, and treat it as a serious appointment. You can also use some of the pleasure-postponing devices mentioned elsewhere; e.g., "I can't do what I want *until* I finish 600 words."

Is it possible to sustain long works this way? Can one write, say, a hundred thousand words through sheer willpower and true grit? Sure! But nobody said it was easy, and it won't be quick. Managing yourself will nearly a full-time job.

A second choice is to adjust your goals, so that you can sustain enough effort to get things done. For example, some people focus on books, but there are a lot of ways to get published, including short essays or short stories, which may be easier to get done through external demands. Or you can write lots of small chunks that can be pulled together into a single document later. A significant percentage of this book is made up of essays, speeches, and the like I pulled together under the overall umbrella, and edited together.

A third choice is to try and hook your existing motive into your work, and that is the intent of the sections above: describing reinforcers for each motive. I like this approach, though it takes a certain amount of refinement in your self-management, because it gives you a longer-term source of energy, making your effort sustainable over time. See below for more on this.

Another choice is to find something else to do that does motivate you. That's not a failure, that's an intelligent approach to making the best of your gifts. On the other hand, I tend to think that having a dream helps you, and the evidence backs me up on this: ambitious, challenging goals that inspire you can help you keep going over longer periods. Often the process of writing or being creative involves being blind to the realities around you, and I think this can be a strength. If you have read this far, you can probably write at least a little. Write short-shorts or something that only requires short bursts. Build up your stamina.

A fifth option is to change yourself. Not the easiest task, when you remember that people's motives typically remain stable over ten-year periods. But it can be done.

In the next section, we'll take a look at how you can manage yourself and your writing.

CHAPTER 9: BEING OVERMOTIVATED OR UNDERMOTIVATED: THE YERKES-DODSON LAW

"Writing is a solitary occupation. Family, friends, and society are the natural enemies of a writer. He must be alone, uninterrupted, and slightly savage if he is to sustain and complete an undertaking."

—Lawrence Clark Powell

"An incurable itch for scribbling takes possession of many and grows inveterate in their insane hearts."

—Juvenal

I know what you're thinking: "What a problem to have! I'll deal with it when I get there." That seems reasonable enough, but you may not realize what is happening until too late to moderate it. While most of this book is obviously aimed at raising your motivation, we should also look at what being overmotivated means.

Remember that motives as we discuss them here are unconscious, emotional drives. That means that they do not necessarily work with your conscious motives, or even your self-awareness. They help shape your conscious actions, but they can also interfere with your conscious choices if they get out of control.

I have seen an experienced, confident adult unable to stop his hands trembling in a simple task—taping cards together, in fact—because of supercharged Achievement motivation (it's a long story with special circumstances). While writing may not seem to be the kind of activity that would get you to reach that particular level of arousal, for some people the excitement of a story can definitely get in their way, let alone the context in which someone must have to write.

One outcome you can expect to see is a level where the drive to write begins overwhelming everything else, as Juvenal (a Roman satirist, apparently commenting on himself) noted some centuries ago. You get distracted from other tasks when you could be writing; you find other activities uninteresting or at least less interesting than writing (troublesome when you are dealing with your significant other—unless he or she also writes); and you may feel guilty when away from the keyboard. For her first book, Kelly Tate set goals that were "too aggressive," and in her desire to meet those goals (Achievement driven, in this case), she exhausted herself. She consistently met her goals—but at a cost to her health and her daily functioning.

I said earlier that motivation can become an addiction —withdrawal symptoms and all. This is where *management* of your motives comes in. You can make them work for you. The first step is to get your motives engaged, aroused, and firing up your writing. The second step is to make sure they do not run your life without your conscious, reasoned permission.

While the typical person will not get to the hand-trembling stage of motivation during the writing process, you may find that strong emotional engagement can interfere with your functioning. If you find yourself to be particularly clumsy, or the words just aren't flowing the way you want, the backlog of emotional energy can become particularly frustrating, and even drive a form of writer's block. Ever fumble in a tense situation?

For example: you are out on a date with a particularly impressive member of the species. This person jams the meters to their pins—just what you want. The pressure is on! You want to look cool, calm, and collected. As you put on your coat, you miss the sleeve. Grinning coolly, you realign your coat and slam your hand through swiftly, ripping the lining. The grin wavers, but you hold firm and ignore that. You whip out your gloves without looking. As you smile in a dazzling manner, you struggle to put a left glove on a right hand. As your face reaches fire-engine red, you try harder, and things just get worse.

Why is this? That question was answered by two primate researchers named Yerkes and Dodson much earlier in this century. They put food-deprived monkeys in a cage within reach of a short stick, which in turn was within reach of a longer stick, which in turn was within reach of a banana. To get the banana, the monkey had to get the short stick, use it to get the long stick, and use the long stick to get the banana. A well-fed monkey was disinterested in the whole process. Why bother, right? A somewhat hungry monkey (say four hours) could and would get the banana, thinking pretty hard for a monkey. But a really hungry monkey (deprived of food for twenty-four hours, for example) could not find a way to get the banana. Instead, he would grab the reachable stick, bang the bars with it, or even throw it at the banana. The hunger – the aroused *motive for food* - clouded his thinking.

Yerkes and Dodson had discovered something very important, one of the few things that psychologists probably should dare to call a law—the Yerkes-Dodson Law, in fact: The relationship between motivation and performance is not a straight line—it is a bell curve[1]. In other words, *moderate motivation leads to the best performance*. Neither excessive arousal nor underarousal will lead to outstanding outcomes. And so we return from monkeys to motivating writing.

The Yerkes-Dodson Law illustrated

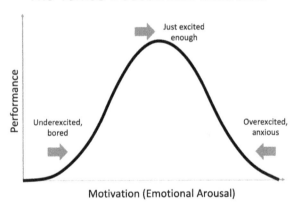

In writing terms, you may have a brilliant idea, and you feel you must get it on paper before it fades. Perhaps time is short, putting on additional pressure. That is the moment when your right hand shifts over one key, and instead of "it was a dark and stormy night," you write "ot was a darl amd stpr,u mogjt." The process of backspacing or deleting seems to take forever. You leap onto the keys, and three words in discover that the first is misspelled. And so forth. As motivational pressure increases beyond the balance point, your ability to function decreases.

So too much motivation can impair your life and your effectiveness. How do you take care of it? And is it possible?

Of course. In the research section below (don't worry, it isn't too gooey), I'll tell you what I found in real live published writers, who suffer just as much as anyone from all the various problems and obstacles described here, including overmotivation. Where do you think all these descriptions came from, anyway?

When asking how you handle overmotivation, think in terms of what tools you can bring to bear. Internal motivation is the problem here, not the solution (unlike most of the rest of this book), so we cannot use that. Other internal traits may assist, including the ability to manage yourself or restrain and focus your motivation, but we will talk about that element later. The other major approach is to use things external to yourself. In other words, control your environment so it helps you. Some of the clues given here around each motive can work both ways. A publicly posted word count, for example, can energize your Influence motive, but posting *both* your accomplishments *and* your goal can help restrain you. Being held accountable to your goal can rein in your target somewhat.

We'll discuss all these things in more detail later, but let's pick out one key thing: You can also try to get outside yourself, and watch your actions. At the extremes it should be easy: on your wedding anniversary, forget about writing and celebrate! What is tricky is when you have choices. That is, you have no special occasion *forcing* you to pay attention. Then you need to find a way to focus your attention. To judge this, I recommend that you consider your records of performance. If you have not written anything in a while, you should probably hit the desk. If you have been writing day and night, you can probably take a break safely enough.

Just remember that there is more to life than writing. (Really!) Once you get properly rolling, you can afford to stop. If you get severely sick, for example, don't worry about missing your daily (or weekly) dose. Get well instead, or substitute a minimal task—noting an idea or doing basic proofreading for half an hour—so that you can say you have done your writing for the day. Otherwise your motivation may rise past the point of being able to work.

On a larger scale, Kelly Tate found herself in a situation where she had to deal with a divorce, two kids, selling one house, buying another house, packing and moving— and she found herself unable to write. So she gave herself a vacation. Rather than winding herself up tight and worrying about it, she said she would write nothing until September 1. (This was July, so she took off the rest of the summer.) By that time she had moved, largely unpacked, and was packing the kids off to school. The date also had personal significance from a lengthy schooling of her own: September is when you get back to work. So she did. She let herself relax instead of ruining herself. Note also that she did not just stop for an indefinite period; instead, she identified a specific interval to hold off writing. She controlled the interval. Not only that, but she made an implicit assumption: that writing was the normal state, and this was a limited time off. She wasn't making it too easy on herself, but she was giving herself permission to take a reasonable break.

The same applies to important family events, vacations,

and so on. Isaac Asimov wrote around 500 books, it is true. But he also hated vacations and had been known to write on a beach. That's fine if you and your loved ones can stand it. Do be sure to *ask* them first. I have no desire to come between you and your family.

Remember we do assume too much motivation here. None of this applies if getting started is your problem. Giving yourself a vacation when you haven't been writing at all is not exactly a positive step (unless you're suffering block from motivational pressure, perhaps). The issue here is that being overmotivated can get in your way.

The Yerkes-Dodson Law and Writer's Block

Opinions about writer's block generally fall into two categories: It's real, or it isn't. Obviously I think it is a genuine phenomenon, but I'd like to take a slightly more nuanced and hopefully encouraging view of the subject, with the help of Yerkes and Dodson.

I think that writer's block is a real issue, but it is a symptom rather than a disease, and indeed something we can treat. When people call it "writer's block," there is this sense of it being a black box, something incomprehensible, which is visited upon you like a plague of editors.

If "The Muse" is a divine creature that gives you your creativity as a gift (see the chapter on The Seven Deadly Myths of Creativity, below), then writer's block is therefore the Anti-Muse: the mysterious removal of your creativity, or at least your productivity. I think there are many kinds of block, and the reasons for it can be made clear enough to help you break it. I've already put a few under each motive, but I want to discuss general principles that you can apply in many ways.

At this point, you know that implicit motivation – emotional drives – keep writers writing. There are two key points beneath that one which may explain how many experience writer's block.

For example, what drives many book-length, mainstream-published writers is, simply enough, the desire to have someone read you, meaning the Influence motive. This means that people with this motive think spontaneously about what makes people tick and how to affect them — obviously good things for a writer, right?

But this motive is not conscious. If I ask you what your motives are, you are likely to give me something different, because what you consciously value as important is different from what emotionally engages you or find fun, and that means you are not always aware of what really drives you to do something.

As a consequence, the very motivation that empowers your writing can also sabotage it, by pushing you towards some other activity that seems just as much fun, or is a more instant form of gratification, such as writing posts on social media (in order to get quick "likes") rather than writing your story.

The other main driver of writer's block is, I believe, the Yerkes-Dodson Law. We've already summarized this above, that the relationship between aroused motivation (or emotion) and performance is a bell curve, not a straight line. What does that mean, practically speaking?

Some people think that the more you push people, the better they respond. If you set very high goals, people will work harder to get there. Reach for the stars!

Except we know it won't work. *Moderate* emotional arousal leads to the best performance. If you are under-aroused, well, you don't even bother to perform. If you are *overaroused*, or overexcited, your emotion gets in the way, or, in some cases, people simply reject the effort it will take to reach a goal, because they already know they will fail. Why bother to wear yourself out in order to fail?

What you want is an edge, but one that you don't fall off of!

So what does this mean for Writer's Block? Let's put it in Yerkes-Dodson terms: sometimes you get blocked because you are not energized enough to write, and sometimes you get blocked because you are <u>too</u> energized (or anxious) to write.

Two cases in point: I interviewed one writer of romantic thrillers. She wrote to escape an abusive marriage, and in her books the evil man would get his comeuppance, usually in a rather satisfyingly violent and awful way. At last she got her big chance: a six-figure advance on her next book, which gave her the ability to leave her husband and take her child with her...after which she became totally blocked, and ceased to write any fiction for years thereafter. The motivation was removed, and so was the writing. Since that time, she wrote a good deal of short nonfiction, like book reviews, wrote several books of other nonfiction and is sneaking back into fiction again, so there is a happy ending here – but she had to find something else to write about. That is the low end of the Yerkes-Dodson – the pressure came off, and she fell down the bell curve.

The high end is familiar to anyone with a contract or a deadline. A deadline energizes people. Why? Because it raises their emotional arousal. But what if you fall behind? Then people start feeling more and more anxious – the goal becomes a stressor instead of a motivator as you go over the top of the bell curve.

I know a science fiction author who wrote one highly praised, award-winning book, but the experience was so stressful that this author never wrote another novel – though this writer was very comfortable appearing on panels to *talk* about writing, even ten years after she had published this novel. Even thinking about writing a novel pushed this person far over the bell curve.

This can couple with Imposter Syndrome, because every time you succeed, you feel more anxious about being "found out" the next time, or one's Achievement motive, because every time you meet a goal, you want to exceed it the next time.

One mystery writer I know well refuses to repeat a plot point, setting, motive, or twist. That's admirable, but when one has written nearly 20 novels and over thirty short stories, you've already hit so many that you might need to repeat one! What's more, this writer tended to elevate it – a minor variation on a plot point wasn't enough, it had to be unrecognizable. My advice was to combine the repeated point with something else that was *not* repeated, and not to interpret a *similar* device as an *identical* one. The self-set goal was getting too high, and was blocking the author from writing until possessing something unique. Even Shake-speare didn't insist on that. And in the mystery field, given that Agatha Christie repeated certain character types dozens of times, and she outsells every book but the Bible, it's probably okay to repeat *some* aspects.

In a related point, T. S. Eliot feared winning the Nobel Prize, because he thought nothing good was ever written by someone who had won – or was he just setting his own expectations too high? In fact, he produced a number of works – good works – after winning in 1948.

While this may seem oversimplistic, what I am

proposing here is that writer's block has two major categories, with various subcategories beneath. Keep these in mind, and it will help you manage your motivation to avoid writer's block – or if you do feel blocked, check this list and see if anything looks familiar:

1. Being undermotivated

a) Because you don't really like the story and are writing what you think you should instead of what you like

b) Because you are having more fun doing something that takes less work, patience, and self-restraint

c) Because you are writing for a personal reason that no longer exists

d) Setting goals that are too low!

2. Being overmotivated

a) Stressing yourself out with your own expectations

b) Letting a change in the outside world lead you to conclude that something is wrong with you

c) External deadline pressure

d) Other internal pressures, e.g., setting goals that are too high

Remember: When the pressure is too high *or* too low, it becomes difficult to think or focus on something. If you take on too many tasks, the pressure mounts; if you lack energy to act, you won't.

SECTION III

HOW WRITERS SEE THEMSELVES

"Artists are meant to be madmen, to disturb and shock us."

—Anne Rice

"An artist is a creature driven by demons. He don't know why they choose him and he's usually too busy to wonder why."

—William Faulkner

"The trade of authorship is a violent, and indestructible obsession."

—George Sand

CHAPTER 10: WHERE WRITERS ARE COMING FROM

Values (and Motives)

"Every asshole in the world wants to write."

—Judith Rossner

Before we get further into the issues of motivation, we should discuss your values. Do you consider writing important? I don't mean that you consider your prose to be deathless wisdom for the ages; just that you think it is important to you to keep doing it. If you don't, if you are not convinced that writing has any meaning for you, quit now!

If, on the other hand, you are writing now and the very idea of quitting makes you snort with derision, then you value writing. The definition of a value (called an *explicit* motive to distinguish it from the unconscious *implicit* motive) is "something you consciously consider important." There are dramatic differences between values and implicit motives.

Implicit motives are primitive emotional structures. It appears likely that you can find something like motives in nearly any mammal. Can you see your typical dog as being happy about a relationship, or a cat upset when they can't influence you? Values, on the other hand, appear to be limited to those animals fortunate or unfortunate enough to have very complex thinking abilities: *homo sapiens sapiens*, and quite probably some of our simian cousins.

Values are cognitive in nature, meaning that they are conscious thoughts. They may go back a long way in your life, but at the core they can bend and change much more readily than motives. College students who refused ever to compromise with "The Establishment" have become lawyers and bankers; H. L. Mencken, the supposedly permanent bachelor and witty critic of marriage, changed his tune when he found the woman of his dreams. When people become parents, many new values appear, as a product of the equally new demands on them. Suddenly developing whole sets of tasks and rules become necessary, and your priorities shift dramatically.

There is nothing wrong with that. Things change, and the things you value can change with them. Values are adaptive structures—they allow you to roll with the punches, and decide what is important for this time and this place. The values of a single twenty-year-old are very different from those of a married forty-year-old with children—and that is right for both of them.

I'm not speaking on behalf of ethical relativism here; I'm talking about your priorities. When I initially wrote this, I had a three-week-old in the room across the hall. Before she was born, I had a list of priorities of importance; she has now abruptly been inserted into the list ahead of many other things. My core values have not changed, but the relative importance of some have. When she cried, I dropped whatever else I was doing.

This shifted again when we had a second child with medical issues. Until the issues were resolved (which they were by 10 months, in case you were curious), she occupied a larger percentage of our focus than she would have otherwise. We felt equally *loving* of both children (and still do, now that both are in their twenties), but we had to prioritize our time and efforts to address critical issues. We added a new value, which we could phase out after the issues were resolved.

As I have noted, both values and motives are kinds of motivation. My focus in this book is primarily on the deeper emotional ones, because, as they are *not* as flexible, your life may flow better if you learn how to live with them than if you try to change them. In addition, motives sustain behavior better than values—motives provide emotional energy, but values cost energy and effort. Yet a strong-willed value can put the kibosh even on a strongly motive-based action, because values constrain which behaviors are acceptable, regardless of implicit motivation.

A motive, being general and primitive in nature, gets no more specific than "I feel good knowing I have had an impact on others" or "I feel good when I have done something better." They are, after all, built into our brains to some extent—into the hardware, so to speak—which means they should be relatively simple. Values can be far more specific and complex because they are formed above the level of basic brain biology—in the software, to continue the analogy. They *focus* the energy the right way.

If you wish to be a writer—or if you just wish to write —you should sit down and think about it. It does not matter what other people think of writing—only you. But if you cannot convince yourself that it matters to you, why should you bother to read this book, let alone make an effort to write?

> **Remember:** Value your writing! Your writing should be important to you.

If you have read this far, it seems likely that you do care to some degree—at least a good eight to ten pages worth, at least. Then you can take this chapter as a cautionary note. There are people who will pooh-pooh your efforts, ridicule your ambitions, and even dare to criticize your writing. Avoid them. They're just jealous, because they don't think they could write themselves, or they have an exaggerated sense of the talent needed. Maybe they just don't like you. Why should people spend their time preventing you from doing something you want to do, which hurts no one and may contribute something worthwhile? Who would want to wound someone that way? As my mother used to say about people who were rude to me: "Consider the source!" And get yourself away from it. You need to stay focused on your own values, and no one else's.

Many writers had people make fun of their ambition. Some of them grow up, get rich and famous, and get their revenge. Agatha Christie had an unhappy first marriage to a dashing RAF officer, and a happy one to an archeologist. Note how many mean, rotten characters in her books are dashing young officers, and how many nice archeologists you find in the same books. Many mystery writers of my acquaintance take the opportunity to bump off people they don't like in their books—suitably disguised, to be sure. You can satisfy your motivation in many ways!

Our purpose in this book is to crank up your existing

unconscious motivation so it pushes you to write, and that is an easier task if you have some conscious values pulling from the other end. The types of motivation described below—the needs for Achievement, Affiliation, and Influence—can all be put in value terms as well; some people think it *important* to meet and beat goals (for example), but do not really get *turned on* by it. These people have the Achievement value, but not the Achievement motive. Contrariwise, some enjoy having an impact on people (Influence motive), but think it is bad or manipulative to try to influence others (low Influence value). These people have a negative value associated with influencing. This is a common attitude in the United States, for example. After all, the Americans threw out the power-mongers in 1776, right? (Of course the same attitude is prevalent in the United Kingdom as well!)

Try to line up your values and motives, or even have them both tugging on the same task, and you will have an enormous well of energy on which to draw, both from your heart and your head. Make it easy on yourself to write, because then your head will be saying "I think it is important for me to write" while your heart says, "I enjoy writing."

Does this always work? No, if only because life is complicated. You may have equally important, mutually exclusive values. You may have immediate needs (like eating, or crises) that take over your longer-term desires. This happens to everyone, every day, and that is why it is useful to have both values and motives—one can pick up for the other at times.

But don't forget one can *block* the other, too. "I want to have an impact and write" (motive) but "I should spend more time doing my bills" (value). Or: "It is important that I write tonight to stay on schedule" (value), but "I want to talk to a friend who is in town for a limited time" (motive). This is why I recommend you ignore or avoid those who criticize your writing practices. They will create a new value in you, if you let them.

To be clear, I do think that *professional* critics serve a highly valuable purpose in helping maintain standards of what writing should be, and no writer should assume total mastery of his or her craft. But for some people, criticism equals rejection. If you are a person who thinks that way, then stay away from critics, at least until you can develop a thicker skin.

> **Remember**: Values are conscious thoughts, motives are emotional drivers. Try to link them where you can.

Self-Image and Social Role—Thinking About Yourself as a Writer

> "The aim, if reached or not, makes great the life; Try to be Shakespeare, leave the rest to fate."

> —Robert Browning

The motives are among the deepest and the most driving characteristics of people, shaping their entire lives. However, that does not mean they cannot be shaped, diverted, redirected, or even thwarted. Your expectations of yourself or your role can influence even the power of these emotional drives.

If you see yourself as ineffectual, you are less likely to act, because after all, it won't work, right? Why take chances? If you see yourself as master of your own destiny, you may be willing to take more risks, because ultimately you believe it will work out, despite the many obstacles and opponents you may face.

In this section I want to trace back where writers come from (who were they before they were writers?), how they see themselves, what impact it has on them for good or evil, and then take that to how you might see yourself. Finally, when you have accomplished something, do you see it as inevitably yours or as a happy accident? This, too, relates to how you see yourself and the fruits of your labors.

Here are the questions we will answer or discuss as we go:

- Where do they come from?
- How do they see themselves? Does it help?
- How do you see yourself?
- How do you attribute your successes and failures?

The Background of Writers—Where Do They Come from?

"When I read my first book, I started writing my first book. I have never not been writing."

—Gore Vidal

"Boozing does not necessarily have to go hand in hand with being a writer, as seems to be the concept in America. I therefore solemnly declare to all young men trying to become writers that they do not actually have to become drunkards first."

—Nelson Aldrich

"Why did I write? what sin to me unknown
    Dipt me in ink, my parents', or my own?"

—Alexander Pope

As noted elsewhere in this book, a myth persists that writers are party animals working in the wee hours of the morning because they spend all their other time drinking, partying, or sleeping off the hangover. I know many people love to pore over an author's biographical notes to see what kind of checkered past he or she brought to the work, and I've done it myself, which brought up the question of whether there is a "best place" to come from at all. Where do writers come from? Most writers today do not start out as writers, because they cannot afford to unless they had a large trust fund (like Larry Niven, who thanks a family member for just that in one book, because it enabled him to write and to get rejected—and to learn—for a solid year).

My study of writers indicates that no single job is "required" as a prerequisite for a good writer. In fact, you could argue exactly the opposite (and some have): that "real world" experience strengthens your writing. All experience becomes grist for the writer's mill. I have collected a few professions followed by published writers at some time in their lives, and sometimes at the same time, since writing isn't particularly well paid:

Accountant, Actor (Lauren Bacall wrote her own autobiography!), Advertising professional, Agent for MI-5, Anthropologist, Artist, Astrophysicist, Biologist, Cartoonist, Chicken Farmer (Douglas Adams), Chemists of all stripes, Computer scientist, Egyptologist, Engineer, Financial

Advisor, Historian, Jockey, Journalist (okay, so this is sort of cheating), Lawyer, Librarian, Magician (Houdini was not a gifted writer, but he published!), Mathematician, Medical doctor, Mother, Navy officer, Neurologist, Nurse, Ophthalmologist (Sir Arthur Conan Doyle—he didn't get a lot of patients, so he wrote instead), Philologist, Philosopher, Priest (including Pope John Paul II, who wrote poetry), Psychologist (yes, besides me), Senator, Speechwriter, Stripper (former stripper, in Tony Fennelly's case), Technical Writer, Therapist, Veterinarian, Zoologist.

Almost any job can contribute to your ability to write; at the least, you have experiences on which to draw. Jobs that require you to produce material on a regular basis (e.g., journalism, advertising) will blast you out of reliance on a muse, because if you cannot write to deadline, you are out of a job in minutes. This also builds up your self-image as being able to write on demand.

Some writers like a writing-related job such as editing a magazine, because they stay attached to publishing; others like manual labor, because it has nothing to do with other people's writing, and their minds are freed to think about their own.

Be what you are for your day job. It does not have to affect your writing, except in a positive way. Or as one writer said when asked how long it took him to write his most recent book: "my entire life."

CHAPTER 11: ASSESSING SELF-IMAGE

"Why should a man who loves good painting, good wine, and good food, living in a happy and well-deserved retirement, suffer in the evening of life what all writers must suffer—in Masefield's phrase 'The long despair of doing nothing well?'"

—Graham Greene

"The act of writing puts you in confrontation with yourself, which I think is why writers assiduously avoid writing. The number of alcoholic writers makes a lot of sense because if you're going to be face to face with yourself, maybe it's better if you don't recognize that person."

—Fran Lebowitz

Writers, like all people, struggle with who they are. A writer who is unpublished wonders if she is really a writer; a stay-at-home parent questions priorities of kids versus writing and then wonders if he is really cut out to be a writer; someone who gets rejected thinks she is really no good as a writer.

Being published doesn't always help either. The paperback writer doesn't feel like a real author; the genre writer doesn't feel literary enough; the successful writer wants to be a bestseller; the bestseller wants to sell to Hollywood; the writer with dozens of movies produced from his books wants creative control or to be a director like Clive Barker.

Some people know they are writers, but some do not. Some, like Robert A. Heinlein or Kurt Vonnegut, stumble into it—the first, because he was in ill health, needed money, and it seemed easy work (it was, for him), and the second because he had a personal story he had to get out but needed to learn how first. Some are obviously writers, but do not take either the profession or themselves seriously. And some want to be writers, work to be writers, study to be writers, but always question whether they can really do it, even after they have a shelf-full of awards. And a few people think they are writers, then change their mind as they become better educated and realize how far they have to go. Many stop there, but a few, like Robert Silverberg, take that acquired humility and use it to drive them to work all the harder. The same self-image can propel different people in different directions. In this section, I am hoping that I can help ensure that you always see yourself as a writer first. You may prefer to see yourself as a writer in training, but still—a writer first.

There is one literary conference on speculative fiction in Massachusetts, known as Readercon, which I have attended for years. For several years running they had a panel called "Hacks vs. the Art Police." Some writers proclaimed themselves proudly to be hacks. They defined themselves as writers who did not obsess with literary attention, but just kept writing books people wanted to read. Other people would take that label and use it to whip themselves. They turned the label of "hack" into a symbol of success. And remember that Shakespeare, Dickens and Coleridge could all be considered hacks by some standards.

I have collected a number of words people have used to describe writers below. Not all are complimentary, but remember that most words can be used in more than one way. The question to ask yourself is "which of these are me?" After that we can decide which might be helping you and which might not. Just try out the directions below:

Using the Writer's Self-Image Sort

1. Read the list completely, and ask yourself the question "what resembles me as a writer?"
2. Sort the list into two groups: "more like me as a writer" and "less like me as a writer." They do not have to be the same size, but you should try to have at least fifteen in each group.
3. Sort each of the two groups into two more groups, again: "more like me" and "less like me." This time, try to have at least seven in each group. You should now have four groups, each from seven to twenty words.
4. Take the topmost and bottommost groupings and select the top and bottom six items. Force the choices if necessary.
5. Compare the top six to the bottom six (the top

15% compared to the bottom 15%—okay, 14.3% really). What do you see?

This kind of thinking tool helps you to get a grip on a complex issue: how you see yourself. There are no "right" or "wrong" answers, only the answers you identify. However, the comparison might help to see what kind of person you think you are and what kind of person you feel you are not.

Don't just do the "like me" list. You need contrast for the most revealing results. For example:

Top Six	Bottom Six
Artist	Failure
Creator	Hack
Catalyst	Untalented
Growing	Amateur
Persistent	Literary
Wordsmith	Struggler

What kind of person does this sound like? Yes, it is a real person. Does this person sound confident? The kind of person you have to force away from the typewriter? Well, perhaps not entirely. This person sees him/herself as persistent and growing, but not necessarily obsessed or a craftsperson. This person might be susceptible to the "muse" myth or the "artistic temperament" myth.

Be alert to what you put in, and what you do not. This person considers him/herself talented and artistic, but not literary. This could be an innovator, or it could be an eccentric who doesn't feel the need to see what others have done.

Don't treat this list as comprehensive; there may be more. If you find it hard to agree with any of these items, come up with your own. Identifying your self-image is very valuable to choosing your next steps. The next section discusses particular aspects of self-image that seems epidemic among writers I have studied; keep your short-list in mind as we stroll through the minds of a few writers.

Table 1: The Writer's Q-Sort

Advocate	Entertainer	Plugger
Amateur	Expert	Popular
Artist	Failure	Professional
Avoidant	Gifted	Reliable
Catalyst	Growing	Sporadic
Challenged	Hack	Storyteller
Comedian	Important	Struggler
Crafts-person	Impulsive	Success
Creator	Laborer	Talented
Dilettante	Lackadaisical	Teacher
Disciplined	Literary	Untalented
Dogged	Missionary	Wordsmith
Doing a Job	Obsessed	Worker
Educator	Persistent	Writer

Fooling the Watcher

> I fear these stubborn lines lack power to move: O sweet
> Maria, empress of my love! These numbers will I tear,
> and write in prose.

> —William Shakespeare

Remember our earlier discussion of extrinsic versus intrinsic motivation? The expectations of others or yourself can inhibit your motives to write. At one literary conference I attended a panel titled "Fooling the Watcher." The entire panel of people—several award-winners among them, who had sold short stories, novels, and movies—discussed the difficulty of writing past or around their own internal critic, the voice of doubt. One member of this panel was so fearful of self-doubts that she wrote inside a trash can (that is, she put a pad inside a clean plastic bin on her desk) so as to avoid actually seeing the prose she wrote, and thus defeat the doubting voice within. Another panelist described turning down the brightness of the computer screen so she could not see the actual words. To my amazement, everyone on the panel and a number of people in the audience all nodded in agreement. "Yes, I understand that," they seemed to be saying. Some even said, "oh, that's a great idea!" This is a surprisingly common feeling. That panel helped propel this book as much as any other single experience I have had.

One way to defeat "the watcher" is to establish your own sense of self-worth; others, such as those above, simply found ways to avoid the watcher, unfortunately up to and including alcoholism and drug addiction (not recommended as an approach, by me or that writer).

Please note that the watcher is not a complete avatar of evil. This same panel agreed that sometimes you should invoke the editor and critic, or your work will never achieve competence. The question is when. If the critic emerges before you finish your first sentence, you may never reach the second, no matter how powerful your motivation.

In fact, a poor self-image can enlist motivation to prevent positive action. Take, for example, the Influence motive. It focuses on having an impact and sensitizes people to the reactions of others. A strong and positive self-image coupled with a strong Influence motive leads someone to face a crowd and say "what an opportunity to have an impact!" The same degree of Influence motive chained to a poor self-image will think "what an opportunity to embarrass myself!" One sees the positive potential for impact, the other sees the negative potential. The same applies for other motives: Achievement motive drives perfectionism and dissatisfaction with one's skill; Affiliation motive drives the fear of rejection by others. Who is right, the optimist or the pessimist?

Both are right. But the optimist will take the opportunity and possibly get advantage out of it, whereas a pessimist might withdraw without ever having a chance to gain from it. If you do not believe you can write and publish, I guarantee you will not, because you will not bother to try. If you try, you may fail, but if you don't bet, you can't win.

That last sentence exemplifies a risk-assessment, and a value around what one's best choice: "Better to have written and failed than never to have written at all." If you do not believe that, it will be very hard to write and do something with it, because it can undermine or even corrupt your own motives to try. You may have read the statement that the person who doesn't read has no advantage over the person who can't read.[1] Similarly, the person who *doesn't* write has no advantage over the person who *can't* write.

You may wonder why this feeling appears so prevalent, and I assure you it is so common that I can stand in front of any group of five or more writers and refer to the "watcher," and easily half the heads nod in agreement, even if they have never heard the term before. I believe it is because the critical observer is an essential part of the creative self. (See Section IV: Creativity for a discussion of the "generate and select" mechanism of creativity.) This is how you get better: Generativity without selectiveness produces gibberish. Note, for example, the many self-published or online-published cranks with theories about how Einstein was wrong (for example) or how medical science conspires to contaminate your body. Many such screeds show a lack of editing. So do "flames" on the Internet—writing which comes straight from the emotional center but did not stop at the mental editor on the way out. To balance both halves of your creativity requires a good deal of thoughtful effort.

Again, it is worth spending some time analyzing how you see yourself. It may take some time. To help you think about it, let us discuss what I have seen in terms of self-expectation and self-image that affects the ability to perform.

Writing on Demand and to Demand ("Can I Write on Demand?")

Writers who are overly concerned with the quality of their writing may refuse to finish, or edit over and over again. There are several reasons for this, primarily a lack of confidence in their own writing.

"I used to take a long time with my writing, because I was afraid if I wrote quickly, it would not be good. I discovered when I had to write on demand, that my prose did not change."

—Geary Gravel

"I love deadlines. Deadlines are the only way I get anything done. I don't worry about the quality, because, hey, I didn't have time for that. I had a deadline."

Ellen Kushner

"I love deadlines. I love the whooshing noise they make as they go by."

Douglas Adams

This is the quality of *letting go of self-criticism*, and some people cannot do so without an external source. Their own high standards/lack of confidence force them to rewrite until stopped.

The concept of a deadline or indeed of any external demand intimidates some. Several reasons apply here. First, a deadline is an *extrinsic* motivator. A deadline can establish in your mind the image that your writing belongs not to you, but to someone else. Therefore it lacks fun—you are not writing for your own pleasure, but because it is just a job. Technical writers may not feel that way, because they always write on demand, so they might be able to get past that; likewise, reporters at least get personal credit for their work, which means it is theirs despite editing. Nevertheless, if they draw too clear a distinction between their personal writing and their work writing, the same effect may occur. Ideally, you can use deadlines to arouse your motivation rather than delegating responsibility and ownership to someone else. With or without a deadline, your work ultimately belongs to you. Good goal-setting creates an external motive that supports your own.

Another issue here is that the pressure of the blank page may inhibit starting the book at all. The expectations are too high even beginning. Some people find ways to give themselves permission to be bad. One writer I interviewed referred to his "zero draft" — the draft before first draft. This writer being a very meticulous and methodical person, I suspect that subconsciously he felt he had to be as meticulous on his first draft. He cites his discovery of this approach as being very important for his writing.

CHAPTER 12: THE IMPOSTOR SYNDROME ("AM I REALLY A WRITER?")

"I'm never going to be famous. My name will never be writ large on the roster of 'Those Who Do Things.' I don't do anything. Not one single thing. I used to bite my nails, but I don't even do that anymore."

—Dorothy Parker

The expectations of others also raise fears in a person about whether or not one is any good. "I'm just an impostor," someone thinks. "Now they'll be sure to find out." Having others waiting on one's own work makes one feel inadequate to the task, because the threat of failure outweighs the promise of success. Failure is easy to imagine, since there are so many ways to fail. Anticipation of success requires a strong self-confidence, or at least an assurance born of experience.

The imposter syndrome has been written about elsewhere, including in this book (see the Seven Deadly Myths, below), but it merits some more discussion: in brief, it is the belief that you have fooled people into thinking you are good. In the course of observing a panel of writers who all suffered from this to some degree, an audience member asked "how many awards, how many books does it take until you believe you are a writer?" One writer just laughed. Barry B. Longyear, the writer in question, had already won some of the highest awards offered in his genre, and published over ten books, had one story turned into a movie, and he still suffered from this. One of his negative responses had been to drink, because drinking silenced the doubting voice. Motivation studies reveal that alcohol makes people feel strong and powerful—but at a price, including the loss of the activity inhibition that enables you to channel the energy of the Influence motive in the first place. This writer paid the price of alcoholism and rehabilitation, and ultimately a decline in writing ability while intoxicated and an even greater stress while sober.

If you see yourself as (= your self-image is an) impostor, success will not magically change that. Instead, you will just think you have fooled them again, and (implicitly), when they find you out, your punishment will be that much greater for daring to win an award, or publish so many books. Without a clear measurable standard that you will believe, no measure will ever make you "good enough." And too many people tend to decide the measure was mistaken if they reach it, if only because they feel no different. In some ways Hemingway succumbed to his own expectations of himself to be a "real man." When in his old age he suffered physical disability and apparently felt he could no longer "be a man," he committed suicide. We are our own worst taskmasters, and only we can change that.

Sometimes something as strong as therapy or psychoactive chemicals (by which I mean <u>legal</u>, preferably non-destructive drugs) is needed, but in brief one needs a change of self-image. Writers often hold several false assumptions and compulsions, especially (though by no means entirely) those in genres where they can hear from their fans, such as mystery and SF. Here are a few:

1. *I must write another book/article/story/etc.* False. As noted above, some people have one book in them. There is nothing wrong with that, certainly not if it is a good book! I'd guess most people want to avoid the situation described in the song "Number Three" by They Might Be Giants: "I've got just two songs in me, and I just wrote the third." Nobody requires you to write except you. If you have a contract, that's a different matter, of course, but the principle still applies. Just because someone else wants you to write a book does not mean *you* want to write a book. The moral struggles about taking money to produce a book you do not wish to write I leave to you. For many professional writers, the work involved in writing a book they do not wish to write is much preferable to the work involved in being something other than a writer—"honest work," as some have described it. It happens to many people. The good news is that with enough practice you can write a decent work even if it feels like pulling teeth all the way. Joe Haldeman describes one book that sounded like fun when he contracted for it and turned out to be agonizing. When he finished, he was surprised to note that it was actually pretty good.

2. *I must continue publishing to be a writer.* Not so! A writer writes—no more, no less. Publishing is vulnerable to the

vicissitudes of the market, the whims of editors and agents, the presence of money to spend on authors, and so on. Sometimes the best writing cannot get published for years because it goes far ahead of or beyond the current state of the art. William Gibson, now recognized as a fine writer and the originator (if not the only practitioner) of the "cyberpunk" subgenre of SF, shopped around his first short story in that oeuvre, "Johnny Mnemonic," for *four years*. When the story finally sold, it attracted the attention of Terry Carr, an innovative editor who was then assembling a series of novels from new writers. He asked for a novel from Gibson, who wrote *Neuromancer*, the novel that set off the whole cyberpunk movement and coined the word "cyberspace." Eventually this led to the original short story becoming a movie. Frank Herbert took *Dune* to 27 publishers. Richard Bach took *Jonathan Livingston Seagull* to over forty publishers. Whatever the intrinsic worth of each of these books and stories now, was it less when not yet published?

Remember that many people have material and few publishers have holes in their lineup. It takes time and effort to match the two up.

On the other hand, numerous writers have published one book, and no one says to these people "oh, you used to be a writer." No one worth listening to, at any rate. Remember *To Kill a Mockingbird*.

If formal publishing does not matter to you, this will not be an issue at all, of course. The Internet has provided a home for a number of writers who prefer to put their work out under their complete control. (There are disadvantages to this, too, but that's for another chapter.)

3. *I have to write a story that someone (my mother, my friends, my colleagues, my roommate, my spouse) will want to read.* No, the only person who needs to read your story is you. Of course you want others to read it (or you probably would not be a writer in the first place), but you cannot afford to be limited by one person's tastes. Nor can you be limited by the expectations or problems of those you happen to know. Why are they qualified to judge? Even if they bring some editorial discernment to the task, they may not like what you like. Their motives may well differ from yours. If instead you are just embarrassed by writing (say) a sexually explicit novel that your mother might read, then write under a pen name. Many others have, if only to disguise what they considered their lesser works.

4. *I must do things (live my life) the way X does, or I am not really a writer.* This belief relates to the way you live your life. If there are a myriad ways to write, how much greater are the number of choices for living? Sometimes there seems to be as much fiction about the creative process as there is created by that process: "You must suffer for your art." "Great writers are alcoholics and have terrible lives."

There are even myths about simply being a writer: "You should always carry business cards with your name on it, so you never miss an opportunity to sell yourself as a writer." No, I'm not kidding, that's a real piece of advice—but not from me. It applies more to freelancers who have published work under their belts, and who wish to grab editors and the like on sight. "You should go to conventions and schmooze with everyone in sight." Contrast that with: "Writers can't go out and meet people." "Writers must sit in their office and write for eight hours a day." "You have to get to know the editors personally." Forget 'em all. There is no single pattern to successful writers other than writing. Some habits may assist you in your writing career (e.g., delivering your manuscripts on time), but even then they are not obligatory to writing in the first place.

As for a few writers' lifestyles: Poe was nowhere near as unhappy or alcoholic as he was painted—a personal enemy wrote the primary biography. Eugene O'Neill became a great writer *after* he quit drinking and then wrote *Long Day's Journey into Night*. Isaac Asimov, one of the most prolific writers of our time, was a teetotaler. So was the multi-genre writer Harlan Ellison. Lots of writers are happy as clams, and write all sorts of things. No two are alike.

5. *I should listen to my fans/the critics/the reviewers/etc. and go with what they recommend.* Heinlein's Laws of Writing include: "Never rewrite, except to editorial order." Good critics can help you improve your writing craft; bad ones or even mediocre ones may not understand what you are trying to do. There may be no particular demand for your voice, but if you want to write and publish, you must listen to yourself *first*. Don't let people automatically convince you of their opinions, even those you respect. If you believe they have a point, and that you have flaws in your technique (who doesn't?) then change your technique and keep going. My rule of thumb is: the shorter and less specific the criticism, the less likely it is to be useful. Smart-ass dismissals are for the critic's benefit ("See how clever I am?"), not yours.

6. *I can only write in one genre effectively.* Let's look at the evidence. Harlan Ellison, noted at the beginning of this

book, writes in the genres of speculative fiction, mainstream fiction, horror, fantasy, humor, erotica, opinion essays, movie reviews, and television reviews; and in the formats of short story, short essay, longer essays, screenplays, novella, and novel. Robert Graves wrote fiction (e.g., *I, Claudius*) to support his poetry; so did Mario Puzo (*The Godfather*). Edgar Allen Poe wrote newspaper stories, horror, science fiction, psychological thrillers, poetry, humor, and essays. Shel Silverstein wrote highly sentimental children's books (e.g., *The Giving Tree, The Missing Piece*), wicked parodies of children books (e.g., *Uncle Shelby's ABZ Book*), and highly explicit adult stories and cartoons for *Playboy*. Sarah Smith has written academic works, science fiction short stories, a mystery novel (*The Vanished Child*), a novel set in early 1900s Paris (*The Knowledge of Water*), technical writing, and a computer-moderated "interactive novel" called *King of Space*. Shakespeare wrote tragedies, comedies, historical (what we would now call "based on a true story") plays, and poetry. The concept of a genre is a very recent one, started in the "pulp magazine" era of the twenties, and established for the convenience of marketing books and magazines to a selected audience, not because it represents what writers actually do. Genres have even been invented by a few writers who made them stand on their own. Stephen King has, almost single-handedly, made the horror genre distinct from fantasy and gothics, and even distinguished it from what horror used to be— Poe and Lovecraft, to name two noteworthy horror writers, differ sharply from King. If you enjoy writing in a genre, that's fine. Don't assume you have to do so. In the heyday of the pulp magazines, the only way to survive as a writer was to churn out stories in whatever form would sell, so writers of pulp fiction wrote westerns, science fiction, mysteries, sports stories, whatever would bring them some cash.

For that matter, don't assume that you should not write within a genre, either. Literary snobs tend to forget or overlook the fact that Dickens was a hack, Hemingway was a journalist, Faulkner wrote for Hollywood, and Shakespeare wrote to entertain the masses (using dirty puns and cheap humor). Thinking of yourself as writing in a ghetto does not do wonders for your confidence or self-assurance.

7. *I can only write in one length effectively.* The same applies to length as to genre. Some people will say "you have to start out writing short stories before you move on to novels." Balderdash. Write whatever you want. The choice of length comes about through a combination of personal preference, the requirements of the story or issue, and the availability of a market. The novella is a fine and useful length that is almost impossible to get published, because it is too short for a separate book (in most cases, except for the occasional "double" books, once done by Ace Books and now by Tor Books), and most magazines don't like to fill up that much of their length with a single story, or only one per issue. So few people write *and publish* novellas, at least in paper form. Some think the Internet and web-based magazines have saved the novella as an art form. Of course, if you write only for fun, no problem. Similarly, the novel tends to be more effective economically than the short story, since it stays in print longer and generates more money over the long term, while an experienced writer does not expend that much more effort over a novel than over a good short story. On the other hand, the tight structure of a short story, while difficult for some, may be just what you

need to get something finished properly. Some say that the short-short story is the most difficult form, but Fredric Brown was famous for writing dozens of them, and Harlan Ellison has written virtually nothing else. I doubt that they refused to write "easier" stuff.

People also forget that each length had to be invented. The "novel" was invented only a few centuries ago. The fine distinctions noted by many magazines and awards (novel, novelette, novella, short story, short-short...) came about much more recently.

8. *Only hardcover books are "real" books.* Many mystery, science fiction, and fantasy authors in recent years started with "paperback originals" and moved on to hardcover deals. Sue Grafton, for example, with her alphabet series of mysteries (e.g., *A Is for Alibi, B Is for Burglar*, etc.) started in paperback, advanced to hardback in later books, then got her earlier books republished in hardback! Paperbacks are likely to get first-time fiction authors better sales and more readers, since people are more willing to invest in a paperback than a hardcover for an unknown quantity. More recently, people started by publishing online, in web-based magazines, for example, or through e-book publishers. Some are extremely successful without ever having a book in paper form, let alone between hard covers. Nonfiction books differ, of course, because you can check qualifications. So are books with huge marketing budgets or a unique "hook." Even then that only distinguishes their covers and size, not their quality.

9. *I'm not a real writer if I don't write full time.* Isaac Asimov, one of the most prolific writers of our time, did not go full time for ten years after he began publishing regularly.

He finally did switch to full time writing because he realized that his part-time writing paid as well as or better than his full-time university professorship, and full-time writing would therefore pay more. On the other hand, some people are not cut out to write full time; most people cannot afford it. Either way, it bears no relation to the fact of writing or the role of writer.

10. *I have to write with a pen/a typewriter/a word processor to be truly creative.* A writer writes. Some use computers, some use fountain pens. They may even prefer their tools and perform better with them: Harry Turtledove writes in longhand, Eleanor Arnason only uses a Cross or Parker ballpoint pen, L. Ron Hubbard used a specially designed typewriter with single keys for "the" and "of," Gregory Maguire writes in notebooks, Spider Robinson uses an Apple Macintosh computer. Graham Greene wrote: "My two fingers on a typewriter have never connected with my brain. My hand on a pen does. A fountain pen, of course. Ball-point pens are only good for filling out forms on a plane." Nevertheless, do not confuse the tool with the process. It is an interesting historical note that every time a new device was invented to make writing easier, some benighted "artist" would complain that it took the soul from writing. This has been recorded for the fountain pen (replacing the quill, for Pete's sake!), the typewriter, the electric typewriter, and the word processor. No doubt the first person to actually draw a story in mud bricks was criticized for removing the creativity of the spoken tale. Ignore these people. Use what you like, or what makes it easier for you. John Barth finds neatly typed first drafts "paralyzing," but Ralph Keyes finds the "elastic quality" of computers, where nothing is indelible, reassuring because "mistakes

can be corrected, improvements made, material added."
By the same token, you need not buy the tools these
people use just because they like them. The fact that I
simply adore my Apple Macintosh does not mean you
have to give up your fountain pen. As Fran Lebowitz
noted: "I don't write fast enough to require a word
processor." Isaac Asimov, on the other hand, wrote *too*
fast (and too cleanly) to require a word processor rather
than a typewriter for anything shorter than a novel.
These are the trappings, not the substance. (Although
they may help to circumvent other obstacles; as one
person put it, "if Dickens had had a word processor
[instead of writing in longhand], a degree in English
literature would take eight years instead of four.")

CHAPTER 13: ATTRIBUTION THEORY

"Ever tried. Ever failed. No matter. Try again. Fail again. Fail better."

—Samuel Beckett

"I have not failed. I've just found 10,000 ways that won't work."

—Thomas Alva Edison

Attribution theory is a body of psychological study devoted to people's attributions around their successes and failures. It has been linked to a range of long-range impacts, not least of which is success in your job and in your life. For our purposes this is part of the feedback loop that begins with the completion or failure of a task. In other words, when you finish a book, why do you feel you managed to finish it? Is it due to your ability, dedication, and spunk? Or did you simply get lucky?

I do not refer to how people politely aver when praised, I'm talking about how *you* feel about your accomplishments or lack thereof. It can make a difference to your next accomplishment—or your lack thereof.

It'll Never Be Like This Again...

I have heard one writer talk about her fear of writing a second book. For her first book, she had nine wonderful months where she enjoyed writing. She stopped at one point and said, "This is too good to last." In this case she was correct: a week later, she lost her job, her home, and her time to write. It took two and a half years of Hell (her phrase) to finish. Even though she won awards for that book, her first published, she was afraid to start again, lest it be as painful the second time. (Though I will note that she seemed to thoroughly enjoy talking about writing on panels at conferences, apparently far more than the writing itself. Remember the trap for the Influence motivated is substituting instant gratification for writing!) As of this writing, she has not written another novel in over fifteen years, but she has managed some short stories, a novella, and essays, so she has at least continued to write.

This kind of reaction reminds me of the clinically depressed. One attribute of the depressed person is that they never think things are all that great, and, more importantly, that things will never get any better than this "not that great" state. Part of therapy for depressed people (in addition to medication in some cases) is to help them to remember that they have been happy before, and they have been depressed before, and they have come out of it.

In other words, things change. You cannot assume that your whole life will be like one small portion of it.

You may wonder where attribution theory comes in. Deciding that a single experience will happen all the time is an example of an attribution—in this case, that a failure is due to an enduring characteristic of the task itself. Clear differences in performance between people relate to their attributions. In brief, attributions fall into three dimensions: is the cause of the failure or success internal (me) or external (outside me); is the cause of the failure or success a temporary event or an enduring phenomenon; and is the cause of the failure or success a specific reason or a global one? The worst-case for most jobs is a failure attribution of internal/stable/global: I failed because I am no good at all. The attribution is internal (I am), stable (no good), and global (at all). Of course, if you are that bad, then there is nothing you can do about it, is there? Or at least that is what you think.[1]

Optimistic people do the opposite. "This time, in this place, it was not possible for me to succeed." In other words, it was time-specific (this time), situation-specific (this place), and external (it was not possible—it wasn't me). Some research I participated in suggests that it may be appropriate to make an internal/temporary/specific attribution, when the focus is in improvement. For example: "It wasn't my doing, but I'm responsible, and I'll fix it." Change is a normal part of our world. People grow, and alter, and the world alters as well. If you condemn yourself to a certain state, saying, "that's just the way I am," you are not allowing yourself to get any better. In a business where you can spend years getting rejected, it helps to remember that editors don't reject you; they reject little pieces of paper with writing on it. George Scithers, the former editor of *Isaac Asimov's Science Fiction Magazine*, said that, so presumably he knows what he is talking about. Especially since he helped a lot of good, new writers get started.

In a case such as the writer described above, it is easy to assume that the next book will be the same as the first. But a moment's reflection will reveal that this is almost invariably not true. Presumably you will have developed your craft, so that things that were hard before will be easier now. It may also be that you pick a harder task, but getting past the first book often resolves a whole host of problems that will therefore not emerge in the second. In addition, the other, external events in this writer's life have nothing to do with writing a book per se; but even well-educated people can fall prey to strong negative associations, whether logical or not.

Many have written about the phenomenon of learned helplessness; a person deprived of effective action long enough loses belief in his or her own efficacy. Let's look at publishing a book the first time in this context. First, you write day and night, whenever you can, with very little outside support (unless you are lucky). People will cheerfully tell you that you have no chance and that you are wasting your time, or they will ask you if you are published yet, making you feel like a failure if you reveal that you are not.

Finally, you finish. You send out query letters and samples to agents and/or publishers. What happens? *Nada*. People you have never met send you criticism of your work, to which you cannot respond and which you cannot be sure is accurate. (One writer I saw on a panel brought an inch-thick stack of rejections for her first book, including these comments from two rejection letters for the *same* book: "characters not convincing," and "wonderful characters.") You are beset on all sides, and people who know you are trying will ask you if you are published yet, and if not why not?

Then you sell. You get your pitiful advance (average $5,000 for the field *including* people like Stephen King), and your friends and coworkers assume you are filthy rich, because they think the average advance is $50,000. (Don't laugh—it's happened *twice* to my wife.) Then you have to start all over again, and maybe do your own marketing for the first book in the bargain, because otherwise you won't even earn back your advance.

This is an ideal setting for learned helplessness. The antidote is intrinsic motivation. You don't write to get that pitiful advance (which is an extrinsic motive, outside yourself, not an intrinsic one), you write because you want to write. You may write for yourself and no one else, but that is enough.

Writing is one of the few avocations that people do not allow you to pursue as an amateur. Many people are amateur painters, actors, even magicians—but when was the last time you heard of an amateur writer? If you dare to tell a person you are a writer, their first question will invariably be: Are you published? Or, even worse: Where are you published? It takes strong internal motivation to deal with this. Even if you <u>are</u> published, that's when people say things like "are you a bestseller?" or even "I've never heard of you."

To Hell with everyone else—if they don't understand, that's their problem, not yours. That is an example of external attribution for failure. Practice it: The editor had a bad day, the publisher is full of books, the market is bad, they have no taste. Just keep going. Every failure is that much closer to success. It works for sales people, it will work for you.

Remember: Don't blame yourself when there are plenty of other things to blame!

And one last word in this section before we get into specific motivational thoughts for the writing process: Don't let anyone tell you their "one way" to write. There is one way—but it must be yours.

I am sure there are many other things you will hear on how to define yourself, who you are, and how you should do what you do. Just remember: *they don't apply to you.* Period. People will try to "help" you, out of the best of intentions, and only mess you up. Whatever works, works.

CHAPTER 14: THE PROBLEM-SOLVING MODEL--INSIDE A MOTIVATED THINKER

"An artist is only an ordinary man with a greater potentiality—same stuff, same make up only more force. And the strong driving force usually finds his weak spot, and he goes cranked, or goes under."

—D. H. Lawrence

We have discussed the core driver within the motive, but now it is time to talk about the elaborations around the motive: the subcategories. Motives do not manifest in a pure rush of emotion or impulse; in adults especially they are filtered through your brain and come out in different kinds of thoughts, ranging from the explicit Need statement, e.g., "I really want this relationship," to Instrumental Action, e.g. "They worked day and night on their idea." The pattern of thoughts that manifest around a motive are called the Problem-Solving Model, because they relate to accomplishing a goal, and that's what motivation is about.

In the early days of motivational research, a very interesting experiment was done to discover what motives were about. The researchers studied the most basic motive of all: the need for food, otherwise known as hunger. They took sailors in the US Navy and asked them to fill out a Picture Story Exercise, without telling them its true purpose: to discover how people thought who were hungry as opposed to those who were not. Some were fresh from the mess hall (the control condition), but some were at the end of a shift and anxious to eat. What did the hungry men write about, when given ambiguous pictures (so they could write whatever they wanted)? You might think: they thought about food!

Not quite.

They thought about getting to food. From an evolutionary standpoint, you can imagine why that subtle difference is crucial to survival: someone who simply thinks of food when he gets hungry doesn't get fed. Someone who thinks about obtaining food does. That's why the model, below, has only one category about visualizing the need (called, appropriately enough, Need), and eight about getting to a goal or failing to do so.

The Problem-Solving Model in Easy Stages

Remember this diagram? I had different text in it before:

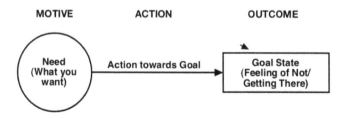

This is actually the problem-solving model at its simplest: motive (energizing thought or need), action, and result—accomplishing or failing the goal. The difference between Achievement motive and Influence motive is *inside* the boxes: are you working towards an improvement goal, or towards influence on others?

However, if motivation is about *getting to* your goal, this simple model isn't enough. Successful people don't just think/act/receive. They do some other things, too.

One key element of effective problem-solvers is *looking ahead*. Anticipating how hard it will be to achieve a goal, or how likely it is to succeed or fail, can have a big impact on what you choose to do. This is one of the reasons why strongly Achievement-motivated people don't often become writers: it's too much of a long shot! Achievement-motivated people tend to take moderate risks that have a good chance of achieving a result. Influence-motivated people, on the other hand, are anticipating the impact when they take a risk; so long shots just increase the impact from their perspective. Either way, anticipation is a critical element to motivated action.

So we add in "Anticipation" to the model, as a dotted line arcing over the action.

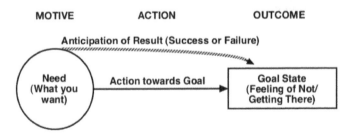

But of course when striving to a goal, all is not smooth. You don't always have the option to see what will happen, nor do you always succeed in action. There are obstacles or blocks to your success. In this model, we define two: *external* blocks, things outside you; and *internal* blocks, things you yourself have. If you are trying to influence someone and they are never home, that is an external block. If you are trying to influence someone and you are incompetent at it or even just hesitant, that is an internal block. Both can prevent you from success.

People aware of blocks are better able to circumvent them; so again, it is important to capture this thought in the model of motivation. We'll put it in:

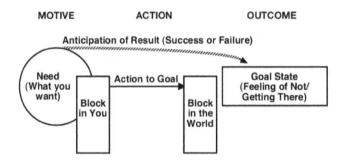

That covers almost everything. There is one other useful element to problem solving, and that is external assistance (like this book, or a writer's group). This is known, simply enough, as Help. This is (sometimes) how you get past those obstacles.

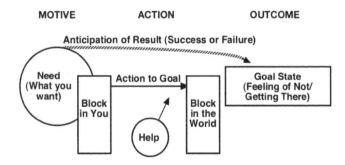

And that is the entire Problem-Solving Model!

Remember this came from the study of numerous *successfully* motivated people. This is a blueprint for thinking in a motivated way. We'll take parts of this for a lot of different uses, but to be clear, let's go through the subcategories again verbally, with a brief, writing-oriented description for each, sorted out by person, action, and result:

The Person

Need: Explicit statement of the goal, e.g., "I really want to impress the critics with this one."

Block in the Person: Obstacles to success in the actor, e.g., "I can't do it. I can't seem to finish a whole novel--I can't remember it all!"

Anticipation of Success: Just what it sounds like. "I think I can pull this off. If I just write another thousand words, I'm done with this thing!"

Anticipation of Failure: "I'm afraid I will fail. I'm afraid I can't end this book."

Outside the Person

Instrumental Activity:	Action towards the goal. "I have worked day and night on this."
Block in the World:	Obstacles to success in the world at large, e.g., "My printer is out of toner!"
Help:	Outside assistance from another person, e.g., "My writers' workshop buddies all came over to help me with this section."

Around the Goal

Positive Goal State:	"I did it, and I feel fantastic!"
Negative Goal State:	"I'm really disappointed in myself for this."

This came from motivational research, but it describes exactly how to solve problems and accomplish goals: know what you want, work towards it with an awareness of what might happen and how to avoid blocks, and know when you get there!

Most people don't show all of these all the time, or have a particular pattern that may be missing an element or two. Here are a few examples of how people behave with only a few subcategories going strong:

- Instrumental Action without Anticipation or

Blocks: "Ready, fire, aim!" Or just "Fire!"
These people jump into action, but do not think
about the ramifications.

- Anticipation of Failure, Block in the World:
  "Why bother? I'm just going to fail." These
  people see all the reasons not to do something
  —writers are ill-paid, people steal your ideas,
  and only a few people get published any year—
  and as a result never begin anything.
- Need alone: These people know what they
  want, but don't know how to begin to get it.

And so on. We'll come back to this in several places,
including a discussion of plotting and how you set goals for
yourself. For now, just consider that writers don't just have
raw motivational emotion—you need to elaborate on it
a bit.

We'll come back to understanding you and your
motives, but first we will look at the act of writing.

SECTION IV

CREATIVITY

"If we pretend to respect the artist at all, we must allow him his freedom of choice...of innumerable presumptions that the choice will not fructify. Art derives a considerable part of its beneficial exercise from flying in the face of presumptions."

—Henry James

"It's kind of fun to do the impossible."

—Walt Disney

"Everyone is a genius at least once a year; a real genius has his original ideas closer together."

—Georg Lichtenberg

CHAPTER 15: MOTIVATING YOUR CREATIVITY

"Unfortunately, an author's creative power does not always follow his will; the work turns out as it can, and often confronts its author as it were independently, indeed, like a stranger."

—Sigmund Freud

"The fun is the creative stuff, when you're sitting out there and you say, What the hell happens here? And all of a sudden *Pow!* And you're just lifted out of your chair by it. That is sensational!"

—William Kinsolving

People see the fruits of creativity as a pure, white light, shining brilliantly through the fog. Creativity is a magical thing, a precious thing, something beyond the tawdry efforts of a mere mortal. "You feel like God on the seventh day," wrote legendary mystery and religious writer Dorothy L. Sayers.

This feeling—and seeing the output instead of the process—clobbers motivation for many people who could otherwise be highly creative people. "I know I can't do that." But what if you can?

Imagine a prism, if you will. Usually we see the white light broken by the prism into all the colors of the rainbow. But the reverse is also true: white light combines every color of the spectrum, the entire range. Ironically, the "purest" color of light is actually the most commingled.

So it is with writing, or indeed any creative task. Many, many different parts of a person come together to create. Inspiration alone could not be enough, or your average kindergartner would equal Shakespeare. People forget this is true, because like anyone else who knows their work, a good writer makes it look easy. The next time you read smooth, apparently ordinary dialogue, compare it to a real discussion, where people stutter, fumble, pause, wander, insert "um" and "ah," and generally throw a lot of friction into their prose. If you ever read a verbatim transcript, the clumsiness of ordinary speech will surprise you.

Look at the task of reading. We largely take this ability for granted—note how much of what we do depends on it, from work to storm warnings on television to our daily news. And yet it is so phenomenally complicated that behavioral biologists point it out as the product of *exogenous evolution*, meaning we had to evolve to do it—though we did so accidentally.

Reading requires you to coordinate your eyes together, have them make short "jumps" called *saccades* to read a few words at a time (a task so difficult that 10% of first-graders —a six-year-old animal—cannot do it), read the shapes, interpret those images as words, link them to their definitions, do a grammatical analysis, link them to related memories, and, oh yes, make sense of the sentences—not to mention remembering plot, character, and setting—and all so fast that you can read an amusing billboard and laugh at it as you pass it on the highway at a mile a minute. Sounds more like juggling flaming chainsaws, doesn't it? And yet most people do it casually, without thinking. In most people the coordination of this myriad of abilities happens so smoothly that one pays no attention to the fact that they must <u>be</u> coordinated.

Creative efforts, such as writing, reflect the same complexity with a wider spectrum required. Writing requires everything reading does, plus a whole set of other actions and skills related to being creative effectively.

The art of motivating your writing has to do, at least in part, with coordinating all the different elements, so that when combined they produce that pure white light.

Creativity is not just one thing! It includes:

- Underlying motivational energy and enjoyment
- Traits of how you think and create
- The way you see yourself, your work, and the world
- Skills of various kinds around work, managing yourself, and managing your creativity
- Key pieces of knowledge about yourself and your work
- Knowing and managing the outside environment to allow the rest to function.

If one piece of the spectrum goes badly awry, the color of the combined light will be tainted—or at least tinted. This happens even to highly experienced and productive writers; if their lives change in some unforeseen way, they find their productivity declining or halting for a time. One key advantage the experienced writer has over the inexperienced is the ability to make up for missing pieces and continue anyway—perhaps going at a slower pace, but still functioning, knowing they can function and can get past obstacles, or edit it later. Every time a writer gets past a temporary block, the more aware they become that blocks *are* temporary.

This book goes into some detail on the colors of this spectrum of creativity, in part to abbreviate the time required to gather sufficient experience, but you should keep in mind that people differ in their approach, so not everything will apply to you. On the other hand, as long as you find one or two things that work for you, that's often enough.

CHAPTER 16: THE SEVEN DEADLY MYTHS OF CREATIVITY

"Writing's not terrible, it's wonderful. I keep my own hours, do what I please. When I want to travel, I can. I'm doing what I most wanted to do all my life. I'm not into the agonies of creation."

—Raymond Carver

Generally in this book I deal with the motivation to write, without commenting on the quality of writing, or how you go about improving it, other than practice. That might be enough if I weren't discussing something like writing. When discussing how motivational science can support and drive art, I have been startled to find people who actively resist this idea. For example, I have had extended debates with a published author who refused to accept the idea that scientific understanding could possibly contribute to the development of art – even though the whole point of science is having proof of what you assert!

I have concluded that one of the chief obstacles to motivated writing is what people think writing is. But creative effort is as susceptible to motivation as any other effort. I'd like to debunk a few of the myths, using some of the science available, so you can get back to the art confidently.

When trying to distinguish writing from everything else, sooner or later someone will say that it is a *creative* endeavor. I do too. But these people use this as a weapon, fighting off those who suggest that creative endeavors are work like any other kind. You can find my response below, but let me quote a few of the weapon-wielders:

First, the mystics: Creativity is mysterious, they say. Mere humans cannot define Creativity (and they usually use capital letters for some reason), for it is like being touched by God.

Then there are the snobs: You require a good education to truly create at the top of your ability, they say. Your IQ needs to be high. Really sensitive work comes from certain social classes.

I find that the former will not only wait for lightning to strike to begin writing, but also they assume every word is pure gold when they hear the thunder—a terrible burden to lay on God, to my mind. The latter are the kind that cannot accept that Shakespeare was common instead of noble, educated in an ordinary school and not by tutors, and likewise assume they write well simply because they have been educated and score well on standardized tests which fail to correlate with performance in the real world, let alone measure anything as slippery as writing.

And finally, there are the humble: "I'm not really creative. I'm no Einstein."

It gives me great pleasure to say that when you look at the evidence, all three groups are incorrect. Some writers work like crazy to hone their prose, others possess neither a high IQ nor advanced degrees, and still others don't think of themselves as creative and yet turn out marvelous work. These are all <u>myths</u>—something many people believe which are nonetheless wrong.

What's wrong with these myths? They can inhibit someone's writing—either that of the person who holds it ("I'm not creative, therefore I can't write"), or a writer near the person who holds it ("You need a degree to really write, therefore you can't, because you don't have one"). In motivational terms, these myths are *Personal Blocks*, internal obstacles to success, and they may be the biggest blockers of motivation to write.

Let me lay down a guiding principle now for our discussion in this chapter: *all* human beings are creative. It belongs to our genetic heritage. Some possess more creativity than others, but I have never met anyone absolutely devoid of the stuff. All these myths, on one level or another, deny this fundamental fact. With creativity as a given, then you can put motivation to work using it.

I think confusion sets in here from setting too high a standard for creativity. A person who takes a set of apparently mismatching clothes and accessories and assembles a stylish ensemble is being creative, in an influence-motivated way (thinking about impact). When you follow your wanderlust and try to identify a new, more efficient route to work, you are being creative in an achievement-motivated way (thinking about efficiency). Helping your kids make posters or jury-rigging that hardware is creative. Once when trying to fix some plumbing (not an expertise of mine), I realized that I lacked a wrench of the proper size and could not unscrew the pipe by hand. Suddenly I thought of applying a rubber jar opener to improve my grip, and it worked. The satisfaction of that task remains with me, and I find no real difference between that feeling of creative problem-solving and the satisfaction of composing an essay, a short story, a simulation, a song, or a sketch.

Creativity is combining unexpected things into something new—but you don't have to set unreasonable standards for what that is. The claw hammer was a marvelous invention in its time (it still is). Who invented those nifty little jewel boxes you put compact discs in? I love 'em. The Pyrex™ dish came about accidentally, when a scientist's wife complained about unevenness in cooking from her metal pots and pans. He happened to work with special laboratory glassware, common enough in chemistry, which was heat-resistant and transferred heat more evenly than metal. He gave her a battery casing made from this glass, and she baked a cake in it. Thus was a new kind of cookware born. While we're on food, trying a new combination of spices and ingredients to create your dinner is creative —even if it doesn't work.

You don't have to be Picasso, or Shakespeare, or Lennon-McCartney. You have all you need. But sometimes you may have an erroneous view of what that means, where creativity is concerned. I would like to puncture a set of suppositions that even highly talented and productive writers may hold. I call them the Seven Deadly Myths, because they can be fatal to your creativity. (There may be others I haven't identified but it sounds pretty catchy this way, doesn't it?) Here they are:

1. Heredity: "Creativity is born, not made."
2. The Muse: "Creativity comes of its own accord —I must wait for the muse."
3. Solitude: "I have to be alone to be creative in a quiet place."

4. Discipline: "I must be disciplined to be creative."
5. Similarity/The One "Right" Way: "I must write the way X does, or I am not really a writer."
6. Completeness: "Creativity must spring full-blown like Athena from the brow of Zeus."
7. Worthiness/Belonging: "I don't belong here; I'm not one of the creative."

Heredity: "Creativity is born, not made."

If you believe that creativity is born, not made, why are you reading this? As noted above, creativity is inherent in the human brain. One theory of creativity by psychologist David Perkins is the "generate and select" theory, which I find a useful and practical framework. Basically, you *generate links* between different things, and extend the links farther and farther out. Then you *select out* the combinations, which work. Take the typical good mystery plot. It may start with:

The butler did it.

That's way too simple, of course. Now proceed to:

The police *think* the butler did it.

Somewhat better, but still pretty obvious. So keep generating:

The police *thought* the butler did it, but decided the evidence proved them wrong. But—aha!—in

> fact the butler *did* do it, and planted phony
> evidence.

See the links? Keep moving farther and farther from the original idea, but you can see the steps, moving from "did it" to "didn't do it" to "did it but looks as if he didn't." That's the generator in action.

The "select" mechanism comes into play when you go too far, or when there are too many choices. If I went on for some length, for example:

> The police think the butler did it, but the detective
> thinks he didn't. In fact the butler did do it, but
> instead of creating an airtight alibi in which he
> didn't (because airtight alibis always appear
> suspicious to the detective), he deliberately set up a
> way to make them think he did it, but made them
> question themselves, so they would be afraid he
> didn't do it and avoid trying to convict him on
> inadequate evidence.

Sounds kind of strained, doesn't it?[1] Time for the selector. Back up a notch, this one's too silly. The selector tells you when to stop, or when to cut to the chase.

That's it: idea generator, idea selector. That doesn't sound too complex, does it? But to generate *effectively* it helps to have a lot of connections to make. This is a legitimate reason why people say to "write what you know." It gives you more resources with which to play. The more you know about a subject, the more complex and interesting the relationships you can establish between pieces.

What motivation does is channel and energize creativity: it controls what you are interested in being creative about. Influence-motivated people think about managing information in a way that creates maximum impact. A classic writing technique is to play on people's expectations, and then surprising them. This comes from knowing how people will react, which is a highly influence-motivated skill. Achievement motivation, on the other hand, may lead someone into be highly creative about better ways to do things—better methods, or interesting ideas. Some science fiction writers have to design whole worlds before they write; this is probably Achievement-motivated creativity at work.

While people do vary in their creativity and where it can be used, no matter how much you have, you can develop it. Numerous books can help you do just that. Furthermore, you can hone it on your own just by using it.

Remember: If creativity is hereditary, you've already got it.

The Muse: "I must wait for the muse."

Creativity is something built into the human brain; it is not imposed from outside. Circumstances can certainly inhibit your creativity, but it is still there. You don't walk when the mood strikes you; you walk because you need to get from point A to point B. Likewise, creativity can work for you on demand.

Like any form of exercise, the more you practice your creativity, the easier it gets. People who write nonfiction professionally, such as journalists or technical writers, find the idea of "writer's block" strange—they have no time for such luxuries. Some fiction writers feel the same way. Tom Wolfe, a journalist and fiction writer, sums it up: "With a gun at my temple, the work is just as good as what I write when I'm waiting for the muse that's never there, who's strumming the harp in the sky." And yet some become hooked into the myth that fiction is different. It isn't really so: the more you do it, the better you get.

One simple cure for writer's block is to form associations that work; if you get into a block, leave your desk at once. Try to ensure that when you sit down at your writing desk (or computer, or what have you), you are accustomed to writing. If you deliberately link productivity with every time you sit down, after a while you will associate the mere fact of sitting down with productivity, and the setting will arouse your motivation to write.

If you associate creative effort with something that does not really contribute to your productivity—say, drinking, or a full moon—then you will be less productive. Don't wait on the muse—she won't wait on you.

Remember: The Muse is you!

Solitude: "I have to be alone to be creative in a quiet place."

Being alone may reduce distractions, but that doesn't make it necessary. Isaac Asimov wrote regardless of what went on around him because he had to. He started writing while working in his father's candy shop, constantly interrupted. Mihalyi Chiksamahalyi wrote about Flow Experience—the most creative period of thinking—taking place after about twenty minutes of steadily working alone, but for some people (known as "extraverts") the most creative time is working with others, trading ideas around a table. You can either block distractions out—some are good at that, or get into an environment that washes them out (like a bus or plane), or simply produce less efficiently. On the other hand, some creators deliberately anchor their work in what they see and hear around them, e.g., cartoonist Derf's "Tales of the City" comics or the songs written by Mark Knopfler of Dire Straits, who directly quoted delivery men he heard in a New York department store for "Money for Nothing."

Jane Austen wrote a sentence or even a phrase at a time into a book set on a sideboard, because that's all she had time for. You'd be surprised how much you can produce that way, if you are willing to work at it. However, those with significant amounts of Influence or Affiliation motive are more likely to be distracted by people around, which is why it *does* take more work and concentration. If you can get solitude, it might help; but on the other hand a writer's group or workshop may help you work out new ideas. Many people find the idea of a blank page intimidating; knowing what goes on that page must come only from them. For these people, a supportive group can help. Groups are not necessary or even desirable in some cases (despite what some people will tell you), but it is a viable option. We'll talk about workshops in Chapter 25. Some people get energized by knowing there are people around, as long as they don't actually speak to them *instead* of writing.

Remember: Solitude is in your head, not in the environment.

Discipline: "I must be disciplined to be creative."

Discipline implies that you have to consciously work at it, or it won't happen. If you enjoy the process of creating, or allow yourself to do so, you don't need discipline. Motivation works better than discipline for most people: motives supply energy, whereas discipline drains energy. If writing is *always* a chore, then perhaps you shouldn't be doing it. Not that you don't have to force yourself to perform on some occasions; but don't confuse regular writing with tight discipline. It's not the same thing.

Here's Carole Nelson Douglas, who writes in multiple genres prolifically (over 65 novels as of this writing): "Discipline doesn't do it. Yes, in a minor way, discipline keeps a writer at the keyboard when there are Nazi midget transvestites on *Geraldo*, or never-before-seen varieties of bird in the backyard. Or popovers in the oven. But the greater factor is stability: in the writer's life situation and in the writer's head. There certainly won't ever be much stability in the writer's publishing climate." In other words, manage yourself rather than force yourself.

Insisting that the only way you should write is through forcing yourself is masochistic at best. As Barry Longyear once said: "Don't beat on yourself." A good portion of this book is about motivation rather than discipline. Where discipline comes in handy is to get you started when you don't feel like it.

Remember: Discipline is for the bad days, not every day.

Similarity/The One "Right" Way: "I must write the way X does, or I am not really a writer."

"There are nine-and-sixty ways of composing tribal lays/And every single one of them is right!" So said Rudyard Kipling. No two writers use exactly the same style. Nor do they have the same habits. Saying, as one writing book does, that you "must learn Latin to write," is dangerously narrow-minded thinking. Joseph Conrad wrote great works in his second language, English (Polish was his first). Poe wrote sentences averaging 45 words long; Hemingway averaged ten. *Bright Lights, Big City* was written in the second person, virtually the only published novel to have done so successfully. Flaubert invented the idea of a single viewpoint for a novel. The ancient Norse used alliterative poetry to tell epic tales, the ancient Greeks a chorus to annotate their plays. Rex Stout plotted completely in his head before setting pen to paper. Heinlein invented some characters, got them in trouble, and tried to get them out, typically using the plot he called The Man Who Learned Better. Philip K. Dick wrote each successive chapter to explain the previous. Tolkien never plotted at all, writing *The Lord of the Rings* as he went and rewriting it later. Some writers outline, others do not, some do both for different works. I've already referred to "write what you know," but that would eliminate nearly the entire *corpus* of science fiction, which is based on "what if" and invention. *Don't limit yourself.*

One student of creativity named "Three B's" of creativity: Bed, Bath, and Bus. In other words, most of his good ideas came in one of those three places. It has been said that Einstein always took great care while shaving, because that is where his best ideas occurred to him, and the jolt of the idea caused him to jerk and cut himself. None of the Three B's help much in terms of training oneself to create *more* (despite humorist Douglas Adams spending inordinate lengths of time in the bath), though on the other hand when fantastically prolific short-story and novel writer Fredric Brown occasionally ran dry, he took a long bus trip to someplace boring so that the boredom forced him into creativity. I wouldn't want to rely on that, though, and neither did he most of the time – it was the exception, not the rule.

That does not mean that other writers haven't learned skills through experience, thought, and training. It does mean that the same skills do not apply to all people—at least where creativity is concerned. I suspect that people feel this way for a number of reasons related to their motives: If Achievement-motivated, people are looking for the most efficient method, and why not use one which works for someone else? If Affiliation-motivated, it might be an issue of trusting someone you like. If Influence-motivated, it might be a case of being impressed by the famous. In this case, I advise you to find what works for you, instead of going with your gut, or relying just on one other person's approach (as opposed to using it for inspiration).

Remember: The only writer you have to write like is you.

Completeness: "Creativity must spring full-blown like Athena from the brow of Zeus."

This myth that creativity must express itself completely and fully (as Athena was born from the thoughts of Zeus) was held by no less a person than Charles Darwin. In his story of how he came up with evolution, he claimed that he had a burst of insight while reading Malthus, which enabled him to identify the process of natural selection. Since Darwin kept detailed, dated notebooks of his daily thoughts and reading, we have the evidence to prove this assertion. Howard Gruber read the notebooks carefully, found the day when Darwin read Malthus and found...nothing. No brilliant insight, no recorded leap of creativity. A continued study of Darwin's notebooks revealed exactly the opposite. Ironically, evolution *evolved* in his notebooks. In retrospect it may have *seemed* sudden, or it may have been a moment when he acknowledge it consciously, but in fact the idea came piecemeal. You don't have to work in "a white-hot burst of creativity," as Alfred Bester put it. Not that it isn't nice when you have it, but for longer works, it can't be done anyway.

Mozart typically wrote in first draft, but that doesn't mean it wasn't thought about first—just that he didn't *write down* his first thoughts. As noted above, Beethoven is equally praised, but he tinkered with his work over and over again. Some people find it easier to put down content and revise it in front of them instead of in their head.

There are those who assume that great work must come spontaneously from the soul, that there is no (conscious) control over it, or that editing would only damage it. Writers who have a particularly lyric style tend to have fans who believe their stories came from such an illumination rather than hard work. I once heard John Crowley (*Little, Big*), a person who writes in such a way, speaking about this. He expressed himself at length—strongly and angrily—regarding this illusion. And it *is* an illusion: he labors over his phrases, adjusting every line and sweating over it. When hearing him talk about this, I got the distinct impression that he resented the assumption that he *didn't* have to work for his marvels, that they appeared before him.

Stanislavsky, the man who invented "method acting," came up with it because he was a mediocre actor watching a great actor. He could not imagine that the subtleties he saw could come from "acting," so he decided that it came from identifying intimately with the character. Unfortunately for him, evidence exists that he was wrong. The man he supposedly studied (but did not ask directly) spent hour after hour honing his craft that made his art possible—rehearsing expressions, movements, and voices.

This may not seem particularly encouraging, but look at it this way: you can make your creative work better, and you don't have to pray for that one perfect moment to come rolling out. No one has to know how much effort you put into it. No matter how many drafts you write, they only publish the last.

This will not surprise achievement-motivated people, particularly those who are more focused on efficiency; incremental improvement comes naturally to them. To the Influence-motivated, however, where big impact is key, this may feel disappointing. Not at all—it means that you don't have to worry about the earlier drafts so much—the final draft will have greater impact. I have also found that newer writers tend to fall prey to this myth more than many; either they think they are bad because their first drafts read like first drafts, or they over-rate their ability and think their first drafts are pure genius already.

Remember: You only publish your last draft, not your first.

Worthiness/Belonging: I don't belong here; I'm not one of the creative."

People seem to feel there is some magic criterion that forever marks you as "a creative person." Furthermore, you don't really belong to the company of other writers unless you bear this mark of Cain.

Some people establish targets, which they think will establish them. "This means I am officially a creative person, an author." People who think this way often get surprised when they reach that point and nothing seems any different. Instead of ignoring the idea entirely, they decide another, better criterion must exist, farther down the line. "When I get an agent." But you still are not published, right? "When I am published." But what if it was only paperback? "When I have my first hardcover." "My *second* hardcover, so I know it wasn't a fluke." "My first award." "When my book is in Barnes & Noble on Fifth Avenue in Manhattan." "When my book is on the *front table* at the Barnes & Noble on Fifth Avenue in Manhattan." "When I win the Nobel Prize for Literature."

When does it stop?

Never. This attitude can be part of the Imposter Syndrome—"I don't really deserve this, and the minute they find out, they'll take it all away. I'm not really a creative person. I have to work very hard to do this." So that makes it worse? You're not naturally creative, so you work twice as hard to come up with something just as good as the "naturally" creative person, so it can't be that good. And you say you aren't creative!

Creativity is a process, not a target. The Achievement-motivated are particularly prey to this concern in that what was good enough today isn't good enough for tomorrow—if they achieve a target, that means it is time to raise it. It is vital to acknowledge what you have done, and set it against its proper context: that most people never even <u>start</u> to write.

Remember: You don't need a creative license!

Forget the Myths

Isaac Asimov once said that if he could be a successful

writer, anyone could. You use creativity for all the arts, but also all the crafts. Writing is a craft as well as an art, and crafts can be learned. You may not be Shakespeare, but we already have a Shakespeare. Furthermore, not everyone likes Shakespeare. Some remarkable people read a wide range of books that are good in ways different from the Bard. My late mentor, the famous, brilliant, and creative psychologist David McClelland, read mysteries for fun. So does President Clinton. John F. Kennedy—a creative writer in his own right—liked (and made famous) James Bond novels.

There is no single criterion for establishing yourself as a legitimate writer—except the one you set yourself. Allow me to present some excuses people could make for "not being a real creative person." Just to drive the point home (or perhaps hammer it into the ground), I'm also going to list a famous creative person who fits that criterion.

Table 3: Examples from History

Excuses for Not Really Being a Creator	Actual Creative Person
"I only wrote one novel."	Harper Lee: To Kill a Mockingbird
"I've never written a full novel, only short fiction, essays, and novellas."	Harlan Ellison: winner of several Hugo Awards, Nebula Awards, the PEN Award, the Writer's Guild Award, the Edgar, the Raven...
"I've only written some plays and poems."	William Shakespeare
"I've only written nonfiction."	Charles Darwin
"I only wrote one book, and it was nonfiction."	John F. Kennedy: Profiles in Courage
"I only sold one piece, and that was to a relative who felt sorry for me."	Vincent Van Gogh

You can write for yourself if you want. You can write for others. But the fact that you are writing at all makes you a writer. Nothing more, nothing less.

Setting additional goals can help you become a more

successful writer, as in having more people read your work, but that means you are a working writer, not a person who is yet to become a writer.

John F. Kennedy said it to Leonard Nimoy, a struggling actor driving a taxi at the time: "There's always room for one more good one."

SECTION V

GOAL SETTING

"There are only two tragedies in life: one is not getting what one wants, and the other is getting it."

—Oscar Wilde

"Obstacles are those frightful things you see when you take your eyes off your goal."

—Henry Ford

CHAPTER 17: OVERVIEW OF GOAL SETTING

"I write when I'm inspired, and I see to it that I'm inspired at nine o'clock every morning."

—Peter DeVries

Much of this material has been incorporated into other chapters, but let's talk about the principles that underlie goal setting and why it matters.

When I say "goal setting," I mean the process by which you identify targets for producing something—prose, a finished edit, a limerick, etc.—before you do it. In other words, the plan for productivity. Too restraining, you say? Too bureaucratic? Why bother with laying out what you plan to do before you do it?

First of all, because goal setting *works*. According to stacks of research, your chance of finishing your book, story, epic poem, etc. improves by doing some kind of goal-setting process.

"Okay, I want to write a 75,000 word book by tomorrow which will be a bestseller."

Perhaps not *any* kind of process, however. In fact, different kinds of goals apply to different situations, and depend both on how much information you have and how far ahead you are planning. Using the wrong kind can actually work against your motivation, because it moves from "wow, this is getting exciting" to "oh, God, I have to do this again." In other words, improperly designed goals become extrinsic motivation, which extinguishes intrinsic motivation – and yes, that's the word in the literature.

For some of this (including the warning!) I am indebted to the work of Richard Boyatzis. The types of goals he picks out are frequently discussed, but I'm using his naming conventions. He identifies three:

- Rational goals (also known as "SMART" goals)
- Direction & domain
- Present-oriented goals (also known as "Muddlin' through")

The first is best for short-range or highly organized goals, like word count goals. The second is better for long-range, more nebulous goals where you know the basic thrust but not necessarily how you will get there: like goals around genre and size of work. The third is not a generally recommended approach *unless* you really have no reason to prefer one choice over another, so you wing it. It is inefficient, but sometimes useful to gather information. It's more exploratory.

Let's spend a little time referring to the work of Boyatzis on goal setting, going in order from least to most specific:

Present-Oriented Goals (Muddlin' Through)

This is really the absence of goal setting: pure trial and error—do things until one works. In the business world, one example of this is the introduction of automatic teller machines or cashpoints (ATMs). When they were developed, no one had any idea how and where they should be placed. How do you set a goal for establishing ATMs when you do not know where they will be?

What happened is that people tried everything. ATMs were placed inside banks, on the outside wall of banks, in isolated kiosks, in special places within malls, in grocery stores — everywhere. With time, it became possible to gather sufficient data to determine where future ATMs could be built—moving to a new kind of goal setting.

In writing, this is not an efficient way to set goals. However, to some extent all writers may *need* to do this, in two ways. First, there are people who will claim that this is the process of art: accidental discovery of a process or style you can make your own. This philosophy assumes that Picasso stumbled onto Cubism through random experimentation, and was bright enough to see its potential or at least intrigued enough to keep using it. The counterargument is that Picasso had a profound understanding of the history and practice of art and worked deliberately to violate certain conventions based on ideas from the pioneering work of others and pushed it until it became uniquely his. I lean towards the latter interpretation for Picasso (you might have guessed), which really puts him in the realm of "direction and domain" goals, but I wouldn't completely eliminate the factor of chance in art, either. Even if you succeed with this approach, "muddling through" is still not efficient once you know what you are working towards.

The second way this becomes forced upon a writer is in terms of getting your work out. If you come up with your own idea, your own direction, the only way to know if people want to read it is to try to sell it. You have to keep sending it around until it sells or you decide to try something different. William Gibson (author of *Neuromancer* and creator of the term "cyberspace") was not able to sell cyberpunk until the market was ready for it — at which point he invented a new *subgenre* the minute his novel was published. Anne Perry wrote ten novels that never sold before selling her British-Victorian-era mysteries. But those first ten were set in different times and places. She just kept writing until something sold—and in the US rather than her native Britain, oddly enough. She said at one point that she would never leave the Victorian setting again, because it sold. It took a long, weary time to find her forte, but she did. Interestingly, as of this writing she also published a fantasy novel some years after becoming a successful mystery writer, so perhaps she felt she could afford to experiment.

One advantage of publishing independently – i.e., self-publishing – is that you can try things that the market may not be ready for. Sometimes the market will pick it up if it becomes successful on its own, sometimes not. Another approach some writers use is to write short stories, which are lower-risk in terms of time spent and more likely to find a market somewhere.

Direction and Domain Goals

These goals are rather more focused, but not what you would call detailed. When you can clear away some of the underbrush you determine the domain. Anne Perry determined her domain (Victorian-era Britain), and could then focus in on that. Many (if not most) writers tend to have some domain focus from the beginning, some area that compels them. A genre, such as science fiction, mystery, romance, or horror, is a domain. A "hardboiled mystery" or "hard SF" or "Regency romance" is a smaller domain. A length (short-short, short story, novelette, novella, novel, series) is a domain as well. People with special knowledge or interest may choose a domain that builds on their strengths: Aaron Elkins, a physical anthropologist (specializing in bones) wrote mysteries starring—surprise! —a physical anthropologist. Elizabeth Mertz, a.k.a. Elizabeth Peters, an Egyptologist, writes mystery novels related to Egyptology. Many SF writers are engineers or scientists: Heinlein, Asimov, Clarke, etc. Domains are delimiters, defining the area in which you want to work, or the playing field for your game. Football, baseball, cricket, basketball? Choose your game.

A direction is just what it sounds like. What do you want to do within your domain? Most writers start with "sell what I write!" But you can also try to extend what you do, or tell a particular story, or extend a lesson. Kurt Vonnegut learned to write in order to tell the story of his traumatic experience of the firebombing of Dresden during World War II; his direction was to get to that point. He did not know, when he started, how many years he would require or how he would get there other than in the domain of science fiction novels and short stories. He certainly did not know he would become a bestseller.

Do not forget that you can pick a *new* domain, too. If you have an interest in a period, for example, no one says you have to be an academic expert already to do well in it. Shelby Foote considered himself a novelist, but his research into the Civil War (for his novels and ultimately for his three-volume history) was so thorough (though somewhat biased) that Ken Burns used him as a historical reference and interviewee for his television series *The Civil War*. Similarly, science-fiction writer Harry Turtledove is a historian specializing in the Byzantine Era, but he has since applied his historical training to so many other times and places that he now has a reputation as a master of the "alternate-history" story, where things diverge from the history we know. He won several awards for the Civil-War era story *The Guns of the South*, and also set a series in an alternate World War II. After anthropologist Aaron Elkins, described above, had success with his Gideon Oliver anthropologist series, he began a series about an art historian.

This kind of goal is very good for long-term focus, since they narrow your direction but do not define it completely, and furthermore can become a framing to manage your inspiration – so you don't extinguish your intrinsic motivation. Where it fails is in daily work.

Rational Goals (SMART Goals)

These goals are rather more concrete and detailed; they are designed to accomplished specific, relatively short-term goals—meaning up to years potentially, but typically a shorter duration. When you have your direction and domain, the logical next step is to start thinking about how to get in that direction. A shorter goal is: write a book. Then you can set up structure around measuring your progress. When done fully, rational goals closely resemble the Problem-Solving Model, and for good reason: they use all the same elements.

These goals have very specific characteristics, and you are likely to run across them in many works designed to help you set and accomplish goals. Let me outline the characteristics:

1. Specific. They need to be precise, not vague.
2. Measurable. You need to be able to know how far along you are.
3. Moderate Risk. The goals need to be challenging but still attainable.
4. Time-locked. A goal needs a deadline.

Ideally, you want some of the first two kinds of goals—preferably together. For example:

Direction and domain goal:

"I want to be a successful mystery writer who writes "tea cozy" mystery series with good characters and who is read by at least a small but loyal audience that follows each book in the series; and I want that audience to grow for each book."

Rational goal:

I will write at least 600 words in a single writing session, four days a week, or at least 2400 words in the entire week.

These latter goals are my restatements of the goals set by my wife, Toni L. P. Kelner, when she got rolling on her Laura Fleming mystery series. Her direction and domain goal is pretty much the same (though she has added others around expanding her scope), but her rational goals have evolved as her abilities have grown—which is as it should be. I'll use her again later, because she is a natural at goal-setting, and I have particularly detailed access to her thinking.

To complete the set, I'll give you an example of a *bad* "muddlin' through" goal: "I want to be a writer some day." Pithy, but useless. Lots of people want to be writers. Few do it, and even fewer publish. A good present-oriented goal might include trying a number of different writing techniques, goals, or styles until one scores for you.

Let's take a look at each criterion in detail. These apply to *any* goal, of course, but I want to give you some solid writer's examples.

Specific

If it isn't specific, you don't know when you have reached it.

Bad example:

"I want to write." Write what? Mysteries? Nonfiction? If you write a letter, have you reached your goal?

Good examples:

"I want to complete a first draft of a mystery novel." A good early goal.

"I will write four pages a day every day." A typical goal, used by many.

"I will finish my short story over this weekend."

Measurable

If it isn't measurable, you don't know how far along

you are on your goal. This is essential to help your progress as well as your outcome—it can help immensely to be able to say, "I am three-quarters of the way finished."

Bad example:

"I want to write a mystery story." Of what length? How much counts? You could write multi-book series, novels, novellas, short stories, essays, short-shorts, limericks, haiku and any would count. Where do you get that "warm feeling" that Heinlein described?

Good examples:

"I will write 600 words four days a week."

"I will generate five scene cards today."

"I will complete one scene written today." (Kelly Tate)

"I will have enough to show my writing group this month."

Challenging but Realistic

This is absolutely key. If you set this well, you are really incorporating the other three criteria. However, this is the most difficult element because the degree of challenge/realism varies from person to person.

Bad examples:

"I will sell a novel this year." Is this realistic if you have never sold before? On the other hand, for an Isaac Asimov it would not challenge him enough. Stephen King wrote under the name Richard Bachman to assure himself that he could sell a book on its own merits and not just his name—a way of checking his ability, but also a way of raising the challenge again.

"I will write some prose people can read and enjoy." This might be so easy that you never complete it—or even start! After all, you could do that any time. This may partially explain those annoying people who say, "I've often thought that if I could just sit down for a while I could write a book." What book? And obviously they don't consider it a challenge to generate 75,000 words of coherent, readable, organized prose—which is why these people are annoying to professional writers, who know just how difficult it is. Not to mention why those people virtually never actually do what they say.

Good Examples (remembering that everyone is different):

"I will write one scene a day." Kelly Tate set this goal (which could include a number of cards of scene description) and her long-range (direction and domain) goal was to eliminate her stack of scene cards. She set this first goal to be time sensitive. When you have no more than four hours a day to write (thanks to kids), you had better set an achievable goal. One scene was about right, and she experimented to ensure this was it.

"I will write 200 words a day on average and definitely 1400 words per week."

"I will write one sentence of my doctoral dissertation every day." This latter was by a graduate student who had a terrible fear of writing. This was the way she ensured that she would *keep going.* One sentence felt safe, even every day. Frequently she exceeded this goal, but her fear made more than that seem unrealistic.

"I will write eight hours a day five days a week and six hours a day the other two, unless forcibly removed from my typewriter." Isaac Asimov, though I don't think he set this goal consciously; it was just what he did. It worked for him.

"I will break out from the limitations and low rates of pulp science-fiction magazines into anything and everything: slicks, books, motion pictures, general fiction, specialized fiction not intended for SF magazines, and nonfiction." Robert Heinlein's goal when he returned to full-time writing after WWII. He succeeded by the end of the 1940s.

"I will sell a novel not under my own name." Stephen King, as above.

Time-Phased

If it isn't time-phased, you won't have a deadline.

Bad example:

"I will write some fiction someday," is so realistic that it isn't energizing. It won't push you until you are on your deathbed eighty years from now, at which point you probably have other things on your mind. Not to mention what will happen if a bus unexpectedly hits you.

Good examples:

"I will write two limericks this weekend."

"I will write 600 words today."

"When I sit down for my four hours today, I will write one scene."

"I will finish 2400 words this week."

As you can see, these goal-setting criteria often overlap.

This is inevitable for the good goals; it is the bad ones on which we need the separate criteria. At any rate, if you can answer "yes" to the question "does my goal meet all four criteria?" then your odds of actually meeting it go up sharply—as much as 70%.

However, before you just copy down some of the goals listed above, let's be sure they are the right kind for you.

CHAPTER 18: GOAL ISSUES--FINDING YOUR BALANCE POINT

"If everything seems under control, you're just not going fast enough."

—Mario Andretti

Now that you know the basic criteria for a good goal, there are other issues that surround the process of successful goal-setting, that enable the precise attainment of that magical balance point or "hot spot" implied by the Yerkes-Dodson Law.

The underlying purpose for a calculated goal-setting process comes from taking the Law and making it useful for you. The art of goal-setting, and indeed of this entire book, is to *identify and use the degree of aroused motivation that leads to maximum sustainable performance.* That varies widely from person to person, making some investigation and thought necessary.

In my experience people often understand the goal-setting criteria above very well in the theoretical sense, then hit a brick wall when it comes to actually using them. So here are Kelner's Rules of the Balance Point, a few thoughts to ponder as you set your goals.

1. Different people need different goals.
2. "Challenging" and "realistic" depend on your perceptions.
3. The balance point of appropriate motivation changes based on external issues.
4. The balance point changes based on internal issues.
5. Give yourself flexibility in your goal-setting.

Different People Need Different Goals

The inverse of this ("everyone should use a single goal") is an extension of the myth above that you should write like someone else. In my research I interviewed people who wrote one sentence a day and people who wrote four thousand words a day (Asimov could theoretically write 40,000 words a day; L. Ron Hubbard wrote more); people who wrote for an hour, four hours, or all day and into the night. Do not be afraid to select a goal that works for *you*, regardless of what anyone else might think. The fable of the tortoise and the hare applies: the person who wrote one sentence a day *finished* her lengthy doctoral dissertation, and that is all that matters. If a goal doesn't work, move it. Anthony Trollope said: "Three hours a day will produce as much as a man ought to write." But Anne Bernays thought it was "shameful" that on her best days she wrote only about three or four hours. Others write eight hours a day. Do not focus on *how much* you do, but what *feels right*, so you can continue to do it. Setting high goals that inhibit your writing will not do you any good at all.

Naturally motivation applies here as well, since motives are about achieving different kinds of goals. The motives you bring allow you to set different goals. If you are highly affiliative, it may not be reasonable for you to spend a weekend alone writing. But you could conceivably do a writer's workshop with your writing friends. If you are highly achievement-motivated, you can set more goals around the process, which may be rewarding in and of itself.

"Challenging" and "Realistic" Depend On Your Perceptions

At one time, my wife Toni L. P. Kelner found herself running behind on a deadline—there had been some deaths in the family and other issues. She studied the time-lines and decided that she had to write two thousand words a day—double what she had set for herself previously, though she had hit that number on some occasions. Toni had been a professional technical writer for years and in the course of having published two books and a short story was normally writing 1000-1200 words a day. What do you think her productivity was after setting this goal? Zero. The goal appeared too high.

But I have a joker here. I said the goal *appeared* too high. Toni turned to me to help her, and I made a suggestion: set *two* goals of one thousand words each—one for the morning, one for the afternoon. You may think, wait, that's still two thousand words! What's the difference?

I knew Toni was perfectly capable of writing two thousand words a day, but I suspected that the goal felt too huge —and daunted her. People cannot reach for an impossible goal. There is a myth (all too often found among coaches and managers) that deliberately setting the goal too high forces people to higher results. "Shoot for the moon, and you'll land among the stars." Besides being terrible astronomy, it simply doesn't work, in the long-term or short-term. People know when the goal is impossible. If you do the best job you can and still fail (and get punished for it) because of an unrealistic goal, why bother to do your best work? It certainly isn't energizing to throw yourself at a job when you know you can never make your target.

On the other hand, some goals *are* possible, but do not *appear* possible. If I went up to you and said: "You have to write a 72,000 word book. You have one year. Can you do it?" What would you say? Probably a resounding "no!" On the other hand, if you break it down into bite-size morsels, "chunking" it, take a look:

72,000 words in a year is...

6,000 words a month for a year, which is...
200 words a day, which is...

the length of the above one-and-a-half paragraphs
from "But I have a joker here" to "do not *appear*
possible!"

That doesn't sound so bad, does it? Let me make this a concrete suggestion: take the big goal and break it down into its components, or you will not be able to accurately assess the degree of challenge. By the way, Toni modified her goals, but not exactly the way I suggested. She set herself a primary goal of 1,000 words per day—her normal goal— twice a day, but at no particular time. Others could do this with an option for a second 1,000-

word goal. She felt she could manage that, and it put the decision back into her hands. She knew she could confidently hit the first thousand-word goal, which meant she had one success a day going into her second, which then became the challenging goal. She started producing again, and in fact usually hit that two-thousand-word mark, but she gave herself both smaller chunks and an out in case she was not able to hit the mark. She caught up her pace again and was only slightly (and acceptably) late.

In terms of the motivational subcategories, this affects your anticipation of success or failure—something worth managing!

The Balance Point Changes Based on External Issues

The amount of time you have available, for example, may not be entirely within your control. Saying you will write twelve hundred words a day is not appropriate if you are working two (other) jobs already and you write slowly. If something happens that throws you off, you may need to reassess your goals, because what was reasonable may now become unrealistic. I mentioned deaths in the family above; suddenly dropping everything and flying somewhere is guaranteed to derange your plans. Consider it a Block in the World; you either need Help, or you need to adjust your goals, but either way you need to adjust an unattainable goal.

The best example I can think of is having a baby. Having a child is one of those changes that is impossible to predict exactly. Your entire life transforms not only in some predictable ways, but also in ways that depend on the nature of the baby and your relation to him or her. All you can do is revert to "muddlin' through" goal-setting, and hope to narrow it down to direction and domain as soon as you can, and keep backup plans in mind.

If you have a baby who goes to bed early, sleeps through the night, and wakes up happy, then you can manage your time well. But what if your baby is colicky? Suddenly you could be up at any time at all, perhaps driving your child around to soothe him or her, short on sleep, and long on aggravation. To make matters worse, this is not a predictable issue; not even from month to month, because infants change rapidly.

What can you do? There is, as you may suspect, no easy answer here. All you can do is *reassess the realism*. Mystery writer Charlaine Harris abandoned her writing for the first five years she had kids; others get an *au pair*, and still others just keep writing at a slower pace. One writer I know worked immediately after the baby was born, relying on her husband to take extra time with the baby while she completed an almost-finished project. It strained them both, but it worked, and she felt comfortable taking time off after that project finished, within the first month or so.

Also remember that things change, and therefore you can change with them. This is profoundly frustrating to people who like an organized life, but sometimes life is like that. Colic usually only lasts the first three to four months, kids go to school, other people can help.

You cannot ignore the potential external blocks. You can try to manage them, if you stay alert to them as they happen. Some even plan for a disaster per month, because, sure as shootin', they will happen. If not, well, add another goal!

The Balance Point Changes Based on Internal Issues

Not only does the outside world change, but you change as well. Remember how much of this book is about individual perception and ability. When you start, 400 words a day for a novel may seem overwhelming. After publishing a couple of volumes, it may not be easy, but it is not overwhelming any more. Your development or re-evaluation shrinks the internal block.

I recall a person who wrote a long and complex doctoral dissertation who said, "After that, I knew there would never be anything as bad again." (Now that I think about it, I think that was me!) At any rate, going through the mill can give you self-confidence. (NaNoWriMo is another way of building that confidence.) Likewise, public announcement of a goal has been found to increase the chance of accomplishment, but that can also increase the pressure so high that you drop over the top of the bell curve and start sliding down on performance, unless you know you can do it. Confidence allows you to use that public announcement, instead of letting anxiety freeze you up.

Greater confidence also usually means you can pick up speed. Furthermore, one *might* hope to get better over time. One day science-fiction writer Geary Gravel realized that he did *not* have to go over his drafts obsessively, that his first draft actually looked pretty good! This meant that a second draft could do almost all his polishing, so he cut the time for a novel substantially. Toni increased her goal-per-day to keep pace with her interest.

I have a friend who occasionally found himself driving late at night—well, early in the morning, actually—in a state of exhaustion. His solution (and no, I don't recommend it) was to increase his speed "until it got interesting again." In a way (a crazy way, to be sure), he used the Yerkes-Dodson Law to overcome his exhaustion: to push himself back up the energy curve until sheer panic would keep him awake. Similarly, if writing at thirty miles per hour no longer challenges you, start picking up speed.

The Yerkes-Dodson bell curve continues to shift upward. What challenged you yesterday does not challenge you today. So move the curve, or you may find yourself losing steam.

Give Yourself Flexibility In Your Goal-Setting

I suppose nearly all the comments above boil down to this single statement. By flexibility I don't mean vagueness or fudging—take your goals seriously and act on them. What I mean is that goals do not occur in isolation. They must fit you, your abilities, the circumstances around you, and so forth. This may be as simple as giving yourself a fallback. Toni set a goal of 600 words a day for four days a week— so she could adjust which days she wrote as needed—but also set a fallback goal of 2400 words for the entire week, so if things went *really* badly she could do four days' worth of writing on Sunday. That is what I mean by flexibility: not compromising your performance, but allowing it to happen multiple ways *when necessary*.

Summary of a Good Goal

A good goal should be:

- Specific, Measurable, Challenging but Achievable, and Time–Phased
- Right for your level of challenge
- Based on your current perceptions of what is challenging enough
- Affected by external issues
- Changes based on your internal issues
- Has flexibility (e.g., fallback goals) built in.

Examples of Things You Can Influence For Goals

- Quantity of writing: number of words, pages, lines, etc.
- Quality of writing: first-draft or free-written material with misspellings vs. spell-checked, grammatical, final draft material
- Quantity of edited pages: number of pages revised/added
- Time of accomplishment: how much over what period (speed of writing)
- Time available for accomplishment
- Fallback goals over longer periods
- External rewards (M&Ms, reading a book you've postponed, sex)
- Internal rewards (emotionally satisfying rewards, e.g., writing fun sections)

SECTION VI

THE PROCESS OF WRITING--HOW IT WORKS, WHAT YOU DO

"Writing is a craft. You have to take your apprenticeship in it like anything else."

—Katherine Anne Porter

"First I get some characters into trouble. By the time I can hear their voices, they're usually out of trouble."

—Robert A. Heinlein

CHAPTER 19: STYLES OF THE CREATIVE PROCESS

"I've got a great idea for a novel. If you just write it, I'll split fifty-fifty with you."

—A remarkably annoying person, speaking to a professional writer

For some people, finding that writing does not just require "applying your fundament to the furniture" comes as a shattering blow. Because we are a verbal species and dialogue composes the majority of most fiction, people come to the erroneous view that all you have to do to write a book is to somehow sit down and "talk to the typewriter," and after sufficient time you will have a volume. Unless you are Isaac Asimov, you probably can't do that. And he's dead.

Mozartian and Beethovenian Processes

There are two types of people in this world: those who divide people into two types, and those who do not. (I fall into both groups, which may be a third type...) Motives divide people into at least three[1], but in this section I want to discuss two basic styles of the creative process: the Beethovenian and Mozartian. Note that we are not talking about "style" in the usual sense—that is, the pattern of words, sentences, paragraphs, and themes that make a writer recognizable. As usual in this book, I am referring to the writing process in which prose or poetry are generated, not what comes out the far end of the pipe. "Beethovenian" and "Mozartian" are nicknames attached to the ends of a particular spectrum of creative practice, which happen to be well represented by the musicians Wolfgang Amadeus Mozart and Ludwig von Beethoven.

Mozart's music sheets were nearly all first drafts, completed music going straight from his head onto the paper, with little or no correction. The *Mozartian* creator does most of the work in their head, writes largely in first draft, and does not require editing. (At least, that's what the writer thinks. Editors and readers may believe otherwise!) Similarly, legend has it that Shakespeare never blotted a line when writing his scripts. His contemporary and friend Johnson commented, "Would that he had blotted a thousand," but perhaps he was just jealous. Rex Stout, the author of the Nero Wolfe mysteries, never put word to paper until he had organized the entire book in his head. He wrote entirely in first draft. Isaac Asimov, who only bothered to use his word processor for novels, also fit into this category. He wrote that "I think at ninety words per minute, and I write at ninety words per minute." His frequent columns and articles were always first drafts, but he organized them well for easy reading, even when dealing with arcane aspects of science.

I have heard Asimov speak on several occasions, and it struck me that, apart from a strong (and somewhat startling) Brooklyn accent, his speech *exactly* matched his prose. It was measured, literate, and precise—and about ninety words a minute. Furthermore, he could extemporize at will; he had gifts that enabled him to quickly produce organized, smooth prose and speak it at once. As I listened, I understood that to him, writing *was* merely speaking on paper. Since he spoke well, he wrote well.

Beethoven, by contrast, fought with his music, trying to make it different from what had gone before—including, and especially, the music of Mozart. Beethovenian creators are the people that agonize over words, who tear up drafts and start over, whose pages are more red ink than black. These writers and creators are the people who must struggle to find the *exact* right word, the right note, and the right color.

James Joyce spent seventeen years writing *Finnegan's Wake*, writing and revising constantly. Award-winning writer (and dyslexic) Samuel R. Delany, in his memoirs *The Motion of Light in Water*, shows a page from one of his books that is virtually all edited. Editor and writer Judith Merril told a story when she had locked herself in a hotel room to complete three writing assignments on a short deadline. After writing steadily all day and churning out whole volumes of prose, her friend Delany came by beaming. Merril, who was in a bad mood indeed, knowing how much she had to do, asked him what made *him* so happy. "I have written a perfectly *wonderful* sentence," he said, "and it took me only *twenty minutes!*" Sitting in her hotel room with stacks of paper she had written *that day*, Merril was caught by the dramatic differences between the two of them, and how fortunate she was. She lacked time, not writing ability or fluency.

"I have rewritten—often several times—every word I have ever published. My pencils outlast their erasers," said Vladimir Nabokov. "I can't write five words but that I change seven," moaned Dorothy Parker. Others, not so driven to change, may simply be unable to keep the entire work in the brain. Some of us, unlike Rex Stout and his mental mysteries, need to write it down and look at it once in a while. People carry around with them a varied set of intellectual gifts, and memory is one of many. This level of memory is helpful (especially for a mystery writer!) but not necessary.

I have often helped my wife as she thought through her mystery plots, and if I made a suggestion she could instantly pull apart the threads of the story and show the links from my suggestion to other parts of the book that were affected. If you cannot do that, you are unlikely to be Mozartian, but I hasten to note that my wife is not wholly Mozartian either. I suspect that it may also be harder for you to be a mystery writer, at least if you feel the need to change your plots after you write them. On the other hand, some rewriting becomes unnecessary once you have the practice to eliminate mistakes.

In brief, Mozartians tend to create all of a piece and more-or-less fully developed prose (or art or music or accounting whatever you happen to be creating); while Beethovenians tinker, edit, revise, and alter their way to completion.

There is no inherent superiority to either type; they are simply different ways of being creative. It would be foolish to say that Mozart's music surpassed Beethoven just because he liked it the way it fell out the first time. Likewise, I am not about to suggest that Beethoven possessed more talent because he took more time to revise. At the end, both were stupendous, and that is what is important: the quality of the final product, not the quantity of drafts. Some Mozartians would benefit from a course in rewriting, and some Beethovenians need to learn when to quit. Time and effort provide the experienced writer the ability to alter approaches as necessary—just one of the massive set of skills that practice provides.

Of course, these two stand at extreme ends of a spectrum. Most people fall somewhere between a pure Beethoven and a pure Mozart, usually rewriting to some degree, but perhaps having an occasional short work pour out of the typewriter (Alfred Bester called these "pianolas," meaning that that they played themselves out without conscious intervention).

Since I have already picked on my wife, let me add that she has clearly moved along the continuum: her first novel went through several complete drafts; her fifth had one complete draft and a thorough run-through editing. By her sixteenth novel, she not only wrote a draft far faster, she had a strong sense of the story arc from the beginning, even though she wrote it out of order (as many do). Furthermore, her prose was always clean and readable, apart from the occasional typo or missing word. In effect, she started perhaps 80% Beethovenian, and moved to be more fifty-fifty, or maybe even more Mozartian, with sufficient practice and skill-building over the course of sixteen novels and some thirty-odd short stories, as well as editing a number of anthologies. Editing well by reading others critically (not negatively, but analytically) can hone your writing skills by giving you both good and bad examples different from your own.

The advent of the word processor has altered this somewhat, in that you can change your words so quickly that you might not even notice you are editing (in fact, one wonders if the word processor in effect expands the boundary of the writer's mind; instead of holding things in your memory, you hold it in your computer's buffer); nevertheless the general rule applies: some people edit a lot, some don't. Some writers ignore spelling, punctuation, even grammar until the second draft; others never let a typo go by, even in their notes. Some don't make typos at all. (Aren't those people irritating?)

You may wonder what this has to do with motivation. Having motivation alone is not enough—"*Now* he tells me!" you think—for it must be fed through your various traits, abilities, and skills. As a result, the Mozartian writer has different problems than the Beethovenian. Often the biggest problem for motivating Mozartians generally is to <u>get</u> going, and then not to lose momentum if they stop.

There is a story that Michelangelo, who sculpted with speed so fantastic that chips flew about him like rain as he worked, quit working on the statuary group that included *Moses* because for once in his life he made a mistake on one of the other works, and as a result chose to abandon the group, never to return. Whether or not this is true (and it probably isn't), it does provide a good example of one kind of Mozartian. For someone who can't put something on paper until it is complete, getting to that point may cause a kind of mental constipation. In motivational terms, the idea of starting over may feel ridiculously large, or perhaps the Achievement motive took over and aroused such feelings of anger or inadequacy that the only approach was to back away, or the public humiliation arouses the Influence motive the same way.

Alfred Bester described having to build up steam by pacing back and forth, gathering the threads of his story, until he suddenly ran for the typewriter. When writing interviews for *Holiday* magazine, he had an area of the office which everyone avoided because he paced back and forth there, presumably building up to that critical point on the Yerkes-Dodson bell curve. But you can also imagine a Mozartian writer like Samuel Taylor Coleridge, who only managed to write the first part of "Xanadu" because of the "person from Porlock" who knocked on the door at that wrong moment, and derailed the drug-induced vision that had guided him.

The problem for most Beethovenians, by contrast, is to *keep* going, instead of editing so often that you just give up. A few Beethovenians do not quit, but they will not stop revising, either. Had friends not forcibly removed the manuscript from his hands, J. R. R. Tolkien would have rewritten *The Lord of the Rings* over and over again, as he did with *The Silmarillion*, over a period of three decades. His Beethovenian perfectionism made it nearly impossible for him to finish a manuscript. In fact, *The Silmarillion* was only published because he died! Tolkien rewrote so often that his son's compilations of his earlier drafts and previously unpublished works now far exceed that of his other published works—indeed, they more than triple that number, the last time I looked. This man would not quit. Or there is Dick Lochte's (author of *Blue Bayou*) experience: "Each time I'd return to the manuscript, I'd begin by reworking that first chapter. Before long I had a brilliant first chapter, but I'd grown tired of the book." Beethovenian style can wear you out, especially with too much Achievement motive, which can lead to perfectionism.

As I noted above, this is a wide spectrum of creative styles. In this book you will find suggestions for making your writing process more rewarding in the motivational sense, but everyone's style of writing is a bit different, and

Mozartians and Beethovenians often require different approaches. I have tried to supply suggestions for both sorts. For yourself, I recommend a general guideline: if a tactic <u>seems</u> inappropriate to the way you write, it probably is. Do not assume that all suggestions will work for you, or that if one fails, you should give up. Remember Mozart and Beethoven, and try something that works for you.

Remember:

- Mozart and Beethoven were both excellent, but created very differently.
- Use the suggestions that work, pass on the ones that don't.

CHAPTER 20: STEPS IN THE WRITING PROCESS

Let's take a little time to examine just what writing entails. Here we get into a dicey area, but I'll try to stay objective. Different people write differently, of course, and even those who use this exact process won't necessarily call each step the same names. This are just names to describe certain steps in the typical writing process. Feel free to substitute your own.

FICTION		NONFICTION	
1.	Generate ideas	1.	Identify topic
2.	Plot	2.	Research
3.	Characterization	3.	Lay out material
4.	First-draft writing	4.	First-draft writing
	- description		- prose
	- dialogue		- captions
5.	Editing	5.	Editing
6.	Rewriting	6.	Rewriting

This is a partial, general list. For example, you could write whole books about word choice, paragraphing, chapter breaks, even punctuation, and some have (for example see *The Well-Tempered Sentence*, a marvelous guide to those strange marks that pepper written English). Some people have written whole books about screenplay writing. Some writing endeavors combine aspects of nonfiction and fiction; e.g., historical mysteries or Regency romances require a good deal of research in addition to all the other tasks, enough to exclude the more casual writer.

Why is this important? Because different motives drive different tasks. I have seen far too many people fail to complete a doctoral dissertation because, while they can do research and analyze data, they are incapable of writing or even just completing the writing they have started. Alas for them, you must have a completed document, not just nifty results. As we proceed through the motivational sections, we will refer to these different tasks, but first let's walk through the lists and discuss the nature of each, always remembering that there is nothing magical about the list, and therefore your approach may vary.

Generate Ideas

Unfortunately, this is the easy part. People who fear that editors will "steal" their ideas do not realize that ideas are cheap—good use of them is rare and precious. ("I think it may be said that the more worthless the manuscript, the greater the fear of plagiarism." —publisher Sir Stanley Unwin) Regardless, motivation does come into play here— perhaps not for an initial idea ("Gosh, what if Sherlock Holmes came to the 20th century to hunt a serial killer?") but for the plot complications, subplots, and additional characters that occur in any novel.

Your ideas may also relate to your motive, in that what interests you as a person becomes a driver for what you wish to write, so you can get others to share your interest.

Identify a Topic

This can relate to your motivation, too. Again, many Ph.D candidates never make it because they try to pick an "easy" topic rather than an interesting one, forgetting that they have to live with that topic for years. Professional nonfiction writers may have fewer choices, but they can try to work in an area where most of the topics (or at least some element of them) interest them. Journalists must cover a lot of dull stories, but they also get the excitement of constant change, fast-moving events, and working with people.

Plotting

Contrary to popular belief, this isn't just sitting back and watching a story happen. It includes issues such as pacing, story, character development, and tension-building. Motivation can affect any of these. Someone who likes dwelling on the intimate life of individuals might slow an action plot down to a crawl in order to get extensive, detailed dialogue. Hemingway experimented with the idea of deleting something from the story in such a way that its *absence* would strengthen the rest of the story. What would you choose to delete? Are you more interested in a plot that moves lickety-split, tumbling along, or a plot that moves with smooth and stately grace, building up layer on layer?

Research

For some people this is the best part; for others it is the part you leave until last. A third group uses research to trigger ideas that may evolve into a story. A fourth group manages to avoid it by writing present-day fiction or a certain kind of pure fantasy. Some works require years of research to complete thirty days' writing. To Samuel Johnson, "The greatest part of a writer's time is spent reading, in order to write; a man will turn over half a library to make one book." This kind of thing doesn't come from nowhere. The kind of research one likes to do, and the ability to sustain it when you need it, derive from motives. For some people the very process of research is motivating – sometimes <u>too</u> motivating, in that they never get to the writing.

First-Draft Writing

People fear the blank page — or the blank screen, if you prefer — that mocks their efforts. Others love the pristine whiteness the way kids love a field covered with snow: as a place to leave a mark. Both behaviors come out of your motives. It might even be the *same* motive for different people. The first draft is obviously critical: if you don't write a first draft, you can't have a last.

Some fear the beginning because, once you start, your magnificent vision is reduced to mere tawdry words that fail to manifest your genius. Well, that's what editing is for.

Editing

Do you love tinkering with prose? Adjusting this word here and tightening this sentence there? Or do you dread it, not wanting to damage your marvelous prose? Some people take pleasure (motives, again!) in reading over their own work, knowing that they will make it that much better. Others struggle and sweat over it, to the point that they will abandon their work rather than have to change it. Depending on the degree of change required, almost all writers might have a balking point. Motives can push you past it.

Rewriting

Virtually all professional, published writers rewrite; Neil L. Albert says that he redoes his outline 25 times. Virtually all writers will have to rewrite. Whether you love it and spend hour after hour on it, or you don't like it and do it anyway, hating every minute of it, you clearly depend on your motives to carry you through.

CHAPTER 21: PARTS OF THE WORK

"There are three rules for writing the novel. Unfortunately, no one knows what they are."

—W. Somerset Maugham

Beginning, Middle, and End

"The desire to write grows with writing."

—Erasmus

These are the three toughest parts of a long or short work. Each has different challenges for your motivation. Even after the book is finished, you have not finished your job—you still have to *sell* your piece. (I won't abandon you there, either. There are ways to bridge that gap between finishing this work and starting the next, while trying to stay motivated to do the things a writer must to market his or her work.)

Please note that "beginning" and "end" refer to the process, <u>not</u> to the work itself. You can write a book in any order you wish. Some like to start at the beginning, write until they reach the end, then stop—for example: Rex Stout, who as a Mozartian formulated it in his head first; and Robert A. Heinlein, who tended to follow a story wherever it went, but wrote his first draft in order. Others skip around writing scenes as they see fit, and fill in the gaps later. Still others organize their writing differently: Jeremiah Healy wrote his Cuddy mysteries in reverse order, the same way he managed his cases as a lawyer: Start at the end with the desired result, then determine the immediately previous step needed to get to that end, then the step before that, and so forth. He worked completely backward, one chapter at a time. To confuse matters further, when rewriting, you can write a complete book in one order and then rewrite in a different order. J. R. R. Tolkien wrote *The Lord of the Rings* forward, but then rewrote it backwards. Some outline first, some don't.

We will start with the initial gleam in your eye and follow through to completion of the work, keeping in mind that not all these steps look the same for everyone and also that you may choose to write in some order not described here.

The Beginning

"Every author does not write for every reader."

—Samuel Johnson

First, you have to have an idea. That's your department. I can only suggest areas you might find interesting.
Past studies have suggested that leisure-time reading matter
correlates with motive patterns. This makes sense, if you
consider a book a way to find enjoyment or release. When
you are unencumbered by conscious needs or external
requirements, you will tend to read what you *like*—and that
is strongly influenced by your motives.

This assumes, of course, that you will want to write
what you like to read, like Disraeli: "When I want to read a
good book, I write one." This can be far from the truth.
Many writers are omnivorous in their reading habits;
others explicitly venture outside of their specialty to write.
J. R. R. Tolkien, for example, was a comparative philologist with special expertise in Northern European and
British languages and literature; he drew on this expertise
in writing *The Lord of the Rings*, but spent most of his time
writing scholarly papers and translating works. Although
one may argue that his giant saga only gave him a place to
play with fictional languages, he brought far more to bear
than linguistics. His place descriptions, for example, are so
exact that a professional cartographer had little difficulty
creating an atlas from them.

Values also play a part. As noted from my studies of
professional writers working at novel-length, they typically
feel the impulse to make an impact on others; but the
impact is not usually random. Values provide the focus for
what point they wish to make, whether a moral point, or a
comment on a situation, or any other kind of message they
want to tell.

Others, such as Robert Graves, write novels to support
other writing habits: "Novels are the prize dogs I raise to
sell to support my cats"—meaning his poetry. Mario Puzo

wrote *The Godfather* for exactly the same reason. I know many mystery and science fiction authors who *avoid* reading in their *genre* so it does not contaminate their writing. Alexander Jablakow, for example, finds himself too critical of science fiction to enjoy it anymore. He reads a great deal of history, which ultimately inspires and influences his fictional worlds.

In any case, the purpose in this book is to <u>get</u> you writing—once you get started, and hook in your own motives, *what* you write can be almost incidental. However, it does not hurt to stack the deck in your favor. If you have trouble writing what you have chosen, perhaps it is not your first interest and you need to find ways to make it engaging.

I do not refer to inspiration here, by the way. The idea of waiting around for inspiration to strike is romantic, but not very realistic. (It's the Myth of the Muse, remember.) Shakespeare wrote two plays a year, consistently. Dick Francis wrote a book every year, timed so it would come out in Christmas shopping time. Philip K. Dick wrote and published 26 short stories one year and 27 the next. Inspiration as an outside force had nothing to do with Dick's productivity; eating, on the other hand, had a *lot* to do with it. I am suggesting only that you will find more emotional arousal around an issue that corresponds to your motives, and thus building in some positive reinforcement right at the beginning.

I have to assume you know what you like to read, but you may find another *genre* of interest as well. As we discussed above, research has indicated what kinds of literature people with a given motive tend to read; you may discover a previously untapped area of interest in which to write. I'll repeat:

The person high in Achievement motive tends to read how-to books, nonfiction, and mysteries—books that include or imply goals or include useful facts or means to reach goals. There may also be a concern for innovation and clever ways to solve problems—hence the fascination for a unique method of murder in mysteries. Remember Aaron Elkins reading mysteries because "I *learn* something." Solving puzzles may also be interesting, as a challenge.

The person high in Influence motive reads political biographies, books about scandals, political thrillers, psychology and religious works—books about the use (and abuse) of power, or interaction with powerful figures (including God), or ways in which to influence people or understand how they may be influenced. I hasten to remind you that Influence motivation need not be Machiavellian; the desire to influence is unconscious. The primarily Influence-motivated person may just be interested in seeing how people react, and may well enjoy reading fictional accounts of actions they would never do personally (thus flushing them out of their systems). In fact, one study showed that people who admitted to fantasizing about violence were *less* likely to demonstrate it.

The person high in Affiliation motive reads romances and books with well-developed characters—books about the interaction of people in relationships. It is probably not an accident that romances are divided up into extremely precise types where the protagonists are clearly defined as people: "Woman aged 25-27, little experience with men, modern, dresses well, professional." A person interested in the real guts of relationships thinks about these details, because every detail changes the nature of the relationship.

If you are having trouble writing, it may be because the

subject matter bores you, or because you approach it the wrong way. "Write what you know" is a cliché for writers; I would also add "write what you *like*," because you will be more sensitive on those wavelengths. Some writers talk about writing a "commercial book" to make enough money to write what they like. Some may be able to do this (when they have a choice), but I find it foolish. You will be more effective writing what you enjoy, and more genuine as well. Unless you are a very quick writer who can get published equally quickly, you are unlikely to get in on a current movement until it is nearly over.

When I interviewed Philip Craig, he discussed his process for writing and how he got started. After writing some eight or nine novels, none of which sold, he and his wife sat down and actually analyzed several books then on the bestseller list. They did not enjoy them much, but they did identify a pattern, which included things such as a middle-aged man of the world involved with a younger attractive woman, a murder, an exotic or unusual setting where people would like to go, and so on. So he wrote a novel incorporating all these elements—and he sold the first book of his ongoing series set in Martha's Vineyard. Interestingly, while he stuck to his "formula," he still writes novels that interest him. Having a high influence motive that is very socialized in nature, he has written stories about the *misuse of power*. In one of his recent novels, *A Deadly Vineyard Holiday*, he writes about the young daughter of a President vacationing on Martha's Vineyard, who slips away and embroils the protagonist in a plot filled with secret service men, intrigue, and so on. The book came about because President Clinton came to the Vineyard, and Craig started to mull over the issues of being a child in the corridors of power. He thinks about power, but has a deep ethical distrust of it (a negative value), so that he would not take on leadership roles in organizations willingly. In a sense, his sensitivity to the Influence motive and the nature of power allows him to warn of its dangers more effectively. The formula came from outside—but the plots are his. He gets enormous satisfaction from the process of writing (except rewriting), because his process and product are closely linked to his motives.

Could you actually write a "commercial novel" totally unlike you? I won't be foolish enough to call it impossible, but imagine the challenge of writing in a *genre* in which you find *no* emotional satisfaction at all.

I have read stories written by people trying deliberately to present a motive pattern different from their own—they almost always failed to disguise their own pattern, which emerged all unawares, especially if it was particularly clear-cut profile. Someone who has multiple motives prominent can potentially shift emphasis. Someone who has one strong motive will find it emerges spontaneously.

On the other hand, *writing* in a genre is not the same as *reading* in the genre. Many mysteries do indeed include some kind of mechanism (usually) for committing a crime in a way that makes it difficult to discover, allowing for the Achievement person to try and figure it out. However, making the mechanism the centerpiece of your story leads to a dull story. (Although I met a woman at a mystery convention who *only* read for the puzzle, and disliked characters.) In other words, all work and no play makes Jack (or Jill) a dull writer. Consider that the classic and best-known mysteries have interesting characters—often so interesting that the mystery itself becomes secondary or at least mixed with the story. Dorothy Sayers, creator of the Lord Peter Wimsey stories (and a fine prose stylist), deliberately wrote

Busman's Honeymoon as "a romance with detective interruptions." Her purpose, as stated at the beginning, was that most readers were accustomed to finding the romance as interference to the mystery, whereas the participants were likely to see it the other way around. She intended to show that perspective—and did, quite successfully, while still exploring the mystery. I might also add that Agatha Christie has sold more copies of her books than Shakespeare—and she's catching up on the Bible. While she was famed for her intricate plots, she never failed to have identifiable, if not complex, characters. Hardly anyone alive has not heard of Hercule Poirot or Miss Marple.

Early science fiction writers often made the mistake that, as they were celebrating science and progress, they needed to lecture on the origin and theory behind every technological miracle in their stories, rather than discussing how people interacted with them—a classic example of assuming your audience has the same interests and motives you do (in fact, this is a clue to a person's motives. See below). I don't wish to insult any writer (who after all wrote for their audience and their time) by quoting serious work, but I feel safe in quoting Randall Garrett and Lin Carter, who parodied this style hilariously in their story "Masters of the Metropolis:"

> "He paused to board a *bus* which stopped at regularly-spaced intervals to take on new passengers. The *bus*, or Omnibus, was a streamlined, self-propelled public vehicle, powered by the exploding gases of distilled petroleum, ignited in a sealed chamber by means of an electrical spark. The energy thus obtained was applied as torque to a long metal bar known as the 'drive shaft' which turned a set of gears in a complex apparatus

known as the 'differential housing.' These gears, in turn, caused the rear wheels to revolve about their axes, thus propelling the vehicle forward smoothly at velocities as great as eighty miles every hour!"

You can imagine what the *actual* stories were like. These stories were often written by engineers (and occasionally still are) who found fascination in how things worked—an Achievement-motive-based attitude—rather than the Influence-motivated perspective of having an impact or the Affiliative perspective of enjoyable, sympathetic characters. This need not block good writing (especially nonfiction) unless you also lack craft. Knowing everything about your field is insufficient if you cannot write a meaningful and interesting sentence; and in the early days of science fiction many did not understand their craft. Fortunately for the field, many of these writers learned better, or at least made their lectures entertaining. Since the audience had motives that made them sympathetic to the writers, everyone felt satisfied. As readership shifted, the typical writer shifted too. Stories that would sell in an instant in 1955 would never sell today. The audience has changed, as has the quality of the writing. Nevertheless, you can choose to write whatever you like — as long as the motivation comes from inside, who cares about the genre of the material? — but it is silly not to write what you enjoy writing. Just consider that not everyone has the same motive pattern as you.

Starting Your Flow

As indicated above, subjects tend to line up with motives. But there is another approach which intertwines with the motives, and that may define how you write your stories.

Different things also drive the *story-writing process*. There are several different kinds of dividers, and I do not claim to have them all, but here is a reasonable list of how some stories are driven:

- **Plot**: You work out an intricate or straightforward plot, and that is what interests you or keeps you moving—you want to see it play out in the same way assembling a puzzle can hold your attention for hours. This could apply to power-and-influence-focused thrillers like Robert Ludlum's novels or to an achievement-focused mystery novel like Agatha Christie.

- **Ideas**: You have a fascinating idea: What If so-and-so happened? Commonest in science fiction, for obvious reasons, but also found in mysteries (what if you had a nearly perfect, undetectable murder method: Dorothy Sayers' *Suspicious Characters*, sometimes called the "gimmick" mystery approach), political thrillers (what if the Soviets invented a silent sub, but its commander was willing to bring it to the West: Tom Clancy's *The Hunt for Red October*), medical thrillers (what if a certain virus got loose?), horror (H. P. Lovecraft: what if the Old Gods were sleeping under the sea, and they affected our dreams?) and the like.

- **Characters**: You have an interesting character you want to follow around, or whom you put in interesting settings. In one interview, Donald Westlake described how he came to write his humorous caper novels featuring the unlucky

John Dortmunder; he had come up with a
crime that was basically so silly (stealing an
entire bank that was temporarily in a trailer)
that his regular crime-novel protagonist "turned
it down." He was wondering what to do when
this sad-faced individual turned up and said
with a sigh that he would take it. This became
John Dortmunder, the unluckiest brilliant
criminal you can imagine. The book became
Bank Shot, starting a successful series that went
for many years and fourteen novels. Leigh
Perry's Sid the Skeleton series features a
walking, talking skeleton partnered with his best
friend since childhood, adjunct professor and
single mother Georgia Thackery. The only
paranormal element is Sid, but in and around
the mystery is the relationship between the two
of them and how Sid can engage with a world
in which he must remain hidden.

- **Scenes/settings**: Philip Craig told me that he
wrote one novel in order to get to a scene. He
had grown up in Colorado, and, remembering
a certain cliff, he wanted to have a scene set on
it. He wound up moving his character from
Martha's Vineyard, Massachusetts to Colorado
for one novel just to get that scene written. The
desire to get there drove this whole novel. Some
writers, including Carol Higgins Clark and
Mary Higgins Clark, set a scene in a place they
would like to visit, and visit that place. Dorothy
Gilman's Mrs. Polifax series is written the same
way. In a sense, this is also tax-driven, since it
meant the trip was tax-deductible. You find
your inspiration where you can.

- **Research**: Some writers write their books so they have an excuse to do research. While some find it the most difficult and boring part, others get joy from it. Sharan Newman said that this was the best part of writing for her; she takes great pains to ensure total historical accuracy, supported no doubt by her advanced degrees in medieval history. Sarah Smith dives into a subject for years before starting her books, which range widely in location and time, and cites this as a serious distraction from the actual writing.

Sitting Down and Warming Up

Hemingway's first rule for writers was to apply the seat of the pants to the seat of the chair. Some people sit down and promptly start writing; others need to find ways to warm up to the task. Hemingway himself sharpened twenty pencils before he wrote—which he did standing up, by the way, because of a previous injury. I distinguish these activities from superstitions and the like (which I will discuss later) because they are inextricably linked to the process of writing for their users.

Since these are idiosyncratic, I will group these into larger categories and cite a whole batch.

- **Music**: One writer I met at a conference wrote an entire book to a single soundtrack; he had to put this on to inspire him, and he played it over and over until he finished. Unfortunately when I met him he had been unable to start a second book. I suggested that that music was now irrevocably associated with that first book, that he needed a new score. Many writers write to music—including me, at this moment—and it has been suggested that engaging the right hemisphere where music is processed may "liberate" one's writing, which comes primarily from the left. Along these lines, Harlan Ellison recommended movie soundtracks, particularly those of Ennio Morricone (*The Good, the Bad, and the Ugly*). The advantage of such music is that it lacks lyrics and therefore does not engage the verbal centers of your brain, and distract you from writing words by making you listen to them instead.

- **Inspirational Reading**: Some writers get ready to write by reading someone else. Willa Cather read a passage from the Bible, Stendhal said "Whilst writing the *Chartreuse*, in order to acquire the correct tone I read every morning two or three pages of the Civil Code." Playwright and screenwriter Neil Simon reportedly saw a stage show called *Something's Afoot* (a murder mystery musical comedy, if you can believe it) which inspired him to go home and write the screenplay for *Murder by Death*. I have seen both, and certainly see a family resemblance in theme.

- **Educational Experiences**: Traveling to places or doing something educational (whether deliberately or not) can trigger a desire to work with those places or things in your work. Sometimes it is as simple as looking at a scene and picturing it as a setting for one's work, or imagining "what if…" I published a short story based on my experiences with a particularly horrible CEO of a startup company, which gave me the inspiration for how someone else might approach dealing with that person.

- **Setting Up Targets**: If one of the unconscious goals of a writer is to have an impact (the Influence motive, remember), it helps to remind yourself of whom you might have an impact upon. Henrik Ibsen hung a portrait of August Strindberg over his desk, saying, "He is my mortal enemy and shall hang there and watch while I write." The writer's equivalent of a dartboard with a portrait, I suppose. Beethoven used Mozart as the standard to measure himself against, trying to do things Mozart had not done. The Beatles and the Rolling Stones had a largely friendly competition.

- **Trips**: Fredric Brown took boring bus trips. George M. Cohan actually rented an entire Pullman railroad car drawing room and traveled until he finished a project. He wrote up to 140 pages a night. Some writers take trips to gather material, but they also want to write off the trip on their taxes. Many writers' conferences have been paid for this way. Roger Zelazny describes writing a chess-playing unicorn story ("Unicorn Variations"), selling it in three places, and paying for the Alaskan cruise on which he wrote it.

- **Relaxing in the tub**: Ben Franklin had the first bathtub in America, and liked writing in it; Edmond Rostand, author of *Cyrano de Bergerac*, wrote in the tub to avoid interruption by his numerous friends—arguably an example of removing distractions as well. On the other hand, Douglas Adams took lengthy baths to *avoid* writing.

- **Stimulants**: I considered titling this "drugs," but let's be more tactful than that (I drink caffeinated sodas, after all). Coffee, tea, tobacco, and other stimulants are long-time favorites of many writers, as well as others no longer legally available. Sigmund Freud used cocaine earlier in his career (and possibly longer) and cigars his entire life (as did American poet Amy Lowell, who bought 10,000 of her favorite brand when shortages looked likely in 1915)—even when diagnosed with cancer Freud could not give up his beloved cigars, which he claimed to need to think. Alexander Pope and Balzac drank strong coffee—the latter 50 cups a day; Dr. Johnson could put away 25 cups of tea at a sitting. Please note again that *if* this is invariably associated with writing, then it helps; if not, then it is just an inconvenient and possibly dangerous habit. Balzac's death is partially attributable to caffeine poisoning, after all. You might increase your productivity over a limited time but shorten your lifespan—and I could hardly recommend that.

- **Positioning**: I already mentioned Hemingway's vertical stance, but that was in some ways physically required. Truman Capote, on the other hand, felt he had to lie down, or he would be unable to write. Mark Twain and Robert Louis Stevenson also liked horizontal composition. Lewis Carroll and Virginia Woolf wrote standing up by choice, and we may presume that Jane Austen wrote standing up because she wrote only a sentence or two at a time in passing in a blank book on a sideboard.

- **Rehearsing**: Just get your fingers warmed up and in the habit of typing words. It doesn't have to make sense—yet.

Getting to the Beginning.

This book will not be useful to you unless you are ready to really begin producing prose. It may help to discuss methods to garner and organize ideas to the point where you do want to take action.

The traditional writing method taught in high schools today generally goes like this:

- Jot down ideas
- Winnow ideas
- Make a tentative outline
- Research
- Revise outline according to research (plot)
- Begin writing from outline.

I have yet to meet anyone who actually *followed* this method strictly except in very limited circumstances—such as high school writing classes. (Though I am certain some wildly successful writer out there does exactly this.) If you ask a hundred writers how their writing process goes, you are likely to get one hundred responses, none of which resemble the above. For example, some outlines never get written until *after* the book is finished—in order to submit an outline to a publisher. I am not about to recommend that you start to use this method if you do not now; I am using it as a list of nearly all of the tasks a writer may undertake before writing, and a means for logically laying them out for our convenience here. In that way, we can sort out the options available for you to get your writing started.

Jotting Down Ideas

The Achievement-oriented individual is interested in the new and different—hence the large number of Achievement oriented science fiction readers looking for well-designed futures and mystery readers who seek for a new and innovative crime. Writers in these *genres* need to remember that ideas are not enough, but that a good one can get them going, especially if they have a sufficient backlog of ideas stored up to support it. The classic device for storing fleeting ideas is the "commonplace book," in which you jot ideas, insert newspaper clippings, photographs, anything that triggers your ideas, or may someday. Items may sit for years—but don't worry about that. The idea is to give you a mine for your notions, so that when you need something right now, you can consult your book and find something waiting.

Alfred Bester, a partisan of this method, relied on it so heavily that he satirized himself in a mystery-thriller, *Who He?*, as a person who was completely dependent on his commonplace book and went into a frenzy when it went astray. A commonplace book is a good place to acknowledge your innovative thoughts; as you fill pages with jotted notes, you can measure the number of ideas you have available. Darwin's were so detailed that we can trace exactly what he read and thought on a given day.

For the Influence-oriented person such a book is a place to put things that evoke a response—that have a profound emotional impact. Dramatic scenes, striking pictures (in the days of pulp magazines editors often commissioned stories to fit a completed cover painting), ways to influence people, descriptions of people who influenced *you*. Then you can refer to it to find a description of an effect you desire to make in your own work.

The Affiliative person could put in descriptions of relationships in all their myriad forms, and the outcomes of those relationships.

For all three types, jotting down notes and keeping them is a way to store your motives up for when you need it, in the form of motivating ideas. If they don't have power to move you, then they probably will not help you.

When making a jot list for immediate use, you can use this same dividing line—does it arouse your excitement? Of course, some kinds of writing just aren't that thrilling— but on the other hand a subject that is boring to the writer will bore the reader as well. If you find a topic that requires sections that lack interest for you, perhaps you should jot some ideas for making those sections more interesting.

Freewriting

This is an alternative form of jotting, where you sit down and begin writing about anything that comes to mind. This technique is particularly helpful when you do not know what you want to do, but know you need to start writing. Anything will do: the preamble to the Constitution, "now is the time for all good men," whatever; after a few lines you are likely to get so bored with the task that you start generating more interesting ideas. This is likely to work best for those with Achievement or Influence motivation, but it could work for any. This can be, in effect, a free association session, where you let your motives run wild.

The usual caution on freewriting is that you do not stop to criticize it. It must be *free*, or you will choke off the flow. If you suddenly begin focusing on a specific plot, go with it; do not bother to fix the beginning until the time is right.

Outlining

The Mozartian writer may choose to outline completely before writing a lengthy work, or not outline at all. The Beethovenian, on the other hand, may choose to write and rewrite an outline before beginning, and then still diverge from it. Whatever works is fine. Just do not let anything limit you. Any writing technique that stifles your motivation, no matter how apparently useful, will work against you in the long run. It may appear, for example, that outlining will make your writing far faster, especially if you are the apparently disorganized type that writes your novel or textbook completely out of order. Note that I said *apparently* disorganized; after all, no movie script is filmed in order, for very good reasons that have nothing to do with the plot. If, however, you hate outlining so much that it sours you on the production of prose, then you will have made it impossible to use that outline.

If you like or need outlines (and not necessarily at the beginning, either: some people like to write isolated scenes, order them roughly, and then outline the remaining plot around them), then you should try to motivate yourself to do them as you would your other work. Make sure, again, that the reinforcement is appropriate to your motives, so you will look forward to it. Keep the scope distinctly different from that of prose writing; it is a different process, after all. Do not count hundreds of words; count dozens. Or better yet, count heads and subheads. For the highly achievement-motivated person, make columns listing each level of heading: Roman numerals, capital letters, Arabic numerals, lower-case letters, etc., as below:

Date	I	A	1	a	1)	a)
March 17, '19	4	10	26	23	3	3
March 18, '19	5	12	32	32	6	3

This kind of recording can be easily placed in a spreadsheet, should your mind work that way, and graphed or charted.

Plotting

> "Within the limits of what I do, I can satisfy myself. ... [My stories] do not rely on plot. Mine rely almost entirely on character."
>
> —Elmore Leonard

> "A story is: the king died, the queen died. A plot is: the king died, the queen died of grief."
>
> —E. M. Forster

> "I never work out a plot—I always say that plots belong in cemeteries."
>
> —Kinky Friedman

Outlining can link closely to the process of plotting. A plot organizes your characters, keeps them moving in the right direction, leading (and misleading) your readers. Some basic plot types are so well known that they become clichés:

The romantic cliché:

Boy meets girl, boy loses girl, boy gets girl.

The mystery cliché:

Crime occurs, police are baffled, red herrings distract, the detective penetrates to the truth.

The epic cliché:

Naive protagonist meets mysterious stranger who leads him to his destiny, overcoming obstacles in himself and the world, finally becoming a hero.

And so on, and so on. These plots recur, with numerous twists, over and over again. Why? Why does *Romeo and Juliet* follow the romantic cliché (with the tragic twist that "boy-gets-girl" occurs in death), Agatha Christie the mystery cliché, *Star Wars* the epic cliché? Just how many plots are there, really?

Many people will tell you how many plots there are—that there are a limited number. Scholars of this subject and writers have pegged it at 1, 15, 45, 64, and probably others as well. However, one strong movement pushes for only one. It runs something like this:

- Hero starts quest
- Takes action to goal
- Encounters obstacles in self and world
- Struggles forward despite despair, maintains hope
- Gets help to overcome obstacles

• Reaches consummation of goals

I've missed some subtleties, but I've covered the bases. Now I don't necessarily hold to <u>any</u> theory that limits range (witness Douglas Adams' *Hitchhikers' Guide to the Galaxy*, about "the end of the world and the happy-go-lucky days that follow"), but I think most would agree this Quest plot has power to move. It includes Odysseus, King David the Israelite, Luke Skywalker, Bilbo Baggins, and many others.

Why? Motivation, by gum! Remember the Problem-Solving Model? The model reflects a pattern of thought about getting to a goal. Well, since the Monomyth is about getting to a goal, shouldn't they have something in common? Let's look:

The Problem-Solving Model

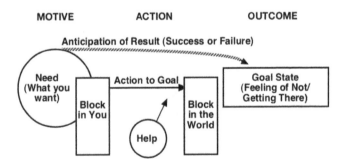

<u>How the Problem-Solving Model compares to the Monomyth:</u>

Monomyth: Motive

Monomyth	Motive
Goal	Stated Need (Goal) (N)
Action	Instrumental Activity (Act)
Obstacles in Self	Personal Blocks (Bp)
Obstacles in the World	World Blocks (Bw)
Despair and Hope (destiny)	Goal Anticipation (Ga+ and Ga-)
Help (Mentor)	Help (H)
Consummation of Goals	Goal State (G+ and G-)

The monomyth is motivational—and I mean that literally as well as literarily. It echoes a piece of our brain...it makes sense. Not that it is necessarily the best plot, but it is a recognizable plot. For example:

Motive Subcat	Romance	SF	Mystery
N	Boy meets girl	Boy discovers truth/destiny	Person discovers crime, must solve
Bw	Boy loses girl	Boy exiled, lost	Person alienated from normal life
Act	Boy seeks girl	Works behind scenes	Investigates
Ga-	Fears lack of merit	Fears death or loss	Fears being wrong
Bp	Loses confidence	Loses confidence	Loses confidence
Ga+	Resolves to go on	Girds loins	Finds purpose
Value	Moral/Selfish	Moral/Selfish	Moral/Selfish
H	Support from friend	Support from secret mentor	Unexpected ally
G+	Boy gets girl	Achieves destiny	Solves mystery
Or			
G-	Loses girl to death (e.g., *Love Story*)	Big Brother wins (e.g., *1984*)	Real villain gets off (various)

Of course, you can (and should) apply this to yourself as a writer:

N: I want to write a book/story/essay

*SA: I think I can do it, imagine my book on the
    shelf, my essay in the magazine*

FA: I'm afraid no one will like it/buy it

Bw: I can't find an agent/publisher

*Bp: I'm no good as a writer, I can't [plot,
    characterize, etc.]*

Act: I'm writing, sending queries, etc.

*H: I have emotional support (spouse/friend),
    writing support (workshop, editor), selling
    support (agent)*

*G+ I've finished! I sold! I have an agent! I'm on a
    10 best list! I've got a hardcover! I've won the
    Nobel Prize!*

*G- It's a bomb. (Ideally followed by "I'm doing
    better on the next one!")*

Don't ignore any of the subcategories—miss one, you may sink your efforts (though some are not good to dwell on, especially Personal Block, World Block, and Failure Anticipation). Note that in addition to the obvious influence motive thinking, positive affiliation parallels the trusting attitude you may need to get it done—that is, that you will be taken care of, that things will work out. God or the universe will provide. This also scores as positive Goal Anticipation (Ga+) and Help (H).

The Middle

Often enough, writers get a perfectly wonderful idea with no place to go. I have stacks of them piled neatly in my computer. I assume that you have gone beyond that stage and instead seek to continue a beginning (or an end, for that matter).

It is at this stage when the motivational writing strategies described above come in most useful: in the midst of a story, with an idea at least partially developed. When the challenge is just to keep going, use these tools.

However, it may be difficult to sit down at the typewriter (or keyboard, or even the quill pen stand) in order to get this going. This is a challenge more for some than others. Many primarily Achievement-motivated people will not stop for Hell or high water once engaged. They are internally motivated anyway (in the sense of not looking for external stimuli to write), so are unlikely to be greatly distracted, except perhaps by nearby individuals.

The primarily Influence-motivated person, on the other hand, may have trouble getting down to cases. Useful tactics may include looking at that big red sign with your word count, talking to someone sympathetic about the book, or just sitting down and staring until you get tired of looking silly. (For the latter, you should think about how you would look to others). You might also refer to the "Sitting Down and Warming Up" section above.

If you are telling a story of some kind, speaking it aloud to someone or even to yourself may be your best tactic. Besides the value of hearing the words roll (assuming you speak well), you will see that your words have an impact on someone else. When they want to know what comes next, you will want to tell them. Make sure they are responsive, or you may kill your book.

Remember that everyone has different tastes—as mentioned above, some of this comes from your motive pattern. If you are reading the wrong book to a person, they will not respond.

The primarily Affiliation-motivated person may do the same, but with slightly different intent. They want a positive impact on the person, or in some cases, a feeling of liking for themselves or even the written characters. A detailed literary analysis is not what they want. They want positive reinforcement and personal support, to reassure them that they are good people, or that they are sensitive and likable, or simply that they belong to something larger than themselves.

Natural Breaks

For many writers, there are clues to when they need a break, or they need to try another take on what they have done so far. These clues range from greater difficulty writing to rage to physical symptoms, so it is difficult to describe them with a single term. I'll call them incidents.

An incident occurs when you should be plugging along and suddenly something happens. Here are some real writers' examples:

A slowdown or stoppage:

> "[I had] A sense of being stuck in doing things — in the assumptions I was making. I felt it. I would sit there and I found it extremely hard to move forward. It takes four hours to write one paragraph."

> —Sarah Smith

> "I just can't do anything. I want to write, but I don't. I just play Pac-Man or solitaire or something. It means I need to think for a while longer and when I'm ready it will go again."

—Toni L. P. Kelner

The characters go awry:

"If something's going wrong the characters go dead."

—Sarah Smith

Driving yourself too hard:

"On my first book, I was kind of obsessive. My goals were too aggressive. I exhausted myself...I hit a wall—I couldn't tell if what I was writing was good or not."

For some individuals, no such stoppage occurs. They simply continue writing. Presumably even Isaac Asimov paused to eat. Eating and typing at the same time is hard, unless your lunch goes through a straw.

Rewriting

"Despite the vast amount of outlining and thinking I do, when it comes to writing there's always new inspiration. My method of work is to get a very good idea of what I want to cover and assign a time percentage to it. I will rewrite each page, and then each few pages, moving ahead very slowly with the handwritten page. When I finish a whole section, I go back and type what I've rewritten. That is an extensive rewriting process—largely with language. Usually it will be taking out much and then getting new ideas to put in. Then I'll read it again, pencil it, and give it to a typist to type. It's not necessary to do much in the way of rewriting [after that]—it's largely a matter of cutting, changing words, catching an inconsistency."

—Joseph Heller, in the October 1977 *Writer's Digest* magazine

"The revision process is fascinating to me. Some of my poems have gone through sixty or more drafts by the time I'm satisfied. I think it's very important for poets to have others read their work, get all the criticism they can as well as be extremely self-critical."

—May Sarton, from a 1989 profile by Lois Rosenthal

Some enjoy rewriting. Many do not. They feel that the pure joy of generating prose is somehow compromised by the tedious backtracking and tinkering. For those people, it is important to keep motivation high—because unless you are Isaac Asimov, Mozart, or Shakespeare, you will probably need *some* rewriting. We are not discussing quality here; we are discussing the process of writing. Even the best prose needs rearrangement, tinkering, or removal to another book.

Obviously, many of the tools described above to motivate writing do not assist rewriting. Counting "new words," for example, might work against you if you tend to overwrite and edit down at the next session. Here are some different approaches:

Internal Measures of Progress

These are particularly helpful to the Achievement motive.

- Count the number of pages you have rewritten. Each time you rewrite them you can count anew.
- Keep track of the number of words reduced (works best if you are a person who overwrites and then cuts).
- Count the number of lines altered in any way, right down to the comma.
- Edit from beginning to end in order, and keep track of your page numbers. Set goals for pages covered, either by deletion or by addition (i.e., you can either edit five pages, or edit one page and write four additional pages. I did that on this book for my first full edit pass.)
- Track the percentage completed. You can do this two ways: percentage of old text covered (that is, I have rewritten my first 30 pages of 300, or 10%, even though I expanded them to 60 pages), or percentage of the total that is now done (60 done out of what is now 330, or roughly 18%).

When I began rewriting this book for this edition, I tracked the overall word-count each day I worked (starting with the original draft), the daily incremental changes in word-count, the cumulative change in word-count, what page I reached in the edit pass (I went from beginning to end), how many I covered in a given session (which set expectations for me to meet or beat), the total number of manuscript pages, what percentage I had completed, and what percentage of the content was new. Each of these indicators had some importance to me: how fast was I editing and writing (pages by date), and how much additional content was I providing (new words and pages) relative to the original work. It also allowed me to graph my progress:

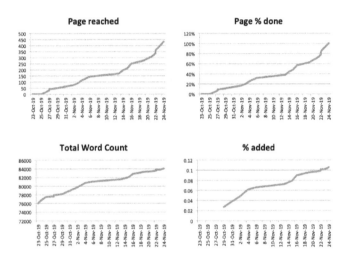

External Measures of Progress

These are often helpful to the Influence and Affiliation motives:

- Get an outside person to praise you for how much better it is.
- Use a writing group, telling them your progress.
- Do your editing in bright red ink, set yourself

> specific time goals for specific chapters and post
> your progress and/or show your pages.

Rewriting may appear to be a trivial point, but in fact it
may be the single biggest differentiator between those
who sell and those who do not—both because of bad
rewriting, or because of not rewriting.

As mentioned elsewhere, Dick Lochte never finished
one novel because he kept rewriting the first chapter. So by
the time he had a perfect beginning, he had lost interest in
the rest of the book. By contrast, Philip R. Craig never
sold his first eight or nine completed novels because he
would send one out, get a rejection, and rather than try to
rewrite he would start another book. Craig gives credit to
his word processor, for making rewriting more interesting
and easier for him. Tinkering with words on a word
processor, where all the formatting and refitting is done for
you, greatly reduces the pain of rewriting.

In a few years the concept of "draft" may well be obso-
lete except in arbitrary or external terms—that is, the first
draft is the one you send out for rejection or happen to
print out, rather than the first one you write out on paper.
Many writers find it easier to tinker with a document
online than to have to red-line by hand and re-type. Since
you can track changes on most applications these days, you
can even reward yourself by seeing what changes you have
made.

An example of how one writer uses her PC to write
and rewrite is below:

> "I generally start by reading over a little of what I did
> the previous day, then keep writing. I often go back and
> change little bits in previous stuff I've written. It

generally takes one 'write' and 150 rewrites, changing things around, which you can do with a computer."

—Sarah Smith

As you can see, rewriting can be very important indeed: Lochte failed to complete a book because he did too much too soon; Craig failed to sell a book (or eight) because he did not do enough. Beethovenian writers are clearly more vulnerable to this kind of issue; if you know yourself to be one, get prepared to do a lot of rewriting. If you think you are a Mozartian writer, remember that Philip Craig got a lot of rejections for non-rewritten books. Be sure you really <u>are</u> Mozartian. Perhaps you just (ahem) possess a great deal of self-confidence. After all, Mozartian writers (or any other kind of creator) are relatively rare, especially at book length. Even Isaac Asimov needed his word processor for his novels. As someone once said: "It isn't writing—it's rewriting." Or, as Peter DeVries put it: "I love writing—it's the paperwork I can't stand." Rewriting is the purest form of paperwork. Be ready for it.

Approaching the Denouement

"Finishing a book is just like you took a child out in the yard and shot it."

—Truman Capote

There is a curious phenomenon observed in some writers: they find it difficult or nearly impossible to finish anything. If they genuinely have no end, well, that happens often enough. But what of those who have an end in mind, or at least a completion (I do not assume you write from beginning to end), and cannot bring yourself to put it on paper?

There are many reasons for such behavior; some may lie in the realm of clinical or therapeutic rather than motivational psychology. For our purposes here, I can propose some reasons that can be understood in motive terms, and dealt with.

The most obvious is that, once writing has become rewarding, you do not want to stop: that the end of a work (be it short story, essay, text, or novel) symbolizes the end of writing and the end of the enjoyment thereof. This is irrational, but no one said people had to make sense. The solution is neat enough: Start something else before you stop. It need not be much; just knowing you have more writing to do might be enough. Writing is a discontinuous process: starting, stopping, and starting again. But if you keep some process going, the discontinuities will not affect your writing motivation. Do avoid getting so involved in the next work that you neglect the first, though—I can just see a writer surrounded by nine-tenths-finished volumes churning happily away at the next. And lest you think this is a fantasy, listen to Erica Jong:

> "I went for years not finishing anything. Because, of course, when you finish something you can be judged...I had poems which were rewritten so many times I suspect it was just a way of avoiding sending them out."

The End

> "Writing every book is like a purge; at the end of it one is empty ...like a dry shell on the beach, waiting for the tide to come in again."
>
> —Daphne Du Maurier

> "For me it is torture when I finish a novel. The good time is when I'm writing. When I am finished it's no more fun."
>
> —Umberto Eco

Umberto Eco wrote large, very successful books. For you, the words "The End" may be wonderful words indeed, because you have **FINISHED YOUR BOOK!!** Now what? Well, it is awfully easy to lose your motivation to do anything more when you have reached an obvious stopping place like an ending; so I recommend (as noted above) you find ways not to stop. Shift gears: for example, start looking for an agent or a publisher before you finish.

It may be quite difficult to consider marketing before you are even finished—unless you have a high need for Influence, in which case you may find the idea of marketing more alluring than writing. But when the book is finished, it allows you to keep moving.

If you already have an agent, publisher, or other platform, start the next book or story. After completing a manuscript, you may not feel like writing ever again; but in most cases this feeling will pass. Do not feel you have to work *hard* at it. Remember that the idea here is to engage your enjoyment. Fool around—write something completely different. Hunter S. Thompson started *Fear and Loathing in Las Vegas* as a brief article for *Sports Illustrated*, who rejected it savagely, as he would say. So there he was: a professional journalist working on a very heavy straight story (the murder of Chicano journalist Ruben Sálazar) that could conceivably get him killed, who unwound at night by letting his fingers run wild over this bizarre, comic, semi-fictional story. Thus was Gonzo Journalism born—or at least acknowledged. Other creative people like to use a different medium entirely: painting, or acting, or something else. Woody Allen, who writes, acts, *and* directs, plays jazz sax in Manhattan for fun. As long as you feel consistently creative, do not worry about it. You will come back when you want to.

And let us not forget that some people need the mental rest that playing around can give. After a sufficient time, you may begin writing of your own accord. If not, go back to the beginning and work on jump-starting yourself.

Some studies indicate that people find restoration in switching hemispheres—of the brain, not the Earth. That is, if you are doing something primarily left-hemispheric like writing or editing, you should alternate with something right-hemispheric—drawing, sports, whatever. One study even suggests that you can jump-start one hemisphere into primacy by blocking a nostril and breathing on one side for a while. Again, a single action like that is too simplistic for practical use for anyone, but the basic principle is applicable everywhere: alternate kinds of tasks. When you exhaust your brain, go exercise your body.

The Next One

Some writers talk about the "second book problem," meaning that you may have said all you had to say in the first book, and can write no more. If this is so, quit! You are in excellent company. Miguel de Cervantes wrote only one novel of note: *Don Quixote*, which happens to be the single most significant and influential work of fiction in Spanish to date—more so than any single work in English, including Shakespeare's. On a less prominent note, *To Kill a Mockingbird* was the only novel written by Harper Lee (though not by her childhood friend Truman Capote) and apparently she felt pretty happy with that very successful and award-winning book, play, and movie.

But that is not true of many writers. They get hooked, and that's it. Once you learn to write and become able to keep writing, it is hard to stop, no matter how little you may feel you have to say. After all, Shakespeare had only a couple of mildly original plots in all of his plays. It didn't bother him—don't let it bother you.

When moving on to the next work, if you set your standards too high, you won't achieve them. For maximum accomplishment, you should set a moderate but challenging goal. Don't expect to write your second novel immediately. Expect it to be harder. It may not be, but be ready for it. Take your time; set your daily goal lower if you have to—but write something, even if it is gibberish. Write enough, and you will begin to force yourself to make sense of it.

Whether you choose to outline first or not is a matter of taste. Some swear by it, but on the other hand, J. R. R. Tolkien wrote his three-volume novel *The Lord of the Rings* over ten years with no idea where it was going. Of course, good plotting would probably have made it shorter—but who knows what we would have lost?

I have said it before, and will again: there is no one best way to write, no easy answers. You must work to make writing something you want to do, and whatever method you use is fine.

Mozart went from his head to paper with virtually no changes. Beethoven went through many, many drafts and edits on his music. These two styles can be applied to virtually any kind of creative endeavor, whether writing, drawing, writing music, etc. Don't let the *other* type of person sway you in the way you choose to go about your work. Including yourself! The second book will certainly be different from your first, if only because you have had practice. You might find yourself unexpectedly better.

CHAPTER 22: MOTIVATE YOUR SELLING!

"You must put your work before an editor who will buy it."

—Robert A. Heinlein's Third Law of Writing

"I don't want to take up literature in a money-making spirit, or be very anxious about making large profits, but selling it at a loss is another thing altogether, and an amusement I cannot well afford."

—Lewis Carroll

Until now, I have primarily focused on the actual process of writing. I have tried to give a comprehensive view of the different issues you bring to the task of writing. In one sense, my job is done. However, yours will not be. If you do in fact have the motive profile shared by most professional writers, you will not be satisfied by having finished a work —you will want to publish it.

Today's publishing industry makes it virtually certain that you will have to spend a significant amount of time working on selling what you have written. After all the work you have done to actually write, it can be very depressing to know that you have only just begun the process of publication.

In the course of studying writers, I inevitably became familiar with the process of selling and marketing as well. I see no reason to stop with the writing if I can contribute to the publication—as I noted earlier, I read too—and certainly given the daunting obstacles facing the writer who wishes to be published, clearly motivation is essential.

However, the market has changed a lot since I did my initial research. In some ways, it is worse: major publishing firms and magazines aren't paying better than they did 20 years ago; it's even harder to break into the field. It's no better for other creatives as well; some famous musicians have commented that had they started out in the 2010s, they would have given up and gotten a real job.

In other ways, it is better. There are actually far more publishers now, though most of them small, and it is possible to publish entirely online; there has also been an explosion of online e-zines which may pay poorly but provide an accessible outlet for people to publish. Many are run by highly professional editors who can help a writer get better. Some have chosen to publish their own works, which can be risky – there's a truism that the lawyer who represents himself has a fool for a client, and the same may apply to someone who goes into doing their own publishing blindly. There are a lot of issues that should be addressed thoughtfully.

The Internet is your friend, when it comes to identifying places to publish, or how to publish, or who to use to help you. You can also find support groups that are enormously helpful for any of those things. Furthermore, if you spend a little time, you can also find warnings against the unscrupulous who want you to pay them to publish your work, or who want to profit from your unpaid creative effort. But let's focus for the moment on what is still the basic problem: getting a publisher.

Realistically, thousands of people are out there competing for an editor's attention. Editors, being only human themselves, have their own personal likes and dislikes, which may cause them to fail to appreciate your unique brilliance. Calvin Trillin tells of soliciting stories for a book called *Authors' Atrocity Stories About Publishers*. He received enough material for a twenty-volume series but couldn't find anyone who would publish it. He was kidding (more or less), but there is a real truth there. People become sensitive about their ability or lack thereof to publish.

If you sell your book, it is the unhappy truth about publishing that, with a few exceptions, you must then go on and spend time selling the book to readers. Many writers spend almost as much time marketing as writing. Some spend more. This is one reason some prefer to just publish themselves and sell themselves – why not shorten the process? The reason is that publishers may have resources, people, and abilities you don't, or don't want to use, but there are people who have been successful doing so. It depends on your objective: are you trying to make money? Or just get your book out there?

I cannot tell you the best way to go about selling as such, though I have some experience and knowledge, if only from assisting my wife in her efforts. But we can discuss the ways in which you can apply your motives to the job.

Robert Silverberg describes this encounter:

> "[A] woman...told me that she had in fact written an entire novel, a detective story, but had never found the courage to send it to an editor. Nevertheless she wanted to be a published writer. I pointed out, not entirely gently, the little lapse of logic in her behavior. Pick a publishing company, I said, and send your book there, or else stop pretending that you're interested in a writing career. ...I figured that was the last I would ever hear of her; but no, no, just the other day I noticed a half-page ad in the *New York Times Book Review* for what I think was her fifth novel, quoting from ecstatic reviews of her earlier books and listing all the awards she has won. She is big stuff, these days, in the mystery field. So she was a real writer after all—with a slight underconfidence problem that I suspect she has long since outgrown."

Heinlein's Third Law, again!

Getting an Agent

At one time writers could sell directly to an editor, who would sometimes hold their hand as they rewrote their works. For some time, no major publishing firm ever dedicated that much time to individual writers unless they produced megabucks, and most of those writers have the clout to demand no editing. Now, with the advent of many smaller book companies, it has become possible to sell directly to an editor again, though it takes a good deal of research and effort to do so, with possibly limited results. It's still reasonable to consider getting an agent for book-length works. For shorter works, there's no need; you can sell directly to magazines or e-zines, or sometimes to editors of original anthologies who announce they will take unsolicited manuscripts.

Today, the agent has often taken up the role of counseling the writer. I'll start here because the process is similar to getting a publisher, and because if you get an agent you can put your motives back to work writing. I didn't call this book *Motivate Your Marketing!*, after all.

The first thing you should know is that you need not reinvent the wheel when it comes to finding a market. Numerous resources exist to support the writer seeking a buyer. That might boost your motivation right there. Many big, thick books list nothing but agents and markets: *Writer's Market* and *The Writer's Handbook* are updated annually. Both include articles on how to lay out a manuscript, how to write query letters, and even how much postage to use if you have to mail something the old-fashioned way. They are available in fine bookstores, online sites, and libraries everywhere. There are also a number of websites that offer free advice, as well as numerous writer's organizations that sometimes provide notifications when a new publisher or magazine is starting up.

If you want more, you can buy or borrow writer's magazines that have interesting articles on the art, craft, and business of writing. Some people may find them inspirational, and often more directly applicable to their work. Others may get mad enough at an opinion they disagree with to propel themselves. *Writers Digest* and *The Writer* are two of the highest circulation magazines available, but you can also find magazines associated with specialty writing, such as screenplays or poetry.

The process of acquiring an agent is as tiring as sending to publishers, and more discouraging, since getting an agent certainly doesn't guarantee publication. However, a good agent will take you on because they believe in you and your work, and think they can sell it. Remember that their livelihood depends on your sale.

This gives me an opportunity to revive a conversation we had earlier about motivational feedback loops. Some agents offer to assess and/or edit your work for a fee. Many imply that their editing will help you get sold, and that they will be more willing to take it on. Let's look at this logically: Does an agent in this position get more money from a) trying to sell your book, or b) charging an editing fee for your book and *then* trying to sell it? Looking at the larger picture, which will provide the steady income for such an agent: the occasional and risky sale of the rare good work, or the sure-fire editing fees from many, many, many hopeful writers?

You get the idea. While extrinsic motivation alone is not an ideal resource for extended effort, it can certainly focus your energies. Agents who charge "reading fees" have no motive to see your work as good, and indeed may not care. Therefore, get an agent whose income derives from selling your work, and avoid the "readers." A goodly number of top editors and agents share my opinion, incidentally, but I'm making the motivational argument here rather than the ethical one.

Maintaining your motivation in getting an agent exactly compares to that of selling your book, except that you know you are one step farther away from actual publication. Set up goals, and send out several. Be careful not to have a full manuscript out to more than one person at a time. The convention is that you can send out as many letters of inquiry as you want—after all, they don't commit you or the agent to anything—but if an agent is serious enough to ask for your entire manuscript, it is only polite to repay their investment of time with your exclusivity until they turn you down or take you on. That is the time to find something else to do. It takes finite time to read a work, and agents always have more than one to read. So find some way to keep yourself focused while you wait.

You have several opportunities here. First: write something else. If you time this right, you can have several works out at once and keep writing, too. Another opportunity is to prepare a list of the next few agents you wish to approach, so you can immediately send another wave of queries. If it depresses you to anticipate failure that way (why else would you need an agent list?), think of it as insurance. If your book doesn't get picked up, you don't skip a beat getting it out again. If your book does get picked up, you can burn the list ceremonially in celebration. If you prefer, you might also keep that list, so you can see the progress you have made. If it depresses you to see a long list of rejections (I'm being realistic here—most writers go through multiple rejections at various points), then be careful about reading over the list except to avoid sending a second query (on a revised version of the same work) to the same person.

Getting Past Rejection

"I discovered that rejections are not altogether a bad thing. They teach a writer to rely on his own judgment and to say in his heart of hearts, 'To hell with you.'"

—Saul Bellow

"I still get stories turned down by editors occasionally, you know, and so does every other well-known science-fiction writer I can think of —if God were a science-fiction writer, *He'd* get rejected once in a while too, editors being what they are..."

—Robert Silverberg

"Cold-calling," which requires you to push yourself in front of someone who does not know you or your product and has no reason to buy what you are selling, sounds like a brutally difficult task, but there are tens of thousands of sales people who love it or at least don't see the process as an obstacle. Top salespeople have certain traits in common; chief among them is the ability to withstand failure or even ignore it.

One method is to consider every "no" as that much closer to "yes." Knowing that, for example, Frank Herbert sent <u>Dune</u> to over twenty publishers before he got it accepted, means that you could get rejected nineteen times without expecting an acceptance—more if you think Herbert wrote better than you. You *will* get rejected, almost certainly more than once; therefore, you want to get the rejections out of the way first. Especially since once you get anything accepted, everything gets easier. You have more connections, more people to talk to, more resources in the industry. After a while, people call <u>you</u> to submit a short story to an anthology, or a new magazine drops you a line asking for submissions, and so forth.

A second method of surviving rejection relates to attributional style. As noted above, psychological researcher Robert Seligman has studied salespeople for years, and finds that when they get rejected, they tend to see the reasons for rejection as:

- External to themselves ("He didn't want what I was selling—I had nothing to do with it")
- Situational ("She could not tell me yes while she was right in front of her boss—she had to tell me alone")
- Time-linked ("I got him when he was about to go on vacation—no way he would buy when he was walking out the door")

Putting this all together, a good salesperson describes a failure happening because "in this time, in this place, this person did not want it." By implication, this means that in the right time and the right place, the right person will want it. In a sense it removes the blame, so that no non-sale (and salespeople have many) feels like a personal failure. Accumulated failure becomes self-perpetuating: people start to believe they will fail, and amazingly enough, they do.

Another part of this relates to the concept of managing your goals. As we have discussed, an overlarge goal tends to crush motivation. If each rejection feels like an indictment of your ability to write, then the goal of selling will begin to appear more and more overwhelming, moving you down the "arousal curve" and farther away from your optimum performance. This is a fancy way of saying that if you get rejected several times running and attribute this to incompetence on your part, it will be hard to keep going.

I remember one study where my colleagues and I compared highly successful versus only moderately successful salespeople, and we found that the most successful people tended not to remember failures, or if they did they did not dwell upon them. They learned from them and moved on. The lesser folk would mull over their failures and re-enact them mentally. Doing that once or twice may help you learn, but doing it repeatedly racks up a larger tally of failure. Let me tell you about one extreme case of overcoming failure. A salesperson had just made a huge sale, so mammoth that he stood to get around a quarter of a million dollars in commissions, as I recall. The sale, which he had in the bag, dropped at the last minute—the day they were to sign on the bottom line, in fact. I asked him what he did. He said, "I went into the bathroom and I threw up. After that, I got up and started calling people to get a new appointment." And that was it!

Try to remember that an editor might have numerous reasons to reject your book, or that an agent can decide not to represent it for reasons you do not know. Do not assume that their rejection of your writing means that *you* are bad. Below I have accumulated some actual reasons for story rejections, collected from various places. Some are easily fixable—sending to the wrong market, for example. Others relate to personal taste—such as whether an agent wants to fight for it. Just be sure and know the difference! Just keep in mind that you can fix fixable things; personal taste varies from person to person. Translate these facts into optimism. For example, avoid "I can't get a publisher to save my life," to "I haven't found the right agent/publisher *yet*." Don't try to rewrite your work unless you have received the exact same criticism over and over again, or you decide as an artist that it is necessary. You must first try to sell it before you should rewrite it!

Actual Reasons for Publishers to Reject Your Work

- They don't publish my genre (e.g., Harlequin Romances don't take westerns).

- They have several writers like me already; they're afraid they can't sell another (e.g.,. a mystery writer with a white female regional amateur detective).
- They have no money to pay for an advance or printing a book because:
- ——They spent their new author budget
- ——They just sank it all into acquiring a big-name writer
- ——They are bankrupt
- ——They are too small
- They only print X number of books a year, and they're booked for the next two years.
- They automatically reject unsolicited manuscripts.
- They have a backlog of new authors.
- They have a backlog of manuscripts in the "slush pile" (unsolicited manuscripts) they are still reading.
- The editor has changed and the new one has different tastes.
- They have eliminated that genre.
- They have reduced that genre list to their biggest names.
- They are eliminating that publishing line and are just finishing out the ones they have already bought.
- The market is saturated; sales are declining on this kind of material.
- They only publish lesbian fiction. (This happened to my wife! Worst thing was, they really liked the book but felt they couldn't publish it because it didn't fit.)
- The editor is unsympathetic with the kinds of

problems I write about, e.g., coming-of-age stories, being some kind of minority in America, intellectual-philosophical-suicidal college students.

- The editor disagrees strongly with my politics as expressed in the work.
- The editor disagrees strongly with my opinions as expressed in the work.
- The publisher's lawyers fear libel suits from my work.
- The topic matter just isn't salable to a large enough audience to justify a major investment.
- The editor had a bad day.
- The editor read three superb ones in a row, and yours suffered by comparison and exhaustion.
- The editor just didn't like it.

Actual Reasons for Agents to Reject Your Work

- The agent liked it, but didn't love it, and in a tight market doesn't feel up to the challenge of pushing it.
- The agent didn't understand it.
- The agent does not sell that genre.
- The agent is overworked and is afraid to take on another author.
- One of the chief agents and other key staff just left to start another firm.
- The agency is understaffed.
- The agency is overstaffed and afraid to take on a writer who is not established (and therefore needs more work to sell).

- The agent died. (Yes, it's been known to happen!)
- The agent didn't like it.

I realize some of these excuses sound lame at best; but you will recall I said these were *actual* excuses, not *sensible* excuses. Pick up the newsletter of any writers' organization and you will find laments about, for example, the trend of publishers spending an entire budget on one blockbuster writer when they could probably have dozens of solid sellers with the same money. Nevertheless, these excuses are no lamer than those the actual people gave. Just be sure not to tell people you consider their excuses inadequate—often enough they are trying to be polite. If they really hated your work, do you really want to know that?

And let's be fair here: do you want an agent selling your life's work in a lackadaisical manner? Do you really believe a publisher should put their entire company (and all its employees) at legal risk for you?

In publishing terms, here are some things you might say to *yourself*, both in terms of attributions and next steps:

- They don't publish my kind of book right now. (I'll check *Writer's Market* for ones that do.)
- The editor hates coming-of-age stories like this one I happened to write this time. (I'll send it to another editor.)
- Their list is full this year, but there are others.
- One agent doesn't like it, but I might be able to send it to another—even another in the same agency!
- This editor does not like it, but maybe he will leave this publisher.

And so forth. As award-winning editor George Scithers puts it, "editors do not reject people. They reject pieces of paper with writing on them." The most important thing is to *keep going*. After getting a rejection letter, one writer I know insisted on identifying a new target and writing a letter to them on the day she was rejected, so she could have a new opportunity for success going immediately.

This lesson applies to many things in life, naturally; having something else ready to go means you never have too much time to brood.

Remember what John Jakes said: "Be persistent. Editors change; tastes change; editorial markets change. Too many beginning writers give up too easily."

Changing Strategies Over Time

Most of the strategies described here are aimed at those just getting started. If you get fired up, you won't need me looking over your shoulder. However, it may be helpful to supply some suggestions for modifying your motivational technique for continued success.

A person with a strong Achievement motive loses patience with the same goals. They should continue to rise. The challenge is not to push them too high to be accomplished. Achievement motive run wild may disable the almost intuitive sense of what is a moderate risk, focusing only on doing more, more, more! So if you raise your minimum word-count goal for the second book, be ready to lower it again if the new level is not working. Try to keep it higher than last time (if that is your chosen tactic), but even a single word is a gain.

The Influence-motivated writer (apparently the majority of book-length published writers, as you will recall) is still trying to impress someone—and therefore may raise the stakes well beyond last time, and make it impossible to deliver. The Influence-motivated would do well *not* to raise the goal unless it will (1) impress someone to do so, and (2) still be a reachable target.

The Affiliative writer still wants to do something nice for someone; it might be a good idea to find out that the previous work has done so. Sending it out to friends and relatives may supply a sufficient store of this satisfaction to continue; if there is a strong response, there may be a smaller need for continual positive reinforcement during the writing of the second work. Reviews are unlikely to be helpful, as few of them are directed toward assuring a writer that he or she is likable.

Self-Confidence

An important point not addressed directly here until now is that of self-confidence. If you believe that you can never write a book (or essay or short story), all the motivation in the world cannot overcome your own thoughts. What may be the best way to convince yourself that you can write (regardless of whether it is good), is to start writing and keep writing. As you grow more certain of your mastery of the writing process (in the sense of continuation), you may need less frequent feedback. Your own internal motives will keep you going fine.

If you think that nothing you write is worth reading, well, you are reading the wrong book. I have to assume you are past that point. Nevertheless, I have advice to offer from other writers: you write for yourself first. The artist has one model and one audience member with him or her at all times: himself or herself. Many books were thought to be unsalable by one editor or another—*Jonathan Livingston Seagull* (more than 40 publishers, by one count),

Dune (27 rejections), *A Confederacy of Dunces*, *Auntie Mame*, and so on. Just take it to another editor. Anne Perry, who writes meticulously researched mysteries set in Victorian London, did not sell a book in ten years of writing. When she did, she sold it in the United States rather than in her home Britain. Years more (and many books) passed before any of her books were published in Britain, and as a consequence she is considered an "American" writer.

If nothing else, you must think that someday you can write something worth reading. Kurt Vonnegut built a career as a writer in order to write one book. Remember that Ray Bradbury commented that he thought every new writer should write a million words' worth of material—to be thrown away. A mere sixty thousand is enough for a short novel, so he suggests you toss away over sixteen novels' worth of material. Why? To learn the craft, nothing more. He does not think your first million words are likely to be worth reading. He speaks from personal experience —he thinks his first million were bad writing, even though some of it got published. Writing is a development process, and no one expects you to be Shakespeare the first time out. (If you are, well, I look forward to reading your work.) No writing work is truly wasted. Save it, think about it, start a new work, and come back to it if you feel the need. John Fowles felt he had to rewrite one of his (published!) novels completely, and he is hardly alone in this: not only have some writers rewritten their books, some have refused to allow early books to be republished. Even the best may worry about their work.

Stephen King chose to write under the name Richard Bachman in order to test himself—could he sell under another name? So don't worry if the first book is a whiz-bang. Just do your best, and with practice it will get better. As John Creasey said:

"Nine out of ten writers, I am sure, could write more. I think they should and, if they did, they would find their work improving even beyond their own, their agent's and their editor's highest hopes."

On that note, let us return to thinking about you.

SECTION VII

DEVELOPMENT--MANAGING AND CHANGING YOURSELF (AND YOUR WRITING)

"The artist is nothing without the gift, but the gift is nothing without work."

—Emile Zola

CHAPTER 23: DEMOTIVATORS

"Another damned thick book! Always scribble, scribble, scribble! Eh, Mr. Gibbon?"

—The Duke of Gloucester
graciously accepting Volume II of
The Decline and Fall of the Roman Empire
from the kneeling author

I hesitated to write this section. Why? Because while awareness of obstacles and inhibitors is useful, getting frightened of the wide range of them is not. Realistically, there are many things that can demotivate you—and just as many that can remotivate you. One of the critical factors is your optimistic perspective of your writing practices; that is, do you believe you can solve the problems and move on?

Nevertheless, it <u>is</u> useful, if only to manage your circumstances to avoid their occurrence. Below I list a few obvious (and perhaps some not so obvious) demotivating factors. And remember they *are* within your control. Don't use these as excuses not to write, just as warnings to plan how to write around them.

The Environment In Which You Write

This can be a myth ("I have to have a quiet office with no interruptions") if overemphasized, but it is fair to note that your writing place occupies a great deal of your time. You should feel comfortable in it. As Kelly Tate told me, it had to be "a place I can enjoy spending some time in." She realized that she did not like her writing room, so she bought some pictures, some plants, some curtains and set it up in a way she found pleasant. If it gets in your way, deal with it. Ellen Kushner was an editor in New York and wrote constantly on the subway, which for some reason was inspirational to her, perhaps because it was pretty much the only time she had, and the pressure propelled her. When she went to writing full time (or nearly full time) the lack of pressure and the large amounts of time daunted her. She started finding ways to take up her time, paradoxically in order to write more. I think this is actually a good example of applying the Yerkes-Dodson Law: restricting the available time raised the target higher, and generated energy.

Creativity expert Mihalyi Chiksamahalyi has studied the phenomenon of "flow experience," when people are functioning at their peak, and for this to occur in a creative effort such as writing typically requires at least twenty minutes of uninterrupted time. I think it is safe to assume that there are exceptions to this, and one probably does not need to be in a flow state to edit or even write decently, but it is worth remembering.

There are more basic and obvious issues, however.

Noise, temperature, smells—all basic senses—can distract you. Key here is not to give up, but to try and manage your environment. So for example: you are in a noisy area and you find it difficult to concentrate. Put on some music (add some "signal" to cover up the "noise") or put on some headphones. At worst, put in some earplugs. One writer with whom I am closely associated has hearing aids, which she sometimes turns into the world's most expensive earplugs by turning *down* the volume so she can't hear anything, or at least enough to screen out most minor nuisances.

If temperature is your bugaboo, deal with that. Too cold? Put on a sweater. Too hot? Write in your skivvies. Way too hot? Go someplace air-conditioned and write there—a library, for example.

Environment is an issue, but it is a manageable one, if you use a little of your creativity on it.

Other People

I've referred to this on several occasions. People can be the worst problem you have, especially those who don't believe in your dream. In some cases their opposition isn't even malicious, merely insensitive. A person may feel they have done you a favor by saving you from failure, disappointment, and low pay. It is hard to tell someone who genuinely cares about you that they have done you wrong. But they have.

Remember: It isn't their place to say.

· · ·

Loved ones, I'm sorry to say, have the worst impact, because you are most open and sensitive to their criticism and influence.

It may be as little a thing as "writing? What do you do that for?" That's what writers generally do, you know. Or the classic "I know if I had time, I could write one of those bestsellers." Yeah, right. Like Stephen King just has more time than you do. To the dedicated craftsperson, this is incredibly insulting. Try substituting their job for "write one of those bestsellers," and see what they say. An artist friend of mine made the mistake of saying "I could write a book, if I only had the time" to my wife, who promptly shot back "And if I only had the time, I could paint a picture." (To his credit, he said "touché.")

Not everyone will agree with me here. James Blish, the noted SF writer, literary critic, music critic and expert on James Joyce, claimed that a thin-skinned writer is not worth having, that there are plenty of other talented people out there. He was a critic in order to improve the quality of writing, and to some extent if you the writer are not willing to try to improve, then you shouldn't try to write at all. However, Blish once said that a certain young writer was never going to get good, and that writer went on to become Harlan Ellison, multiple award winner. Blish, I note, apologized handsomely in print and became a friend of Ellison, who credited Blish with teaching him about the English language.

My point here is that developing a thick skin may be helpful, but also that ignoring the critics and practicing may be just as helpful.

Let's test out a few phrases, and some snappy answers you can give to them, at least until you develop your own.

"What Do You Want To Do That [i.e., Write] For?"

Have you noticed that for some reason everyone feels comfortable asking someone with an artistic job this incredibly rude question? Here are some possible answers to this question:

- "I love reading, so I always wanted to write."
- "I can't help it."
- "It's a disease."
- "I'm a writer."
- "What do you eat for?"
- "What do you do what you do for?"

"Don't Make Much Money at That, Do You?"

- "That's not why I do it."
- "So?"
- "How much do you make at what you do?"
- "Stephen King does all right."

"What Makes You Think You Can Write/Publish, Anyway?"

- "Effort, study, and practice."
- "Experience."
- "What makes you qualified to judge?"
- "Just look at what *else* gets published!"

CHAPTER 24: SUPERSTITIONS

"I'm no more superstitious than most writers—which means that if I lost my lucky coffee mug, I'd be looking for another job."

—Joe Haldeman

Above I described a myth or two that had to do with the magical nature of creativity and when it takes place. Cross those with your view of yourself and your role, and you may get superstitions. Since most people consider creativity a mysterious and magical happening, who knows what could affect it? Anything may influence the unpredictable. Some people write at night, others in the morning. Some insist on a quiet room, others can write in bedlam. Most of them occur around inspiration, and have been mentioned above. Generally how I am distinguishing a superstition from beliefs and myths is that they often require some sort of ritual behavior, designed to invoke the magic. I have carefully considered the evidence, and my comment on this may surprise you:

Go ahead!

If it helps you write, who am I to tell you otherwise? The placebo effect has its own power and legitimacy. And who knows? Maybe wearing a crystal *does* help, at least for you. Rudyard Kipling required extremely black ink (never blue-black, which he described as "an abomination to my Dæmon"); Truman Capote and Alexandre Dumas *père* required specific colors of paper—yellow for Capote, and rose, blue, and yellow for nonfiction, novels, and poetry, respectively, for Dumas, who was so adamant about this scheme that he had his ghostwriter/assistants use the same colors. Mystery writer Tony Fennelly, who has studied under astrology masters, arranges much of her writing and marketing by the stars. She once sent off a package to her agent at exactly 6:50 in the morning in order to get the proper benign influence (she stayed up late to do it. She is not a morning person). In this case it turned out well.

I do *not* endorse astrology or any other belief here (I believe in keeping my personal beliefs, outside of faith in your ability to write, out of this book); but if you do, you can use it to help you. Invoke St. Clare against sore eyes, St. Vitus against oversleeping, or St. Mathurin for protection from Fools, Clowns, and Idiots (always useful when the reviews come in). Burn incense, or call Higher Powers. Barry B. Longyear, the award-winning science fiction author, uses a "God Box" when he gets a problem; he writes it down on a piece of paper, puts it in the box, and lets God take care of it—that is, for all intents and purposes he forgets it. It works for him, and it might for you.

I have one important caution, however: make sure your belief *helps* your writing instead of inhibiting it. For example: if you think you can only write in longhand in a bus to Detroit, you are making it mighty hard on yourself and greatly limiting your efforts unnecessarily. Even a literary light like T. S. Eliot was not immune to superstition: he was convinced that no one ever wrote anything worth anything after winning a Nobel Prize. Since he had just won one, this did not exactly encourage him. I would prefer you to agree with Toni Morrison when she says "I don't wait to be struck by lightning and don't need certain slants of light in order to write." Superstitions only help you if they support your writing, not when they make it easy for you to hide from your responsibilities. If you don't want to write or are afraid of it, then stop. Don't invoke a superstition to take the blame.

CHAPTER 25: RECHARGING YOUR MOTIVES

"I write whenever it suits me. During a creative period I write every day; a novel should not be interrupted. When I cease to be carried along, when I no longer feel as though I were taking down dictation, I stop."

—François Mauriac

Motives generate energy, but no source of energy is limitless. If, as research indicates, they relate to specific neurotransmitters in the brain[1], you can certainly drain them dry, as it were. You might drive yourself into exhaustion first, but you still face the problem of restarting once you get yourself rest.

Some folks can wipe out their energy on one particular task rather than their motive overall. Just because writing does not require hard physical work does not mean you cannot tire yourself doing it. An extended mental effort is draining in its own right. Roughly half the oxygen your body collects goes to the brain. There is a reason for this.

For those who exercise regularly or who do perform hard physical labor, you don't have aching muscles in your brain from such effort, and certainly physical effort is tiring as well, but tired is tired. If you feel physically tired, you cannot perform physical tasks, no matter how alert you may be. If you are mentally tired, you cannot perform mental tasks, even if your body is in tip-top shape.

Ask anyone who has finished a long doctoral dissertation, for example. Few feel thrilled by the prospect of an immediate return to the keyboard. Mine was over two hundred pages long (of small print), with 62 tables (some three pages long!). Personally, I think the thought of putting any more numbers in columns and rows could have pushed me over the brink.

An extended effort focused not only on one task but one *motive* can drain you really dry—especially if that motive is not your strongest. I saw this once with an individual who was trying to be friendly to others on a professional basis with only the barest shred of Affiliation motive to help. To make matters worse, she had to stay with the same small group continuously for two weeks, day and evenings. By the end of the day all she wanted to do was hide. She knew how to do the *behaviors* of affiliation, but she could not get up the *energy* even to socialize with one of her most familiar colleagues. This issue becomes particularly salient when working out of your weaker motive. Eventually you run out of the "natural" energy and start working harder, draining yourself.

Well, how do you recharge?

First-stage tired: you're just tired of the task. In that case, you might be able to sustain a different task with the same motive. You're tired of writing alone; go out and socialize, or attend a conference of fellow writers and fans. Many find (including me) that listening to others discuss work gets them inspired and excited about moving again, or at least so frustrated by listening to those other bozos that you want to go back to the keyboard and show them what for! A caution: If working out of a lesser motive, try not to drain your motivation in the *wrong* task.

Second-stage tired: you're out of motivational energy. Rest. Take a significant break. By that I do not mean just switching gears and doing something else, if that other task requires the same motive. Do something completely different. Writing that is primarily Influence-motivated could allow you to use the Achievement or Affiliative motives to recover: Solve puzzles. Play solitaire. Go have a picnic. Play with your children. Again, watch what you choose. It should interest and engage you, but not too much. Some studies show that 40% of the activity on personal computers is playing solitaire. I know a writer who had to remove the game from his hard drive after three days because after he bought a computer he literally failed to do anything else with it. I'm not telling you his name, for obvious reasons, but he is a successful published author of a number of books, and had two or three in print when he bought his computer. This story is not apocryphal. His (successful) action falls under the category of managing your external setting, by the way—remove the temptation, remove the concern.

Once you have truly exhausted yourself, don't try to start too soon. In some jobs, a solid two-week vacation is necessary to completely clear the mind of past worries. Why should writing be any different? If the option exists, you might need those two weeks. Several writers (including my wife) take a break after a major accomplishment, such as turning in a manuscript. Especially since deadlines tend to promote high-speed, high-volume writing, which wears you out that much more.

Sometimes you need a break in the middle, too. In the course of writing a mystery novel, my wife carefully avoids anything current in the field, either reading a classic that won't affect her work, or something like science fiction.

Even then, you might not want to start with the same thing. You might want to shift to option one: try something different for a while. Many writers, especially in the mystery field, write multiple series. This prevents staleness; after living in one character's pocket for months or more, they go to some other character. That way they maximize productivity *and* get a rest from their main character. I don't mean you have to spend exactly half your time some-where else. Take Rex Stout, the author of the Nero Wolfe mystery series: he wrote primarily Wolfe stories, both short and novel length, but periodically he would write a novel about someone else. He filled the majority of the fifty-odd books he wrote with stories about Wolfe, but he also wrote two about detective Alphabet Fox, one about Inspector Cramer (a character who shows up in the Wolfe series), and a few which stand alone. Agatha Christie had several series (Hercule Poirot, Miss Marple, and Tommy and Tuppence), but also some mysteries that stood completely apart from any series.

Or you can do something related to writing and very useful (once you have finished your book). Concentrate on marketing. Go visit bookstores, prepare a cover letter for your press kit, talk to your publisher's publicist, write a blog post.

Other writers do something dramatically different: mountain climbing, painting (Churchill painted as well as writing histories), whatever. Just be aware that if you start back writing and you feel tired just sitting at the keyboard, it might be too soon. If you have had your two weeks or so, you may need to re-energize yourself about writing. In that case you might want to *arouse* your motivation in appropriate ways: inspirational music or movies, for example. Ideally, you should be itching to get back to work. If writing feels like a punishment instead of a reward, there might be a good reason.

As always, this assumes you should enjoy the process or at least find it acceptable work. People who must write for their daily bread either enjoy it, or they don't consider it painful.

CHAPTER 26: MOTIVATE YOUR LEARNING

"All want to be learned, but no one is willing to pay the price."

—Juvenal

Grow or die. It applies to writing as well; you can improve—in plotting, in speed, in confidence—or you can rot away on the vine. Even highly experienced writers sometimes begin to cannibalize themselves, to become a parody of themselves rather than speaking genuinely. To prevent that requires learning. Most people, sadly, think of learning as unpleasant work. They have lost the gift of children to simply absorb. But when you are learning about something enjoyable, you may find you forget it is learning.

When I was in college, we called fun courses "gut courses," meaning that we could do it from the gut rather than from the head. I recall examining the required reading list for one such course and realizing that it had nearly a thousand pages of different texts, some quite difficult—but the class was so much fun that people could not see it as being real work. That is what we aim for, and for good reason.

Writing, or indeed any creative endeavor, does not come from nowhere. Not even from the muse. It comes through work, practice, and learning from your mistakes. Can you be born with talent? Of course! But if you were born deaf, don't expect to be an opera singer. You simply lack the tools to do the job – or, more fairly, have major obstacles that most people cannot overcome. The best potential writer in the world who does not read might as well have a bucket over their head.

Some might think I am being overly optimistic, that it isn't possible to get better than a certain degree. Here's Kurt Vonnegut, Jr.'s view of that: "This is what I find encouraging about the writing trades. They allow mediocre people who are patient and industrious to revise their stupidity, to edit themselves into something like intelligence."

Elsewhere in this book I refer to the "nine-and-sixty ways" to write. All of them depend on learning how to use the tools of a writer, but they can be learned.

It has become a common insult that the modern artist "doesn't know how to draw." People make jokes about Picasso's distortion of "obviously" correct proportions. People forget that any two-dimensional image of a three-dimensional object must have translated the information in novel ways. What modern audiences see as "right" is no more true to reality (whatever that is) than Picasso's work. Furthermore, Picasso was a very fine representational artist when he chose; I remember seeing an exhibit of his drawings, one of which came from the period when Cubism was at its height. It was a beautifully detailed, highly realistic pen-and-ink portrait of a friend, done for a birthday. To break the rules, you must know first what they are.

I mention this because the process of being continuously creative often is coupled with constantly learning. Again, we have a need for motivation. Why learn at all? Why not repeat one's own expertise? Well, it can be boring, for one thing, and that isn't good for motivating oneself to write. The Achievement motive is aroused by challenging oneself.

In any case, if you are not a published author, your best chance is to learn the craft well enough to sell. Yes, there are authors who were good but underappreciated; an entire book, *Rotten Rejections*, chronicles some of the worst rejections of the best authors and stories. But I prefer to think like Pasteur: "Chance favors the prepared mind." Or, if you prefer, Thomas Jefferson: "I find that the harder I work, the more luck I seem to have."

Given that, how do you keep learning? I will remind you again that Bradbury thought you should write a million words to be thrown away. He sold a respectable chunk of those first million words, but he did not consider it good work, especially once he learned more. Please note that "salable" is not the same as "good." Likewise, Robert Silverberg became a selling machine in his earlier days. He once told the "dean of science fiction," Robert Heinlein, that he had sold two million words in the past year. That's at least 26 novels! Heinlein's comment deflated him somewhat: "There aren't that many words in the English language. You must have repeated a few." With time, Silverberg realized that he had enough quality to publish, especially in a market that was desperate for readable, competent material, but he lacked the quality to do more than that—to really engage people. He was fortunate enough to get advice from several gifted people, and used it. But how in the heck do you keep working, how do you know if you are good enough? How do you get through those first million words, if that is what you need?

Answer: Link the learning with the natural process. Many writers see their lives as if they are writing, transferring their experiences into fictional terms in the same manner that Picasso could transfer a three-dimensional image into a two-dimensional canvas. It has become habitual. As Dorothy Sayers noted of her fictional writer Harriet Vane in *Gaudy Night*, "In that unpleasant habit of the novelist, of turning over the memory in her mind to turn it into a scene in a book..."

Robert Silverberg, the award-winning science fiction author, editor, and essayist, has this to say about learning: do it! He recommends books and reading. Well, if you didn't read in the first place, you wouldn't be writing, would you?

Some like to use different techniques, however, such as workshops or even brute force. For example: several highly prolific writers consider their success to be due primarily to hard work rather than talent, including Stephen King, Robert Silverberg, Kurt Vonnegut, and Isaac Asimov. In *Robert Silverberg's Worlds of Wonder: Exploring the Craft of Science Fiction*, which is intended as a textbook for beginning science-fiction writers (among other things), Silverberg describes in detail the various books he read (H.D.F. Kitto's *Greek Tragedy*, *In Search of Wonder* by Damon Knight, *The Issue at Hand*, by "William Atheling, Jr." (actually James Blish), Thomas Uzzell's *Narrative Technique*) the mentors he had (James Blish, Damon Knight, H.L. Gold) and various turning points in his career, such as the time when he realized that though he was selling everything he wrote—which at one point was "two short stories a day and a novel in two weeks"—and realized he still was not writing as well as he should. Ultimately, he describes an endless process of learning from multiple sources, and he recommends this: "The process of becoming a writer involves discovering how to use the accumulated wisdom of our guild, all those tricks of the storytelling trade that have evolved around the campfire over the past five or ten or fifty thousand years. Others can show you what those tricks are. But only you can make a writer out of yourself, by reading, by studying what you have read, and above all, by writing."

Alfred Bester discovered how to write *mostly* by writing, and by making mistakes. He credits comic books with giving him "a place to be bad" — a place to sell and survive but at the same time learn. At one point he describes a conversation he had about discovering if you had two plots play against each other, saying it was "tremendously exciting!" The other man, an experienced writer, stared at him and said, "you mean you have never heard of plot and counterplot?" He does not describe it as an *efficient* way to learn, but he did learn. He also cites a mentor, something that, when it happens commonly to people, can greatly accelerate one's development. Robert Bloch cites Lovecraft as an influence, for example. Bester's case indicates a couple of patterns: you learn if you keep doing it, and a mentor helps.

Asimov loved stories so much that he started to write his own down in a copybook. Being the kind of person who loved an audience, he often read stories aloud to his friends, so he read his own story. To his amazement, the friend treated it like any other story—he wanted to know what happened next.

Sharyn McCrumb tells that in her very Southern family all the women tell stories in the kitchen, and that they were very refined in this art. Her own writing has its roots in this tradition of storytelling, and the desire to be able to tell your own stories by learning from them.

Kurt Vonnegut, as mentioned elsewhere, became a writer in order to write *Slaughterhouse Five*, but it did not happen magically. He worked at his craft, and experimented with approaches. His sophistication changes markedly from his early work to the point he thought he was finally ready.

Philip R. Craig not only learned an approach, he determined what the approach was first. As an academic, he took the logical approach: he bought a stack of best-sellers and studied them. He developed a list of things that were necessary, and then used them systematically. Some people may say "yuck! how constraining!" Go ahead—but he sold that book, and a lot of books since.

Hemingway was a journalist who worked quite deliberately at his craft of writing. As a professional writer, he did not expect the muse to strike. In his letters he spends a good deal of time talking about his techniques and experiments. He thought about ideas and then tried them out.

People have studied the process of how to learn, and not everyone learns the same way. David A. Kolb has identified four learning styles that most people tend to fall into. However, you need not limit yourself to one; in fact, the best learning comes from using multiple styles in rapid succession.

What does this look like when learning to write?

•Concrete experience (Feel):

Just start writing, and see what happens. Many writers start this way—just trying to tell a story.

•Reflective Observation (Watch):

Listen to writers at conferences, read writing books

and memoirs, observe writers at work. Many science fiction fans-turned-writers did this through fanzines, reading criticism, and study. Robert Silverberg was one.

•Abstract Conceptualization (Think):

Create a pattern, principles, lists of steps; create a set of concepts. Phil Craig did that when he compiled his list of what a bestseller looks like.

•Active Experimentation (Try):

Apply learned principles to one's own writing. Hemingway would experiment with ideas by applying them to a story.

Or put them in a row! Try writing an exercise for fun, then take it to a writer's workshop where people can tell you what to do, work out for yourself what you think the key principles are, and apply them to your story.

Another example: Go to a conference where writers talk about their craft and listen; organize their descriptions into a list of items; do a writing exercise trying something out; start fresh with trying something out.

Or do it backwards! It doesn't matter; just do it, and you will learn more effectively.

In any case, you can apply these principles to anything —not just writing. If you use it to research a topic you need to write about, you will retain more of the information. Sharan Newman set her fourth Catharine LeVendeur mystery novel on a 12th century pilgrimage, and she wound up taking the pilgrimage path herself. It is a commonplace that when you immerse yourself in a subject, you learn it faster. To this day I recall the Spanish word for an overhead cable car (transférico), which I learned nearly twenty years ago, because I was in Madrid and was looking for one. It takes me a good week to get back to basic conversational Spanish, but I remember that word now.

Basic Principles of Personal Change

1. Change only happens if you want it.

You cannot force yourself to change if you don't really want to, and neither can anyone else—for the long term, anyway.

2. Change can come from inside and from outside.

You can change yourself or you can change your environment in such a way that your ability to write is enhanced.

a. Creating internal change: develop, shift focus, learn something, set a value, make a decision. Use the Competency Acquisition Process.

b. Creating external change: set a structure, arrange for someone outside you to affect you. Organize your environment so it organizes you.

For example:

• Learning how to set a schedule for yourself is an internal skill; setting the schedule is creating an external change method.

• Having to write only by the dark of the moon because of superstitious dread of moonlight could certainly limit your output. Internal change: break your fear of moonlight. External change: write in an inside room with no windows so moonlight can't get near. So it's the bathroom—so what?

In the somewhat silly second example, you can choose either to change yourself or change the environment to support you as you are. But you can do both: use the "write inside" option to smooth the path as you eliminate your phobia. As long as it helps, do it!

When smokers quit their addictive habit, it works better if they have an array of tools: nicotine patches, rubber bands, hypnosis, whatever. Likewise, the more supports you have the better.

3. Change can come in many ways.

If one does not work, try another (or more than one).

Remember that there is no one way to write. Likewise, while there are principles for personal change that are reliable, the exact best methods vary from person to person. In studies of the effect of therapy, the single most important predictor of success is the therapist-client relationship itself (with some exceptions, particularly around phobia treatment). Similarly, if you find one technique or one particular writer's group fails to help you, change it. Don't assume you can't do better.

4. Change can be painful and slow.

Expect it, and prepare for it.

People generally do not wish to change. The intellectual acknowledgment of a need to change is not the same as being able to change, and it certainly does not make the change process any less painful. If you are unleashing your existing motivation, you may find it highly pleasurable as the floodgates open, but if you are imposing structures on yourself, you may chafe a bit. Remember the intention, and your own commitment.

CHAPTER 27: WORKSHOPS

"The best book is a collaboration between author and reader."

—Barbara Tuchman

"The primary distinction of the artist is that he must actively cultivate that state which most men, necessarily, must avoid: the state of being alone."

—James Baldwin

Many writers participate in groups called "writer's workshops." They vary widely, from support groups that meet to read each others' stories and eat dinner, to carefully-structured organizations with a charter and a set of by-laws, to "online" organizations. A related idea is the "amateur publishing association," or APA (pronounced "apa"), which goes the extra step of not only choosing to create, but to publish on their own, too—a much less difficult step than it once was thanks to inexpensive desktop publishing, Web-based forums, e-zines, and e-publishing houses.

Practically speaking, both groups tend to overlap in function: to provide a support group of fellow writers, artists, and creators, which often provide some kind of feedback on performance. As John Hall Wheelock noted: "Most writers are in a state of gloom a good deal of the time; they need perpetual reassurance." Workshops also exist where professional writers or creative writing teachers provide this feedback for fee-paying participants.

Many writers swear by workshops; one of my acquaintance once critiqued a story by saying "this is good enough that you should find a workshop for it." The recipient of this note was astonished at the assumption that a workshop would be the obviously necessary next step. Those who rely on workshops may use them at every step of their writing process: ideas, outlines, rough drafts, later drafts. Others may get some limited criticism (say at an early stage) and leave it at that. Others have no interest in them at all.

Workshops can be a powerful tool. The Inklings, which included C. S. Lewis and J. R. R. Tolkien, was a kind of workshop. The Mañana Literary Society was a group which included what would be some of the best names in science fiction, including Robert A. Heinlein, Cleve Cartmill, "Anthony Boucher," and others, though its avowed purpose was "to permit young writers to talk out their stories to each other in order to get them off their minds and thereby save themselves the trouble of writing them down." The Algonquin Club (known to the members as the Vicious Circle) gained fame for its quips, but a good deal of real work was accomplished there as well; people tend to forget that the legendary Algonquin Round Table members were all nobodies when they started their meetings. Harold Ross got the capital to start *The New Yorker* from winnings of a poker game hosted by the Club. A mystery-writers' group met at Kate's Mystery Books in Cambridge, Massachusetts for years. I have seen numerous groups on social media, working on writing exercises to a fortnightly challenge (e.g., "Theme Park," where everyone who wants to can try writing about a particular theme), short stories, and even novels a chapter at a time.

What can a workshop do? The answers vary. The only thing more complicated than understanding one person is to understand two and the relationships between them. Nevertheless, the workshop can have profound effects, because they support <u>all</u> the three motives, under the right circumstances, and help you manage them as well.

Benefits of the Workshop

Here are some of the things a workshop can provide:

- Temporary arousal of motives you need; bringing out the Achievement motive, for example, when you are ready to start cutting prose, or the Influence motive when you need to consider the impact of a scene more closely.
- Engaging the motives you have: the impact on others hooks the Influence motive, meeting a challenge (even just producing your share of prose) snags the Achievement motive, meeting with and helping people you like and trust pulls in the Affiliation motive.
- Training of the behaviors and thoughts of a professional writer focused on actual practice. There is a way to develop a characteristic that

sounds painfully simple when stated, which you should remember from the section on developing your motives: first, learn to *recognize* it when you see it demonstrated well. Second, *understand* what is going on inside and outside the head of the person demonstrating the characteristic. Third, *assess yourself* against what you have seen. Next, *experiment* with doing it yourself. As you master it, *practice the skill*, and get objective *feedback* on how you are doing. This practice was used to develop Achievement motive, but it applies to any characteristic. A workshop allows all the steps to take place at one time and another.

- Substitution of other's viewpoint for your own in an area of weakness
- Emotional support (for any or all three of the motives)
- "Fooling the watcher," trying to hold back the self-criticism that can stop you, in three ways:

1. "It's just for them, not for real." Writing for your trusted group instead of the anxiety-provoking "professional market" can lower the perceived level of the challenge—you could not possibly satisfy the reviewer for the *New York Times*, but you know your fellow workshoppers.
2. Shoring up self-confidence by getting "real" feedback instead of the "watcher." Shut up the self-criticism by the feedback of others. For some people, outside feedback can carry far more weight, especially if it comes from a professional. Even negative feedback may feel better, if you focus on something that you can

improve rather than on something
insurmountable, as self-criticism tends to zero
in on ("I don't have the soul of a writer.").
Remember good attribution is time- and place-
focused. A group can focus on the prose rather
than on vague self-perceived inadequacies.

3. Unconditional support when necessary to
silence the watcher.

- Hard feedback on performance: supporting the
  Achievement motive's desire to know "how am
  I doing?"
- A chance to show off and impress people:
  supporting the Influence motive's desire to have
  an impact or influence over others
- A "safe" environment to try an experiment in
  new fields.

Dangers of the Workshop

The workshop has three main dangers:

- Reinforcing the wrong things
- Tearing itself apart with its own strengths
- Seducing people away from their writing

First is that it can reinforce the wrong things. Workshops that give positive support for a fledgling writer help
that writer spend enough time to develop the craft. Workshops that give only positive feedback, or tend to see everything as outstanding, do their participants a disservice.
While it may support your motive to write (over the short
term), it does nothing for your ability to write, or may even
reinforce the wrong things. This may be prevented by

having a balance of feedback. As noted above, studies have suggested that ideal performance feedback should be at the ratio of three or four positive to one negative. Indeed, there is reason for this beyond the issue of quality (which is not part of the scope of this book—or of motivational psychology per se, for that matter): Unabated praise starts to lose its force. People cease to believe it as genuine, at which time it fails to motivate. "Well, he liked it, but he likes everything. Maybe he just has bad taste."

When I was an apprentice in a summer stock company, I worked as an assistant to the prop mistress. She asked my opinion as we selected furnishings for the sets. I would dismiss something I found inappropriate as "tacky." Unfortunately, I limited my critical vocabulary to that one word. She turned to me once and said, "you know, I don't know if you have great taste—or no taste at all." After that, I became specific as to what I liked and disliked, and we could actually discuss the quality. "I think the light-colored Scandinavian style furniture would be inappropriate for this family of characters, not only because they are Edwardian English people, but also because they are ostentatious people and therefore are more likely to want large, ostentatious furniture." She decided that I did have some taste, after all. The same principle applies to feedback.

I do not suppose I have to delineate the demotivating aspects of entirely (or overwhelmingly) negative feedback —if one has a fragile ego, it can be nearly destroyed by ongoing abuse. If one has a strong ego, it might be shaken, or at least over time faith in the other person's critical judgment is bound to falter. Both of these essentially push someone the wrong way on the Yerkes-Dodson bell curve – off the peak.

The second danger of the workshop is that its strongest force—the varied dispositions, talents, and motives of the

group—can tear it apart. A group without careful management can and *will* disintegrate—or explode—from the
conflicts it must inevitably engender. Remember that the
motives are *nonconscious*. That means that people may not
know the forces driving them. A quick and strongly
Achievement-motivated person, impatient with a slow
exposition, may finish sentences for an Influence-motivated
person who wants to let the words roll out impressively.
The "obviously deliberate insult" in turn incenses this
latter person. The former cannot understand what
annoyed the second: "but it's faster." The latter cannot
understand why the former would do such a thing. "Did
you consider my feelings here? I'm trying for something
more than speed of downloading."

Dissimilar levels of talent can inhibit as well. Different
people have various gifts. Two people may have equally
exceptional final products, but reach them through their
own uniquely meandering paths. If one misinterprets a
single gift as representative of them all (for example,
someone who writes speedily seen as someone who writes
well *and* speedily), one may set an unrealistic goal for
oneself. Resentment follows.

The same applies to relative time before pecuniary
success. One person may sell their first work. Another may
sell their tenth, or hundredth. Neither is necessarily supe-
rior to the other, but a great deal of resentment can build
up between the "amateur" and the "professional." In the
science fiction community this has produced the odd
phenomenon of the "dirty old pro." Fans—who may write
stories, essays, even poems that are published in their own
"fanzines"—have turned on a fellow fan who dares to
publish professionally. The implication is that you have left
the ghetto—and how embarrassing for those left behind! A
good group can share in success (see below), but even so you

have to allow for human feelings. One can only go so long congratulating your luckier (or more talented) fellows with a genuine smile. After a while the felicitations are uttered through clenched teeth. Anger propels some people to produce, but others only become anxious and depressed. One obvious defense: Leaving the workshop, temporarily or permanently. Remember that this is not failing as a writer. No matter how much workshoppers like their practice, *it is not the same as actually writing.* If you think a workshop will help, find another group whose chemistry supports your own. The single strongest variable predicting the success of therapy is the relationship between the therapist and the patient—if that does not work, you should find another therapist, not give up on the problem. Likewise, other workshops are available to help with your writing problems—or none. For many writers, workshops would only get in their way. Dickens didn't need a workshop; Stephen King doesn't either.

The third kind of danger is the seduction of the workshop. When taken to extremes, it becomes a serious obstacle; for example, when you can write no other way than for a workshop, the orientation of your audience has altered. Belonging to a workshop then becomes a superstition: "My work won't be any good unless they look at it." The workshop can also remove the sense of personal responsibility for the work: "I'm afraid to try alone," or "I can't do it without them. I'm not good enough." In this case, people may have lost the self-image of being a writer, instead, seeing themselves as only *part* of a writer, the remaining part supplied by the workshop. This does not mean that the workshop may not provide elements a person may find difficult to supply him or herself; instead, it means a person may choose to give up all elements of writing without that one key piece, and that can sink your long-term motivation. Fanatic workshoppers to the contrary, many great works of writing never went near a workshop, and never needed to.

A final kind of seduction may come about when people can get hooked by their motives into activities that do not produce writing, e.g., editing. If you are editing someone else's work, you are not writing. Period. You may hone skills that assist your writing, but no more than that. This seduction is particularly treacherous if the workshop has not put guidelines in place to prevent it. One writer of my acquaintance has apparently made a hobby of critiquing new writers' first novels. She reads thoroughly and well, making numerous helpful observations, suggestions, and notations. Fortunately, she is still writing also—though more slowly than her fans would prefer. She appears to be much faster at editing than at writing. In my perception, she has three reasons for this: First, she does intensive and thorough historical research, which can absorb a great deal of time before ever touching a keyboard; second, she rewrites frequently, testing out alternatives or linking units so much that when writing, she always has 24 windows at once open on her computer. Third, she spends a lot of time being a one-woman workshop; I can recall three novels she read out of the goodness of her heart for which she wrote a total of thirty pages of single-spaced criticism. This is a gift from heaven for the unpublished writer (one of whom was published shortly after taking large chunks of advice), but can be a deadly danger for the published one giving the advice. You will note that I do not reveal the name of this author, if only to avoid burying her under unsolicited manuscripts!

This can seduce people of any motive pattern; hence its danger. The Achievement-motivated person may be tempted by the ability to *make something better*. A person with this motive may often think about the costs and benefits of his or her effort, and in these terms helping others scores high. If you can take personal pride in someone else's accomplishment (and some do), then for the cost of perhaps an hour or two, you can feel you have pushed a story from unpublishable to publishable. Great benefit—minimal cost.

The Affiliation-motivated person may feel the appeal of doing for others, and basking in the warmth of others' thanks—depending on how positive the feedback is, of course. The affiliative person may be tempted to be more positive than is indicated, to get just that response. The social nature of a gathering may be irresistible to the affiliative person, and this could keep them coming—but not writing, if the rules of the group do not manage the output.

The Influence-motivated person can know he or she has affected someone's life and work—and possibly gotten that person visible to the world by helping the writer write publishable material. Furthermore, a workshop is a wonderful opportunity to display one's own talents and person to a more-or-less captive audience; the person higher on Personalized (selfish) Influence may like the idea of being on stage and in charge far more than being the victim of the process. Again, a motive to avoid writing.

And perhaps a fourth danger: workshops can slow you down! Good workshops put limitations on the amount that is read, both to be equitable and to ensure that people critique a reasonable quantity. Very fast writers then must wait for their critiques, if they really want to use the feedback. This only applies to very fast and capable writers for the most part; that's why I don't see this as terribly serious.

Small Group Research

Many people have studied how small groups and what processes occur in them. Robert F. Bales made one of the best descriptions, using the system he calls SYMLOG, for SYstematic Multiple Level Observation of Groups. He found, as had others, that groups tend to *polarize*—that is, form small, focused groups sometimes in opposition—but he went further and found a way to observe how a group changes over time. In brief, he found that there two groups typically form: one group that is positive, group-focused, and willing to go along with authority for the sake of the task; and another loose coalition of those who are more individualistic and rejecting of authority.

You can think of these as the "let's go along with the gang, huh?" group and the "why should I do what you want?" group. As you might expect, extreme polarization prevents a group from complete and effective functioning as a whole.

Polarization need not last, however. An extreme focus will frequently shift and flow, thanks to people who move into the *Moderator* or *Scapegoat* roles: the former works to bring the groups together, and everyone loves to hate the latter. Either way, the two groups will tend to merge, and perhaps realign because of the moderator or scapegoat, with some joining the moderator or moving away from the scapegoat.

Studies have suggested the ideal array for an effective group and group leader. The group should be positive, group-oriented, and willing to accept authority and focus on the task. None should be overly emphasized. The leader should be the same, but with a stronger dominance to help influence the group.

When working in a workshop it is important to

remember that a group is not fixed, nor can it be made so. An effective group must be a dynamic equilibrium, with enough flexibility to include everyone yet enough rules to correct itself as necessary. Otherwise, the polarization will literally tear the group apart.

Not every group will get along. Nor will the members of a good group always get along. You need not like the people—you need only to work well with them. If you cannot even work with these folks, you do neither yourself nor the group any good.

The band Fleetwood Mac, for example, is famously contentious; at various points none of them liked each other, but they found they could work together to create remarkable albums. Of course, the band also had different members at different points, or subsets of past groups.

Effective workshops, like the Cambridge Science Fiction Writers Workshop, evolve and change. They have turnover (several have come and gone from CSFW, and sometimes even come back), as people find they were not suited for this kind of group work or sometimes have a personality clash that is too strong to allow for functional criticism. There is nothing wrong with this; if anything, it is not sensible to assume that any group of people will invariably get along—yet that is probably the commonest error of a new group. "We all write—we can form a workshop!" But if one person despises the other's writing, or does not respect the other as a person, it will not work.

You need not like everything they write. You must admit that this is your taste, not some standard chiseled in stone. While I (and many others) believe in minimum requirements for writing craft, there is always a point where two people can never agree, no matter how similar their tastes in other respects. When you hand over your pride and joy to be hacked and bloodied, you may feel as

Abraham did in sacrificing Isaac. But like Abraham, it can be important over the long run to bear it.

Still, nobody said you had to *like* it.

Things to Watch

When looking at a group, watch several things. SYMLOG tells us that people express certain values and behaviors (which may not match) around the three dimensions of dominance-submission, positivity-negativity, and forward-backward, and that these interact with each other over time.

Motives tell us that different people like different things, and may have different emotional or unconscious agendas in what they do. They also are essential to understand what drives people.

Writing styles come into it as well: some people like to outline and find it rewarding. Others write at apparent random as the Muse strikes.

And always: *people want to be good writers*. Criticism hurts when untempered by respect for the individual as someone trying hard to learn a difficult craft and turn it into art. Remember: there is no one way to write! If you cannot accept that, *never* join a workshop unless they all resemble you exactly—an unlikely possibility, especially since writers often change as they move from new to mature.

Below is a list of ten process guidelines taken from those participating in successful workshops, and from the field of group psychology. I hesitate to call them the Ten Commandments of Effective Groups, especially after the Abraham reference earlier, but it sure is tempting:

1. Trust in others' abilities.
2. Mutual respect for each others' efforts.

3. Mutual respect for each other as people.
4. Enough self-confidence.
5. Willingness to protect and maintain the group as an entity.
6. Awareness of the ultimate shared goal.
7. Knowledge of what you like and don't like.
8. Clear and fair expectations of each other.
9. Someone to manage the rules and/or do the work.
10. Desire to grow and improve

The alert reader will already have noticed a pattern here. The first five are all about *group cohesion*. In other words, what keeps the group together: trust, mutual respect, and willingness to believe one is part of the group. The next four (6-9) are about *clarity of purpose and practice:* understanding what the group is doing and how. The final item stands alone, but is far from the least important: *focus on improvement*. We will come back to this pattern below, but let's look at the specifics first.

1. Trust in others' abilities.

Not that you consider everyone to be outstanding, but that you trust that everyone is good at *something*. Ideally, you should be able to state that thing, e.g., "Joe knows how to plot well," or "Jane can target inconsistencies in characters every time." This may take some time to establish. At first, you may want to keep an open mind, and watch what strengths people show.

2. Mutual respect for each other's efforts.

The first item tells you to trust that people have ability. This one tells you to respect what they do with it. A workshop is an opportunity to develop one's writing. Therefore, you should not expect deathless prose in a first draft. Respect the effort, not the outcome. A Beethovenian writer is no less competent than a Mozartian writer—in the long run. Some people write much slower than others whereas Dickens churned out mountains of prose. As someone once said, "if Dickens had had a word processor, a degree in literature would take eight years." By contrast, James Joyce spent seventeen years on *Finnegan's Wake* alone. I once heard writer and editor Judith Merril talking about a bad period, when she was hiding in a hotel room working frantically on three different assignments and churning out stacks of paper, and Samuel R. Delany walked in beaming. She asked him what was so great, and he replied that he had just written "a perfectly *wonderful* sentence—and it only took me twenty minutes!"

3. Mutual respect for each other as people.

You must go beyond basic respect for the work to respect for the person, or you will not be able to work together over the long term. You do not have to *like* each other— but you do have to respect each other. This is good advice for life in general, but worth repeating here. If you see a fellow workshopper as scum of the earth, I doubt you will be very helpful to that person—and if he or she knows your feelings, don't expect helpfulness in return. This kind of conflict can also polarize a group in the ugliest possible manner.

4. Enough self-confidence.

The members of the group must have enough self-confidence (or support) to deal with the time when one person sells and one person does not. This is critical, considering the wide range of speed at which different people produce their work, let alone the idiosyncrasies of the publishing world. Either personal self-confidence (if you are the slower one) or good emotional support of others (if you are not) and preferably both are needed. A good group can share in the success of any member; everyone had their part to play, even if it was just to force the other person to come up with a new way of saying things. I see many people thanking their workshops in acknowledgments these days.

5. Willingness to protect and maintain the group as an entity.

From time spent with members of the Cambridge SF Writer's workshop (and others), as well as interviewing several of the members, I observed a tendency to protect the group for its own sake. If someone applied to the group and one workshop member hated the submitted sample, no one would push to get that person in, even if they liked that person. Furthermore, they did not all get along with each other; people joked about each others' styles of criticism (though not of their writing) and personality quirks. Many would avoid going to parties together. But they were willing to put up with each other to protect the mysterious gestalt of the functioning group. This is important. If individual problems outweigh the focus of the group, then the group will collapse into individual squabbles. You have to be willing to put up with some eccentricities for the sake of the group. Since looking at CSFW, I have seen the same behavior among other groups and self-managed work teams in business as well.

Now for the items about clarity of purpose and practice:

6. Awareness of the ultimate shared goal.

Keep in mind your goal: to generate publishable, quality written material. Not to create your kind of written material, not to change the world. Set a goal that you can all agree on, and remember it. Make sure that goal lines up with writing, rather than just being nice to each other, for example. See my comments on practices that support writing rather than stand alone from it. If you get together as friends also, be sure to manage the time so you can move from social to practical easily.

7. Knowledge of what you like and don't like.

This applies both to you and to the other members of the group. Being objective makes you effective. If you hate "coming-of-age" stories, then you might want to moderate your criticism, or at least make it clear that you dislike the subgenre so much that Shakespeare himself could not write one you liked. Likewise, if you know another member of the group dislikes the type of story you have written, you can shield yourself from the fallout. (Some people see this as a challenge, of course: "if I can write a story of this type that even *this* person likes, it must be good!"

8. Clear and fair expectations of each other.

Resentments build rapidly if there is a perceived inconsistency or inequity. In dealing with people, your intentions mean very little; the perception of the *other* person is what counts. Objective expectations will help keep personalities out of the mixture. Some examples include:

- Everyone edits, everyone writes. It is tempting, as noted above, to get hooked into just editing, or just writing. Some online writing workshops, for example, actually kick you off if you do one and not the other exclusively. It is not fair to criticize and not get criticized, or vice versa. It produces an imbalance of power.
- Be no meaner to others than they are to you. Some people can take brutal feedback without blinking. Some only pretend to do so. Some can't even do that. Try to respect the other person's feelings. Some groups are good at providing and receiving tough feedback calmly; others (with more Affiliation motive) need friendlier and warmer feedback.

9. Someone to manage the rules and/or do the work.

Every effective group has one—a person who monitors the process, or who keeps track of who is applying and handles submissions, or who maintains the rules. In the case of CSFW, it was David Alexander Smith. He liked the job, he as good at it, and others wanted him to do it so they didn't have to. For groups where no one wants the work, rotation may work as well. Sometimes no one wants to be the banker in *Monopoly*. I hasten to note that if that person is a writer, special care must be taken to ensure that their writing and criticism time does not become overly hampered by their facilitation duties. Cut this person some extra slack. I have seen groups give extra benefits to the coordinator (including extra royalties on shared books) to keep that person happy and part of the group. It's usually worth it.

10. Desire to grow and improve.

A group is at best a dynamic equilibrium, not a stable object. The more willing that participants are to accept changes (in people, process, etc.), the better your chances to sustain the effectiveness of the group over time. In this manner you can grow together, and also self-correct. Part of this derives from the Achievement motive desire to improve, but part of it also derives from the willingness to be open and trusting that the group can move.

Note the pattern again. Three categories: The trust and respect that goes along with (trusting) Affiliation motivation; clear understanding of intent and approach, and Achievement motivation. In other words, the combination of two motives and one external factor. Let's look at one real example of a group and see whether this holds up.

Case Study: The Cambridge Science-Fiction Workshop

As part of the research for this book I interviewed and measured the motives of three of the eight members of the Cambridge Science-Fiction Workshop (CSFW) at that time: Sarah Smith, Alexander Jablakow, and David Alexander Smith. Each had distinct impressions of the group and what it did for them. Since the whole is often not just greater but qualitatively different from the parts, this case study focuses on how the group works, not how the individual members as such react to it.

The group was founded about 1980; it has gone through several iterations, but one relatively constant group has stayed with the group for around ten years. Currently, only one of the four founders is part of the group, but some have gone and come back. They use techniques derived from other successful groups (*e.g.*, the Clarion workshop) and developed themselves through years of testing. They share their experience with participants in mini-workshops at science fiction conferences, and when they do they give people a set of tools:

- Names and addresses of participants
- A "critiquing manifesto" which lays down the principles of the group, e.g., "Why Are We Here?" and "How Do We Critique?"
- Organizational notes, including the logistics (e.g., monthly meetings) and how the agenda is set
- Specific critiquing rules for a session
- Variations from the norm (e.g., doing a novel rather than a short story)
- A list of useful vocabulary accumulated over the years from the group and others, e.g., POV (Point of View), "nowism" (putting something current into the future, such as a wristwatch on Captain Kirk) and so forth.
- Writing aphorisms: useful things that have been said and done which may not have direct application but could be inspirational.

I would like to quote some of the CSFW's notes, with annotations based on some of the concepts we described above. As always, different groups operate differently.

1. Why Are We Here?

We're here to help one another produce our best fiction. "All other goals are subordinate to that. If you want to work out personal issues in your fiction, that's fine, but if the results are bad fiction, you can't defend yourself by saying your life happened that way.

This exemplifies the "Affiliation plus Achievement" criterion described above, with a dash of socialized (for the common good) Influence. "Help one another" is Affiliation; "best fiction" is Achievement. Note the example used for the excluded: working out personal issues can be construed either as self-centered (and thus not group-focused), or anxiously affiliative. It is also a clearly shared goal and guideline that can help determine the rules of engagement.

2. How Do We Critique?

...[A] two edged commitment: (A) Tell the truth, (B) Criticize the prose, not the writer.

As a *critic*, comment on anything that moves you. Line edit if you want. Argue with the character motivation. Question the rubber science. Suggest alternate plot lines.

At the same time, *you must respect the author's right to tell his own story*. Figure out what the author's objectives are, and then figure out how to help the author achieve them. You may not like heroic fantasy, but if you're critiquing an author who does, you have to provide suggestions for making it more fantastic or more heroic. You're not here to demand that an author change his agenda. You can suggest other agendas, but if the author declines them, you must help the author go his way, not yours.

This lays down the specific role of the participant: anything is fair game, but the author is the final determinant of the story. It is not a collaboration. This allows for Kipling's principle, but also focuses on Achievement (make it better) over Affiliation (be nice to people by holding back criticism) implicitly. It also includes the issues of Mutual Respect and Know What You Don't Like, and how they apply to the group. Finally, it has a component of Influence as well, as you are empowering the author to make an impact of their own.

Several points follow from this:

A. <u>You Must Do the Work.</u> You're not here reading for pleasure. You're here because other people have agreed to work on your material. And they won't do that unless you work on theirs.

A clear statement of equity and fairness: do mine, and I'll do yours. Also reinforces the goal: to help one another create their best work.

B. <u>Be General First</u>. If something bothers you over and over, state the general issue first.

A good guideline for coaching overall: state the largest issue, or the one that will have the biggest impact, in general terms and in a way that will enable someone to avoid the specific examples for themselves in the future.

C. <u>Then Be Specific</u>. "Why do you feel it's slow?..."

An essential partner to the above point, and related to goal-setting. The critic should not say just "it's too slow" because that is too vague a comment for specific improvement. Instead, try this: "I found the long descriptions of scene bored me and interfered with the action." Then you must cite a specific example, both to illustrate and to allow editing to take place at once: "In the scene with the executive, you spent an entire page to describe the contents of the desk and the office, but only four pages on the entire scene, which was critical to establish the relationship between the protagonist and the executive." To put it another way, good coaching does not include summary statements of what the person is, but instead tells what the person specifically does, and what impact that action has, so then can change the action to change the impact. This is far more "actionable."

> The author, of course, doesn't have to take your suggestion, but the act of examining an alternate story line is enormously helpful. All too often, writers see their stories as having no options—they <u>must</u> occur a particular way.

A vital point. Respect the other person, not only as a coach but also as a participant: realize that another perspective may assist you. Not stated here but stated to me by CSFW participants: hearing other options may help you understand what you *like* about your choice, and how to strengthen those traits, whether or not others like it.

3. <u>How Do We Listen?</u> As an author, you must absorb what is said to you. That doesn't mean you accept it or reject it, it means you listen to it. You take it seriously as being motivated for your benefit.

Being critiqued in a roundtable workshop is no fun. You sit there, naked and exposed, as someone goes over your flaws with a microscope. Ouch! And a bunch of other people who've also read your material agree with the critic. Double ouch! ...but intellectually you're realizing that a good chunk of what's being said is dead right. So you don't even have the normal defense of rationalizing that your critic is full of beans.

How do we get through this and come back for more? *Because the prose gets better.* Just like exercise...

...wouldn't you rather hear the problems from a few folks in private, than have editor after editor recognize them, reject your story, and never tell you? Or worse, have your story published with the flaws there for all eternity, for hundreds of people to notice and cluck over? [Note the Influence motive here! "Better" sounds like Achievement motive, until you hear why.]

That's why in our workshops:

A. No outsiders. You can't be vulnerable with other people if there's somebody who can take free shots.

Interestingly, the CSFW follows this so scrupulously that even when doing mini-workshops most of the CSFW members will submit a piece, even though they are the teachers more than the students. Of course, they do believe in this technique, which supports an egalitarian philosophy, so from their point of view more people might equal more benefit, even for them.

B. Everyone must submit periodically.

Equity again; you can't just do the parts you like, or hold yourself aloof.

C. You have to build trust. You have to come to believe that people really are trying to help you, otherwise you'll close up to the comments.

Positive affiliation: you can trust that people will help you.

D. Things are written down. You can react to them later, after the pummeled feeling subsides.

Memory is a poor servant of accuracy. Studies indicate that 80% of the witnesses will be flat wrong about an event they just witnessed. A person who has just seen a crime—a dramatic, memorable event—will be mistaken as to the height, dress colors, hair colors, build, and actions of the criminal if asked to state them, even immediately after-ward. When under emotional stress (and getting criticized is certainly that!) the ability to recall exact words may get lost under the negative feelings.

E. Over time, we become very respectful of one another. We hold nothing back in terms of identifying and pounding problems...but we're all extremely solicitous of each other's intentions.

A restatement of the honesty-plus-respect, or Achievement-plus-Affiliation goal.

> 4. What about giving away ideas? We've had people get very upset when given ideas or asked for ideas....

> You don't have to accept it.

> As long as things are reasonably reciprocal, everybody wins.

> If you stick with it, sooner or later everybody gets published. When that happens, each person in the workshop can share in that wonderful feeling, because everyone contributed to making it happen.

This latter refers to Socialized Influence—feeling satisfaction on having had a positive impact on another person; or in even more sophisticated fashion by feeling strengthened by the strengthening of another. Reciprocity is key here; they assume that as people get published, they improve in their ability to assist *you* to get published[1].

Note that the CSFW meets virtually every characteristic I described above. This is not accidental. They took rules from other successful organizations, and were willing to experiment to find out the best combination for them, and grow. They protect each other and the fragile creature that is their workshop to maintain effectiveness over time. Even those who are not dedicated workshoppers *per se* acknowledge the usefulness of the group, and they know that.

A Picture of a Successful Workshopper

I've spent a good deal of time on the process of a good working group, and this is important, because the best group of people in the world may ruin themselves without the right process. "Never go into business with friends and family" is a truism, but for good reason. For most people, the nature of a relationship with those individuals is deeper and more important than the immediate business needs, which is good for personal relationships but very bad for the business.

Turning this around, some characteristics support an effective working group, and study into self-managed work teams has identified a number of them. Self-managed work teams are just what they sound like: a group of individuals who can successfully do good work, and reinforce each other's behavior as necessary to improve performance, without a fixed or formal leader. In the ideal state, there is no formal manager at all, though in effective teams one person typically occupies the leadership role at a given time, or in rotation, or when needed. This describes a workshop very well: nobody tells all the other writers what to do with formal authority; no one holds sole individual responsibility for the performance of the group. While this field is highly debatable, there have been some interesting findings, which seem to apply for a host of different jobs and roles.

First, the motives. The Achievement motive is key for getting things done and moving forward; the Affiliation motive (positive) is key for keeping people together and maintaining the group. Both together can act for the good of a group.

A person with only the Achievement motive engaged will tend to act for personal accomplishment—it is easier and more satisfying to control the steps. Such a person will chafe under the needs of a group to maintain itself: "Why should I care about feelings and process? We've got a job to do!" In disgust, they will start working on their own, or jettison the group, or try to force things in a single direction.

Contrariwise, a person with only the Affiliation motive engaged will act for the personal harmony of the group, taking care of the people involved. Since a normal task of a writing group is to criticize, this person may spend more time being nice to people than giving them the feedback they really need. The good of "the group" starts to become paramount, regardless of whether the group gets anything done.

But if a person *combines* both, you get a person who:

- Wants to do well (Achievement motive)
- Likes being part of a group of people (Affiliation motive)
- Wants the group to succeed (Achievement and Affiliation or Team Achievement)

This is the key to getting a group to work effectively. As noted above, the Influence motive drives most writers published in long-form through traditional methods, so while this is a major driver for individual writing, it can threaten a group. If group members focus on the persuasion of others rather than on the improvement of the work, it won't be a group for long. Instead of everyone trying to get the best possible outcome, people will spend time getting others to agree that their work is fine just the way it is—or that someone else's work has to be redone *this* way.

Seems like a paradox, doesn't it? Influence motive often

drives the individual to write, but Achievement and Affiliation enable an effective team. Not many people have all
three high, do they?

Here is where we return to the concept of values. You
do not have to have the motive to carry out the behavior.
You can be laden with Influence motive and *act* as an
Achievement-plus-Affiliation person. Indeed, the well-
socialized Influence-motivated person might want to do so,
because it will have the most positive impact on the group.

I know that sounds circular, but bear with me. Here is
the logic:

1. I want to influence others (Influence motive)
2. Therefore, I want to write (value).
3. For whatever reason, I have decided to join a
   group.
4. To succeed as a writer (influencing others), I
   need to make this group work for me.
5. I can't force people in the group to help me, I
   need to influence them (Influence motive).
6. The best way to get their help is to help them
   and make sure the group is successful
   (Achievement and Affiliation value).
7. If the group succeeds, I succeed, and I get to
   influence people and take pride in my impact
   (Influence motive).

If you already have some combination of Achievement
and Affiliation, the specific issues become different, but the
basic issue is the same: be a good team member by
choosing to act like one.

CHAPTER 28: WHEN YOU ARE NOT WRITING

In the course of this book, it may appear that I blithely assume that you write constantly, or want to do so. I do, if that is what *you* want. In practice, however, few of us will get the opportunity to write full-time. In fact, many people find full-time writing a difficult job indeed, even some professionals. Writing is a solitary activity; those with a very strong affiliation or Influence motive (and as we have seen, many professional writers have the latter) may find it intolerably lonely if forced to do it day after day.

Most writers do not spend all their time writing. Even if they write full-time, they do not spend all their daylight hours producing prose. Science fiction writer Alexander Jablokow (who writes under the name Jablokov) became a full-time writer some years ago. He described his writing process:

> "I work at the same time... morning... sometimes I just sit there, but I am there. I use the old trick of rewriting some of last night's work to get started. Sometimes I'm hot, sometimes not. I usually pick up something to read

—the danger of keeping books in your writing office—
then write a little bit, then wander around, then come
back... if you graphed out my time, there would be a
little peak early in the morning, then a long gap, then a
longer peak, then a gap, then a longer gap. Eventually
I'll catch hold and write steadily. If I write six pages a
session, four of them are in the last hour to hour and a
half, and the remaining two are in the previous three
hours."

Contrary to popular belief, you do not have to churn
out pages every hour to be productive—unless you are
doing it to survive, of course. Six pages a day, five days a
week equals approximately 120 pages a month. A 70,000-
page book-length manuscript will have 280 250-word
pages (longer books will have more, naturally, e.g., James
Clavell's *Shogun*, which weighed in at 1200 paperback
pages, roughly 420,000 words, or over 1600 manuscript
pages). You can theoretically write a first draft at that pace
in two and a third months, which many writers consider
very fast indeed.

Realistically, many interruptions and natural pauses
happen to your writing. Not to overstate the obvious, but
you do have to eat and sleep sometime. You may have to
deal with a day job, as most writers do. You may have to
deal with the needs of children or your spouse. Sometimes,
you may just want a rest from writing. Some writers get
depressed at the end of a novel; others love to get the
monkeys off their backs. Frankly, you may not be cut out
for full-time writing. Even if you are, you may not want to
write every minute of the day, either. So the question here
becomes not the maintenance of a pattern of behavior
(writing), but the care and feeding of yourself (and your
motives) when not writing.

You may want to consider your other motives. Motives are sources of emotional energy. They don't go away just because you have no opportunity to use them; instead, they build up a tidal wave of energy. If they do not find some outlet, you may find yourself irritable, frustrated, or restless. Robert Heinlein tried to retire from writing at one point, before he realized what a source of satisfaction it was for him. Here is what he said in his book *Expanded Universe:* "I retired... This went on for about a month when I found that I was beginning to be vaguely ill: poor appetite, loss of weight, insomnia, jittery, absent-minded—much like the early symptoms of pulmonary tuberculosis, and I thought, 'Damn it, am I going to have still a *third* attack?'" Then an editor asked him to make some minor rewrites to a rejected story, and "I sat down at my typewriter to make the suggested changes...and suddenly realized that I felt *good* for the first time in weeks. ...Once you get the monkey on your back there is no cure short of the grave. ...If I simply loaf for more than two or three days, that monkey starts niggling at me. Then nothing short of a few thousand words will soothe my nerves."

This is an extreme case of writer's addiction in a man of not terribly good health, but it illustrates the cost of suppressing a motive. They are natural forces within you, and you may not ignore them for long if they have great strength. Indeed, they parallel other kinds of addictions. After one has developed a tolerance to a drug, higher and higher doses are required to create pleasure, but one will keep taking it to stave off the pain of going without. Sounds grim, doesn't it? Realistically, most writers are not crazed junkies willing to do anything to get their fix (well, except maybe the late Dr. Asimov). Of course, even if they are, at least they don't wind up selling the stereo to get some more writing done.

Getting back to the subject at hand, the real point of this discussion is that your productivity will increase if you maintain a balance of satisfaction suited to your own pattern of motives. You can't ignore your motives, so you might as well adapt to them and, ideally, use them.

Some people avoid reading within their *genre*, so they can stay focused on writing instead of reading. Alexander Jablokow and David A. Smith do that, because they have trained themselves to be so critical that reading SF is "not relaxing," in Jablokow's words. Philip Craig only came into mystery fiction by accident (there was a murder in the book he was trying to sell), and reads mostly the classics, not current works, with few exceptions. A number of writers I know make a point of not reading fiction at all while in the process of writing their own work, because as one put it: "I would rather finish [reading] a work of fiction then finish my own book." Some manage to read in a different genre —science fiction instead of mystery, for example.

Some of this may be natural procrastination, but I have reason to believe that some of it may be motivationally powered. A motive is what you think about when you do not have to think about anything; remember that externally motivated actions are not the same as internally motivated. Jablokow, who, like virtually all the people I studied in my first group, is largely Influence-motivated, may not find the process of criticism itself very satisfying when he really wants to see a dramatic situation laden with emotional energy. Reading critically lacks a free-flowing nature. Alternatively, it takes a lot less energy to get satisfaction from reading than from writing. Interestingly, in Jablokow's case he continues to read influence-motive material (such as histories of Eastern Europe or psychological thrillers like Ruth Rendell and P. D. James), but his profile is very much dominated by that motive. Similarly,

David A. Smith reads mysteries when not writing SF, generally of the hard-boiled variety, which is also associated with the Influence motive.

You may feel the need to rotate your focus from time to time. This can refresh you, and give the emotional energies time to recharge. The motives can provide powerful energy, but you must use *all* the motives you have sometime. And keep in mind that the way in which you use them may have its own price. Your Achievement motive could propel you to lift that weight just five more times, to use a nonwriting example, but that might be five more times than your stressed muscles can take. By the same token, if you find yourself running a fever or getting eyestrain, perhaps you should lay off the keyboard for a while. Besides, many writers speak of the value of taking time off to learn something that feeds into the writing. "I cannibalize my life," said Harlan Ellison—but he has a life filled with experiences worth cannibalizing, which he did not gather in his office. Isaac Asimov resisted writing an autobiography for years because he thought his life was rather dull. Most of his working life—eight to ten hours a day virtually every day—was spent typing in a small, windowless room. Somehow, he managed to produce four large volumes anyway, but never mind. As long as you produce reliably to a reasonable extent, it is okay to take a break. Anxiety can hamper your output, too. Try to be aware of your needs.

CHAPTER 29: SUPPORT SYSTEMS

"Solitude, competitiveness and grief are the unavoidable
lot of a writer only when there is no organization or
network to which he can turn."

—Toni Morrison

Writers appear as lonely figures, toiling away in a garret at
midnight with no one around for miles. No committees
have gained fame for their masterworks of literature, it is
true, but by the same token no man (or woman) is an
island. Just because the task itself is typically (though not
always) solitary does not mean that you must isolate yourself from all society.

Even if you exclude collaborators, many writers
depend on the emotional and even literary support of
friends and lovers. While Thoreau wrote his salute to the
natural life in Walden Woods, he had Sunday dinner with
his mother every weekend. And a quick perusal of

acknowledgments and dedications will reveal a remarkable number of people "without whom this could not have been written."

People are embedded in a webwork of other people. That webwork can work to your benefit or against you. Your challenge as a writer is to make the best use of it, or shield yourself form the worst.

A large scientific literature exists showing that support systems are vital to emotional health, overcoming adversity, and success in life. At its simplest, a good network can provide information. At the most complex, it can provide jobs, emotional support, financial support, and opportunities to sell your work.

What Is Your Network?

Below is a simple list of categories of people cobbled together from frequent sources of support. You can add to it as you wish. The important part is to mark whether you see these people as having a positive, neutral, or negative impact on you in terms of support. That is, someone who helps you is "positive," someone who makes you feel depressed or angry is "negative." Someone who does not fit into either category (or perhaps both) would be "neutral."

Here's what such a table might look like:

Social Support	Positive	Neutral/Both	Negative
Spouse	√		
Grandpa	√		
Joe Friend			√
Agent	√		
Sister			√
Jane Friend	√		
TOTALS	4	0	2

Normally such a table would be applied to life overall. That is a useful task in itself. I suggest taking it a step further and measuring impact on your writing. Someone who is a positive impact on your social life might be a negative impact on your writing, especially if they say "oh, knock off that writing and let's have some fun!" Someone who wants you to see writing as boring, difficult work has a negative impact no matter how much fun they are otherwise.

Let's put together a table. Below I have gathered a list of obvious and less obvious suspects that can support your work as a writer. Some may be specific to writers. Don't limit yourself to the categories or people I happen to suggest. It can be helpful to have multiple lists, one for each of the categories below:

Family: Parents, grandparents, siblings, children, spouse/significant other, in-laws, aunts/uncles

Friends: Past and present

Work Support: Boss, employees, peers, Human Resources

Community Support: Minister, church members or groups, fraternal organizations

Writer's Support: Agent, editor, publisher, publicist, writer's workshop, other fellow writers, writer's organizations (e.g., Author's Guild, Mystery Writers of America, etc.)

<u>Anyone else you can think of</u>: Teachers, mentors, etc.

I'll put more explicit directions below, but first, put down as many or as few of these into a table as you need. Check where people come out, and add them up. Don't be afraid to add names—we want this to be a complete list.

To use the Support Systems List:

1. Go down the list one at a time, and assign specific people where appropriate. For example: Grandparent might be your mother's father, who encouraged you to write and has a complete collection of your articles in the high school newspaper.
2. For each person, determine whether they provide overall *positive support* or *negative support* or *neutral or no support*. Check the appropriate column. Take time to think about it if you need it. Check two if you must.
3. Add up totals at the bottom. Look at the overall balance. Do you have more positive support than negative?
4. Look at the people you checked as positive. Is there a pattern here? Who are they?
5. Look at the people you checked as negative. Is there a pattern here? Who are they?
6. Add these people to your writing plan: get support from those who give it and find ways to circumvent the negative impact of those who don't. For example: when feeling down, call a

>fellow writer (who is a positive impact, naturally) and commiserate. If you know your mother is coming into town and she will occupy your time, don't set a goal of writing when she is there—it will only set you up for failure. (See Section V: Goal Setting.)

Simply comparing the number of positives to negatives alone may give you a clue as to how easy it is for you to write; it is hard to maintain motivation in the absence of support, and even harder in the presence of opposition.

Note that your motives affect this as well. The Affiliation-motivated person is more susceptible to being "guilted" out of work to be with people. "Come on and be with your friends!" "Um...okay!" The Influence-motivated person might choose to skip writing in order to be visible somewhere, or to appear at a conference or with a group. Only the Achievement-motivated are relatively immune to this, but even they crave feedback on performance that might come only from someone outside them.

That is the negative side. On the other side, a good friend can give the uncritical support an affiliative person needs to keep writing alone ("You're a good friend, and I'm proud of you for your writing. We can get together when you're done."), or the feedback needed to propel the Influence-motivated person ("Cool! This is very impressive; you had me completely absorbed in your work. I want to read your next book—hurry up!), or the Achievement-motivated person ("You're making excellent progress—much better than your previous draft. You want details? Okay...").

The process of creating this list may give you some insight, but remember that this is too simple to really capture the real world. The same person may be a very positive impact or a negative impact, and you may be able to help that change.

For example, many people suffer negative remarks from their families regarding their writing. "What do you want to do that for? You're just wasting your time anyway." Then, when they win an award for their writing, their families fall all over themselves to say how proud they are. Well, you can make them a support instead of an obstacle. Don't make enemies of them by maligning them in your acceptance speech; sigh and be glad that they are turning around.

For many people, they just don't understand. Perhaps their family members are simply not well educated, or they lack a value around reading and writing. You can still recruit them into your support system if you want to, and if you can find ways to do so.

To interpret your Support System List:

1. **Grand Totals**

This section will help you see whether you generally feel supported or not. Questions to ask yourself here include:

- Do I have supporters?
- How many?
- Do I have obstacles?
- How many?
- Do I have more supporters than obstacles? (Positive greater than negative)
- Are most of my supporters mixed?

Think about how many people you have here. Granted, you only need one supporter (and some do without that for periods of time), but it is nice to know whether you have enough of a network that you don't have to rely on only one person.

Also, know your obstacles. The worst obstacles are those people whom you like and care for, but do not help you write. You can hardly write off your family (so to speak), but they might not be helping you either. Those people you have to manage or educate. One writer told me that she had her children trained not to come to her office door unless there was a significant amount of blood still flowing.

2. **Balance of positive and negative**

Questions to ask yourself include: What is the balance of support I have?

If you have three supporters and fifty obstacles, this might be a clue why you are finding it hard to write. Of course, if the three are your spouse, child, and parent while your obstacles are people at work this might not be a problem.

3. **Balance per list**: are some predominantly positive or negative?

Questions to ask yourself include: What is the balance for each list? Are some areas more supportive or bigger obstacles?

This will show you *where* your support is located. As noted above, who is supporting you can make a big difference. If your only obstacles are at work, then don't talk about writing at work. This could become challenging if you are supported everywhere but at home, since most people write at home, but perhaps you can write during your lunch hour or bring your family around.

4. **Key sources of support overall**.

Questions to ask yourself include:

- Who are my best supporters?
- Where should I go to get consistent support?

This is a good time to create a short list of "Key Sources of Support" and "Key Obstacles to Writing." Who makes the biggest difference for you? This list is a good one to keep handy for those down periods—*both* lists. Why? Two reasons. First, when you are down you want to know whom you can call to get back up. Second, many people get down because someone put them there. If you know such a person is on your "obstacle" list, you can just remember what my mother told me: *Remember the source.* Don't take the obstacles too seriously. Forewarned is forearmed.

A Far From Complete List of Writer's Organizations and Websites

- American Crime Writer's League (www.acwl.org)
- Author's Guild (www.authorsguild.com)

- Horror Writers Association (www.horror.org)
- Mystery Writers of America (www.mysterywriters.org)
- Romance Writers of America (www.rwanational.com)
- Science Fiction and Fantasy Writers of America (www.sfwa.org)
- Screenwriter's Guild (www.screenwritersguild.com)
- Sisters in Crime (www.sistersincrime.org)
- Writers Guild of America (www.wga.org)
- National Writer's Union (www.nwu.org)

CHAPTER 30: CHANGING YOUR MOTIVES

"Don't try to teach a pig to sing; it wastes your time and annoys the pig."

—Robert A. Heinlein

You may be asking yourself whether you have the motives you want, and whether you are stuck with them forever. Given that you may see your own motivational pattern as more of an obstacle than a benefit, this becomes a question of large personal import.

Fortunately, the answer is no, you are not stuck—up to a point. You <u>can</u> change your motives, using a lengthy and difficult process. Motives resemble muscles in the sense that if you flex one, it grows stronger. But like muscles, only a repeated, steady effort over time makes a significant difference.

Fortunately or unfortunately, however, no one has ever managed to make a motive go *down*. One study examined people with severe osteoarthritis—the crippling kind. We (I worked on the study) thought it might lead to reduced Achievement motive, since people would be unable to act on their desire to meet goals due to physical incapability. Nope. Exactly the same as the rest of the world. Unlike muscles, motives do not appear to atrophy, nor do developed motives return to their former state. That's mixed good and bad news. If you want to develop a motive, it's good news: whatever you develop seems to stick. If you find a motive blocking your efforts, it's bad news: you're stuck with it, so you will have to find some other way to manage it.

Remember: Motives can grow, but not shrink!

Early work around the world in such places as India, Poland, and urban Washington, DC was devoted to developing the need for Achievement in people. The process was surprisingly simple (though not easy): teach people to see the motive in others, to understand the motive from the inside (that is, to understand how people with the motive think and act), and then to practice thinking in the motive, making sure you get positive feedback for succeeding in the use of the motive. With time, the natural reward systems of your body take over, and you will have a higher motive. I'll lay it out in a list later.

One way to integrate a motive into your normal thinking is to practice writing the appropriate stories. Writing "maximum Achievement" stories gets you into a personal understanding of how an Achievement-motivated person thinks. Likewise, writing "maximum Influence" stories gets you to practice thinking like an Influence-motivated person.

If you know what people of a given motive pattern read and watch, you can do the same to match their motives. Saturate yourself in the appropriate material, and try to find it enjoyable on its own terms rather than the ones you are accustomed to. Remember that everyone has all the three basic motives; it's just a matter of degree. If you spend time building up your motive strength, unlike a muscle it will stay strong.

Before trying to change, however, you should think long and hard about whether you need to do so. We know the commonest primary motive of published writers, but does that mean you cannot write if that motive is a close second in you? Of course not. You may just have to rearrange priorities, or use your values to manage the application of your different strong motives.

Changing a motive is simple in concept, but very difficult in practice. It can be done. I met a woman who set her mind to it and increased her Influence motive by nearly 50 percentile points (below average to above average, in her case) in less than a year. So you can do it, but it demands much. You should not try unless both the requirement and your conscious values are strong and clear. The values, particularly, will carry you over the threshold of change to start making a motive satisfying in its own right.

Before you try to change, you should:

1. Set your values
2. Do your research
3. Find your reinforcers
4. Find your sources of feedback
5. Find your potential obstacles

Set Your Values

First things first: you will work hard, so you must prepare yourself to do so. You must decide that this matters to you enough to make a concentrated effort. Then you can make your plans. You need not inscribe your new values on a stone tablet or even a piece of paper; you simply need to be clear in your own mind as to what you will be doing.

Do Your Research

The second step: start finding out the thinking patterns of the people you wish to emulate. This book is a starting point, but only just. You may find or deduce more, particularly by looking at other people who write what you want to write. Read what they read, or what they would like to read if they were not writing. Watch movies that appeal to your chosen motive-to-develop. I think watching movies in a theater can be helpful because the setting helps ensure strong involvement and emotional engagement. In other words, they don't make movies to bore you, they try to draw you in.

Find Your Reinforcers

Now that you have some idea of what you are doing, the third step is to find ways to reinforce yourself for doing it. All motives are found in everyone to some extent, so you can probably get at least a small amount of pleasure out of the process; allow this to happen. Beyond that, you may well need to create or use other rewards to help you practice the new method of thinking, at least until you master the basics. Link up what you want to do with the most effective reinforcers you can identify. Remember that ultimately you want the motive to operate on its own rather than being dependent on outside sources (e.g., M&Ms), so the best means is to find ways you can fan the flames of your existing motive, however embryonic. I can't dictate any specific approaches; they must fit you. However, I do know this: one of the most effective ways to prevent a person from manifesting their potential is for them to limit themselves. If you are unwilling to take satisfaction from a new kind of behavior, you won't. It can be as simple as that.

Find Your Sources of Feedback

As your fourth preparation step, identify your best personal sources of feedback. This step couples with reinforcement, as good feedback is reinforcement, but finding a *source* of good feedback is a separate problem. Why is this important? People (this means *you*) are often not very good at judging themselves, particularly on motives, which you will recall are nonconscious in nature. Someone whose opinion you trust can support your efforts, both emotionally and practically.

Find Your Potential Obstacles

Finally, know your enemies. By that I mean the stumbling blocks and barriers to your effort, both internal (not wanting to work at it) and external (negative reinforcement from others). The people who give you feedback are a source of help; these are the folks who will prevent you from succeeding.

Changing Your Motives—The Actual Process in Detail

At the beginning of this chapter I quickly described the steps to develop your motives. Immediately above I described the "homework" you must do first, so you go the right direction. Now it is time to lay out the development steps systematically. These are cribbed from the work of David McClelland, and are known as the Competency Acquisition Process.

1. Recognition

In other words, know it when you see it. Observe those who have the trait you wish (in this case, a motive) and see what they are doing that is different from you. "I don't know how he does it, but I can see what he does!"

2. Understanding

Know it from the inside. Learn the inner thoughts of the person with that motive (or trait, or whatnot). Be able to reproduce it, at least on paper. "I may not be able to do it, but I know how she does it!"

3. Measurement of Self

Know how you stand against it. This will be difficult for motives unless you get a more precise measure through a Picture Story Exercise or the like, but you can probably get a fair idea of how much of your life is based on a given motive from the self-assessment exercises included here. "I know how much I have of it!"

4. Experimentation

Try it out, and learn how it feels from the inside. One critical characteristic of science (as opposed to other major human endeavors such as art, religion, war, or agriculture) is that failure is understood to be part of the process—that even negative results are good data. Try to take on the same attitude here. Your objective is not to succeed every time, because that is not reasonable or likely. Your objective is to *experiment*, and expect some failures along the way. Just learn from the failures (which is why science has been phenomenally successful). A fifty percent success rate can be pretty good at this stage. "I am trying it on for size."

5. Skill Practice

Once you can more-or-less consistently produce the behaviors and thoughts you want to develop, then you must strengthen the ability through practice, so it becomes reflexive rather than deliberate. "I am doing it regularly."

6. Integration

Make your new motive part of ordinary life. Once it becomes reflexive, you can move on to using it anywhere and everywhere you want. This step may seem obvious, but I also know about a phenomenon called *state-dependent memory*. In other words, some memories are closely associated with the situation in which you acquired them. This is one reason why some people claim to do tests better stoned than straight—*if* they studied while stoned, they *might* be able to recall better once stoned again. In a more typical situation, you might get into the habit of thinking in terms of your new motive only when you are working on your new motive. It should be everywhere.

7. Feedback

This tells you how you are doing, and takes you back to step three so you can reassess yourself and your progress. *This step is critical to continued improvement.* Feedback enables the process to happen accurately (you don't want to develop the wrong trait, or just find a new way to manifest the motives you have), it allows you to track your progress, and it charges you up to keep going. "I know how well I am doing in my growth."

To develop a motive means that you change the pattern of your thoughts. So above all, practice the thoughts. Everyone has them to some degree, and so do you. Build on what you have, and be patient. It takes a significant amount of time—months before a change in a motive becomes noteworthy. Don't look for instant success, but in time you can build a motive up—assuming you need to.

CHAPTER 31: LAST WORDS

"If only God would give me a clear sign! Like making a large deposit in my name in a Swiss bank."

—Woody Allen

"He who hesitates is last."

—Mae West

Long Term Results

Motives do not predict immediate choices; they predict long-term *patterns* of behavior over time. If this approach works for you, then it should apply over years, not just days. To do so requires hard work, but it will be worth it. This is not a get-writing-quick plan. Fortunately, the characteristics we are discussing can have enduring effects, once you have them linked to your writing practices the way you want them.

In a study of men and women in business, their

motives were measured when they joined a company, and then they were re-examined eight to twelve years later. The single strongest predictor of success later in life (at least for two-thirds of them) was the primary motive of the individuals as measured eight to twelve years before. Thus: Motives can strongly influence your success in certain broad areas.

The individuals who were taught Achievement Motivation in the 1960s were also encouraged to meet in groups to discuss their accomplishments and compare notes. This was a means to obtain feedback, a reality check, and positive reinforcement—not unlike writing workshops. Some groups were still meeting 25 years later, and they were still applying what they had learned. They were, on average, highly successful entrepreneurs. Therefore: Not only can motives influence your success long-term; but also the motives can be learned instead of "natural," and still have a profound impact.

Finally, you get better over time at things you keep doing, and that applies to writing as much as to anything else. If you get your motives properly engaged and you start writing and keep writing, you will find it gets progressively easier.

This is common sense for most things, but—you may ask—what about writing? What about the creative flash, the voice of the muse that strikes by random chance? As Pasteur put it: "Chance favors the prepared mind." Or, as some golfer (either Gary Player, Jack Nicklaus, Miller Barber or Arnold Palmer) put it: "It's amazing. The more I practice, the luckier I get." You are better prepared to hear the muse if you practice listening.

As proof of this I would like to offer an extreme case I have mentioned before: Isaac Asimov. He wrote nearly 500 books in his long writing career, starting in his teens and continuing to the last chapter of his autobiography, which he wrote by hand on his deathbed. Every book was practice for Asimov for writing more. Five hundred practice rounds is a reasonable statistical universe. In examining the time it took Asimov to write each hundred books, Stellan Ohlsson (*Psychological Science*, 1992) found that it fit the standard learning curve perfectly: that is, the speed increased asymptotically. Asimov's first hundred books took nearly twenty years to complete. His second hundred took fewer than ten. His third took fewer than six. His last 190 books took less than seven and a half years together.

This was interesting, because the learning curve had previously been studied only over short periods of time, usually under laboratory conditions. Asimov presented an unusual contrast, because he was doing a highly complex real-life task over many decades, and he nevertheless fit the curve perfectly.

This means you will get better, as long as you keep going. You don't have to write hundreds of books; but you must practice and keep practicing. If you do, you *will* get better.

If All Else Fails

"The mass of men lead lives of quiet desperation. What is called resignation is confirmed desperation."

—Henry David Thoreau

"Just writes to make his barrenness appear,
    And strains from hard-bound brains, eight lines a year."

—Alexander Pope

What if all this good work fails? You do the exercises, you write and write, and still you cannot sell, or even get someone else to read your work? Let's look it straight in the eye.

Mark Twain suggests that if you cannot get paid for writing within three years, you may fairly take that sawing wood is what you are intended for. I don't agree with that, having met too many good, successful writers who took longer, but the possibility exists.

Rather, I would like to leave you with a thought offered by Barry Levinson, the award-winning producer, director, and writer, when he was given his special award for lifetime accomplishment.

He started out writing comedy material, which he could not sell. He spent a long time writing volumes of material that no one would buy.

Levinson's father, a retailer, did not really understand what his son did, but would ask how business was going. He replied that it was tough, that he kept producing material but he couldn't sell any of it.

"Well," his father said, "at least you've got inventory."

You have inventory, too. You bring a unique insight, your own gifts, a lifetime of experiences—and that is before you begin actually writing.

I have mentioned David McClelland, the great motivational psychologist (and my mentor), who gave rigor to the understanding of motives we now have. One of the fundamental drivers of his life and work, rooted in Quaker belief, was the conviction that all people are of equal worth. In my years of study with him and without him, I have never found cause to doubt that every human being has some special worth. Whether you write successfully or not, I would be remiss if I did not reinforce that. Writing isn't everything.

But in any case everyone has a story to tell, everyone has motives, and everyone has inventory in their warehouse. Start there, and apply yourself, and you will write. Maybe not a lot, maybe not a bestseller, but you *can* write, and you will. Now go do it!

Remember: You can write!

"I have described writing as a cross between a religious calling and a heroin addiction. There are a lot of bad things that go along with it, and a lot of ego gratification, grubbing for fame and money—visceral things. But that's part of it. Anyone who says otherwise is a saint or a liar, I guess."

—Eric S. Nylund, author of *Dry Water*

"True ease in writing comes from art, not chance,
As those move easiest who have learn'd to dance."

—Alexander Pope

APPENDICES

APPENDICES

Appendix A: Discovering Motives Using the Picture Story Exercise

Appendix B: Discovering Motives Using Doodles

Appendix C: Case Studies

Appendix D: Sample Development Plans

APPENDIX A

DISCOVERING YOUR MOTIVES USING THE PICTURE STORY
EXERCISE

The basic measure of motives is one with some appeal for writers. It is called the Picture Story Exercise, and asks you to write stories to ambiguous pictures. In this way, you may write whatever you choose to write, and let the motives emerge naturally. It is a difficult measure to fake, since people do not generally know what is being coded or why; even those who are knowledgeable are frequently unable to skew their stories.

On the following pages are a set of pictures commonly used for motivational research. For each, spend no more than five minutes writing a story. For best results, do not study the pictures for more than a few seconds; just get a sense of the image and begin writing.

There are no right or wrong answers, of course; only motivational data. This is a self-analytic opportunity, not a test. Don't worry about your grammar, spelling, or handwriting; the only person who needs to see this is you.

To use the Picture Story Exercise:

1. Glance at picture #1 for a few seconds

2. Begin writing a story. Do not take more than about five minutes. Try to write a story with a beginning, middle, and end. Try to answer the following questions in the course of the story: What is happening? Who are the people? What has led up to this situation? What is being thought? What is wanted? By whom? What will happen? What will be done?
3. Turn to picture #2, and continue.

Pictures

What is happening?	What is wanted?
Who are the people?	By whom?
What has led up to this situation?	What will happen?
What is being thought?	What will be done?

What is happening?	What is wanted?
Who are the people?	By whom?
What has led up to this situation?	What will happen?
What is being thought?	What will be done?

What is happening?	What is wanted?
Who are the people?	By whom?
What has led up to this situation?	What will happen?
What is being thought?	What will be done?

What is happening?   What is wanted?

Who are the people?   By whom?

What has led up to this situation?   What will happen?

What is being thought?   What will be done?

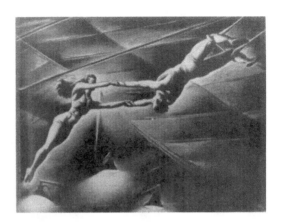

What is happening?	What is wanted?
Who are the people?	By whom?
What has led up to this situation?	What will happen?
What is being thought?	What will be done?

What is happening?

Who are the people?

What has led up to this situation?

What is being thought?

What is wanted?

By whom?

What will happen?

What will be done?

When you are finished, refer back to Chapter 2, "Identifying Your Own Motives," and use the motive imagery found there to examine the stories. Read your stories over carefully for content—or get someone else to do so. Tally how many times you get each kind across all stories, and you can get a rough sense of your own primary motive or motives.

Keep in mind that you are not a trained, expert scorer, so this is only approximate at best. Furthermore, it may be tempting to try and score it the way that suits your values rather than what is actually there – whether you mean to do so or not. There are several ways to try and prevent this:

1. Ask someone else to score it.

2. Underline specific sentences to justify your scoring, and tie them to a specific indicator,
   a. E.g., "attempts at influencing in order to convince others to comply" or "outperforming someone else who represents a standard of excellence

3. Wait a while to score it, so it is less fresh in your mind.

Reality Testing Your Motives on the PSE

While the PSE is a reliable instrument, scorers are not; furthermore, the sensitivity of the PSE is high enough to pick up "noise" from events happening in one's life—accurate representations of your unconscious concerns at a given time, but largely unrepresentative of your life as a whole.

The first half of this section deals with some details of interfering factors ("artifacts" in technical language), and the second with additional data gathered over the years on the behaviors a person may show with a given motive high.

Artifacts

1. Drinking. The need for Influence is associated with alcohol. Studies have shown that drinking more than two ounces of alcoholic beverages (two cans of beer, glasses of wine, shots of whiskey) will start to raise your Influence motivation—and not for the better. Personalized Influence, the need to prove or display yourself over others, gets stronger over time and more booze. After seven drinks (in a reasonably short period, of course), <u>all</u> motives tend to decline. The reasons for this latter finding are obvious enough, but the association of Influence and alcohol has no certainly proved reason.

2. Recent trauma. The need for Affiliation tends to rise after an affiliative stress, such as a death in the family, a person moving out of the house, moving to a new place—all times when you would expect people to be focused on relationships and concerned with how they are going.

3. Exhaustion. This will depress your motives. When you have no energy to spare for anything, why should motives be an exception?

4. Interruption
5. Arousing circumstances. Motives can be aroused over the short term. Repeated arousal can lead to temporary increases.

APPENDIX B

DISCOVERING MOTIVES USING DOODLES

Studies of Achievement-motivated people have indicated that they tend to doodle in certain ways. They tend to make S-curves (but *not* continuous waves) and diagonal lines, varying their line. They also tend to fill pages rather than leaving them blank. This has been applied even to ancient Greek pottery designs, and appears to hold true. Unfortunately the same approach has not been used to identify Influence Motive or Affiliation Motive, but at least you have something.

APPENDIX C

CASE STUDIES

Case #1: Science Fiction and Mystery Writer

Background

Had no formal writing training; sold one book "the hard way"—wrote it all himself without help—and then joined a writer's workshop, to which he has belonged for years since. Several books and short stories published as well as editing a collection assembled by the group.

General Behavior

A very meticulous person, for the most part; a self-employed individual who also acts as the administrator of the writers' workshop when some kind of special work is required. Hates wasting time; organizes his time to maximize his resources. Plans his writing.

Approach to Writing

No structure at first, just wrote as he felt. "Much more difficult than now." Wouldn't go back; didn't want to break the momentum.

Only occasionally does he feel like writing powerful scenes—runs with it when he feels that way.

A true believer in workshops: would not write any other way, and volunteers time to do one-time workshops to get other people involved.

Key Learnings

- Evolution came through assurance and the influence of the workshop.
- Came up with a "zero draft" to relieve stress of producing a first draft: a draft that was purely for creative purposes and lower pressure.

General Progression

Middle

Used lots of structure: wrote an outline then followed it faithfully.

Recent

"I know when to move away from the structure." However, still uses an outline so carefully that when he decides to change elements of the plot as he writes, he goes back and revises the outline as well.

Now

Less time for writing but still wanted to help run the workshop.

Third book "three to four times as efficient" as first book.

Case Study #2: Mystery Writer and Technical Writer

Background

Writing since age eleven or so, originally intended to become a scientist but switched her major to English in college. Became a technical writer and began writing fiction in her spare time. Partially deaf, she learned to read lips but tended to stay in the background in crowds until getting hearing aids in adulthood.

General Behavior

Sometimes perceived as quiet and shy, she is neither; she is an acute observer who is also an irrepressible smart-aleck when in a comfortable situation. Tends towards negativity at low moments and constantly questions herself—not in a neurotic way, but in a self-analytic manner which sometimes inhibits her writing briefly.

Approach to Writing

Wrote science fiction short stories and was rejected repeatedly until moved to a different part of the country and wrote a mystery set near her home. The contrast she saw between her current home and her previous showed her she had something distinctive to say, which she had taken for granted in her home environment. She began writing mysteries set in the present-day, in a first-person, distinctly regional voice. From the beginning, she "just plain enjoyed writing," creating worlds for herself where she could be an adventurer. Will work on a schedule by choice, but knows points where she must stop and recharge; sometimes she finds her self stalled, and invariably this is because she needs to think through her plot and characters further before proceeding.

Key Learnings

- Understanding the endpoint of a novel-length work, so she could measure progress toward that goal.
- Learning to set and track goals for herself
- Learning to adjust goals for herself
- Finding ways to keep going in the face of rejection, for example by sending out new works before the old could be sent back.

General Progression

Early

The first book took the better part of a year, and was totally rewritten at least once, changing plot and language; the second book, using a more organized approach, took nine months.

Middle

Started challenging herself on each progressive book to keep her series (and herself) fresh. Increased speed steadily, but ran into trouble when first child was born: unpredictability of baby's schedule made it difficult to work even when time was available. Increased confidence; when asked to write a short story she said "sure!" though she had never published one before. She has sold a number since.

Current

Much more adept at managing herself around an unpredictable schedule; partially through the use of outside resources (a regular babysitter, husband) but also through a higher tolerance of chaos developed through two children.

Case Study #3: Science Fiction Writer

Background

Full-time writer, but writes only four hours a day or so. Reads pop history, enjoys it as visiting alien worlds. Saw *Shogun* as a "first contact" SF novel. Reads and likes novels where mysteries are posed and then revealed. Likes history of Eastern Europe and Russia (is of Russian descent), ancient history, history of religion, French histories. Rarely reads science fiction because he gets too critical, thanks in part to his workshop experience, so does not find it relaxing. He doesn't think he could write mysteries because he is "too straightforward." Always surprised by the end of a mystery. Likes being in the hands of the author. Particularly likes P. D. James, Ruth Rendell, Dorothy Sayers, Tony Hillerman, and James Ellroy.

General Behavior

Gregarious and friendly, very thoughtful in his discussion, but laughs frequently.

Approach to Writing

Starts with a scene, either a visual hook (i.e., a very vivid image), or a scene with emotional charge. One story he enjoyed writing was entirely a dialogue, with no visuals at all, but the relationship of the characters was important.

After the hook, he goes back to the beginning and writes to get to that point.

He belongs to a workshop, but uses it selectively rather than as a true believer. He gave me the impression that he felt he commanded his work, merely using the workshop as a source of useful advice, and therefore he could easily write without it. Indeed, he wrote one recent book almost completely without the workshop, having only shown an early fragment and then did not return to the workshop to finish. Even before that, he tended to keep a distance from the workshop. While others turn in early drafts or even outlines, he virtually never turns in unfinished work or outlines

His stated reasons for using the workshop are:

- Outside perspective. He uses this to help him find his <u>own</u> way through the story rather than following other's suggestions slavishly.
- People satisfaction: likes scaring people with a whole new novel.
- Gives as well as he takes, and therefore he enjoys the giving.

<u>General Progression</u>
Steadily improving; has won awards for his work.

Case Study #4: Thriller Writer

Background

This woman started writing as an escape from a terrible, abusive marriage. She felt trapped because she did not have enough money to get out and survive, and she had children to support. She felt helpless to fight back overtly. But motives can't be kept down for long: she found a way to feel strong. In her spare time she started writing novels.

General Behavior

Thoroughly enjoyed being around people and had a very outgoing personality. Not afraid to strike a provocative and risqué pose for a publicity shot; had a fine sense of marketing and management of relationships—she was perhaps the only writer I have ever known (of scores) who managed to connect with book distributors, and was very successful in getting them interested in her. Took her work very seriously, but definitely had a sense of humor.

Approach to Writing

She wrote novels that came straight from her feelings: she wrote stories where men were killed in awful, satisfying ways, and romantic stories set far away from reality as she knew it, such as romance/science fiction novels.

Despite what you might think, she set herself daily goals, and tracked her performance day after day, including producing wall charts of her performance. When in her marriage she hid herself away and wrote in bursts.

General Progression

When I interviewed her she had just reached a critical point in her career: she had received not one but two major contracts, one in the six-figure range, which allowed her to free herself from her abusive husband. However, she was totally blocked. We discussed that perhaps she had too strongly identified her writing with escape: with the pressure gone (an extrinsic motive of sorts), she could no longer write. I suggested she start with a very low goal, such as one sentence a day, just to get herself jump-started, which was an idea she had already had. At last check she had managed to publish another book, but had not delivered on her contract. She has since joined the staff of a magazine that caters to her genre and organizes conferences.

APPENDIX D

SAMPLE DEVELOPMENT PLANS

"We need not worry much about writers. Man will always find a means to gratify a passion. He will write, as he commits adultery, in spite of taxation."

—Graham Greene

In this appendix I am going to show you some examples of how to decide what you might need to change. At various points throughout this book are specific recommendations, so I won't attempt to consolidate them here. Instead, I want to focus on the big picture of change: what enables it to happen?

In addition, I have taken a few motive profiles and other characteristics and identified a key challenge of each, and proposed some options for change. These are examples of development ideas, not requirements. Only you can determine the direction of your development; these may or may not work for you, but they may trigger some workable notions that will work for you. Then you can lay it out in more detail and depth, using the Goal Setting principles described above.

The following are sample motive profiles.

<u>High Achievement, Low Influence, Low Affiliation</u>

The Challenge

Might need to develop Influence motive, and has a strong Achievement motive that could either support efforts or block them.

Comment

Achievement-motivated people might well see publishing as a long shot, which indeed it is. The amount of effort that goes into a slender chance of being published looks like a losing deal. The need here is to harness the Achievement motive to support the long-term goal of increasing the Influence motive.

Option 1

Structure: Set up a system of targets and writing goals to keep motivation going independently of publication.

Option 2

Thought: Develop Influence motive.

Option 3

Focus your writing where you have the best (or most manageable) chance of success.

High Influence, Low Activity Inhibition, Low Achievement, Low Affiliation

The Challenge

To successfully manifest and channel Influence motive though writing takes a great deal of AI. Being low on that can make it difficult to apply Influence motive to the task of writing.

Comment

People with the right motive but low AI may find themselves petering out quite rapidly on longer works, or giving up after only a single rejection. Influence-motivated people want to have an impact, but without AI may find it difficult to postpone gratification of that desire when they can go do something easier.

Option 1

Focus on short works: essays, articles, short stories. Hoard your discipline.

Option 2

Structure: Set up a habit, rhythm, or plan to manage your time for you. Invite help to move you along.

Option 3

Thought: Develop AI. Not easy!

High Affiliation, Low Influence, Low Achievement

The Challenge

Writing out of a different motive, or may need to develop Influence motive; to resist the Affiliation motive that may block writing.

Comment

Affiliation motive can easily block writing, since writing is essentially a solitary process, and does not necessarily earn you friends as such, whereas creating any kind of impact can be satisfying to a Influence-motivated person whether they are liked or not. Restraining the Affiliation motive and focusing on writing needs can be quite difficult, as Affiliation is the commonest human motive, and easily satisfied to some degree.

Option 1

Focus on short works: essays, articles, short stories. Arrange your time so you don't have to be away from people too long.

Option 2

Structure: Set up a habit, rhythm, or plan to manage your time for you, with shorter, protected time periods in which to write, preferably supported and defended by a friend or partner as well.

Option 3

Thought: Develop Influence motive. Not easy!

High Achievement, High Affiliation, Low Influence

The Challenge

Use the two motives that are not associated with published writers and which can both block writing efforts, or develop the Influence motive substantially to overcome the obstacles.

Comment

Having two motives significantly stronger than the one you want makes development much more difficult. It may be easier here to reorient the motives you do have, for example by bringing in a team to help you, as this profile is characteristic of effective team members.

Option 1

Structure: Join a supportive and well-structured writer's workshop to help you manage your writing.

Option 2

Thought: Develop Influence motive. Not easy!

Option 3

Structure: Set up a system of targets and writing goals to keep motivation going independently of publication as such, linking both of the other motives, e.g., using friends and goal-setting.

NOTES

Introduction: Motivation And Writing--So What?

1. Or con men who shamelessly take your money, of course.

Chapter 1: What is Motivation

1. Some links have been identified to key neurotransmitters (nor-epinephrine, epinephrine, dopamine) which are largely controlled by the limbic system. You don't need to know this to take advantage of them.
2. In the academic literature, this is known as "Power Motive." In English and German, people assign a negative value to this, even though all motives are neutral, so I'm changing the name for our purposes. But if you want to read the academic literature, this is what you look for.

Chapter 7: Discovering Motives Using Reality Testing

1. For the mathematically minded, there are 23 Achievement items, 19 Affiliation items, and 32 Influence items, so if you want to convert them to the same scale, you can easily make percentages by dividing your checks in each column by the total possible for that motive. For example, if you checked 6 Achievement, 4 Affiliation, and 8 Influence, that works out to 26%, 21%, and 25% respectively, but it may well be absolute numbers are better indicators if you spend the same amount of time on each item.

Chapter 8: Motives, Readers, And Writers

1. I can't resist pointing out (at least in a footnote) that my approach covering the three motives in the previous chapters has turned out to be exactly the right thing to do for this new world of publishing, so about 97% of what I wrote before this chapter is unchanged!

2. For those not conversant in statistics, you can use the standard deviation (SD) as an indication of how off from the average you might be. Since the American mean is 1.75 and the SD is 0.25, that means 2.0 (the mean plus one SD) puts you at about 85th percentile – in the top fifteen percent of the population. Two SD puts you at 98th percentile. Three SD is 99.8%ile. Having an AI score of 18 means, technically, a score of *sixty-five* standard deviations above the mean, which is just ridiculous. Hence my amazement!

Chapter 9: Being Overmotivated Or Undermotivated: The Yerkes-Dodson Law

1. Yerkes RM, Dodson JD (1908). "The relation of strength of stimulus to rapidity of habit-formation". *Journal of Comparative Neurology and Psychology*. 18: 459–482.

Chapter 11: Assessing Self-Image

1. Attributed inaccurately to Mark Twain.

Chapter 13: Attribution Theory

1. This framing is based most strongly on the work of Martin Seligman, a genuine leader of the field, and a good popular writer on psychological concepts as well. I've used his tools myself for research purposes.

Chapter 16: The Seven Deadly Myths Of Creativity

1. Actually, Dorothy Sayers has her detective make this exact point in one of her books, that the *really* clever criminal *won't* have an airtight alibi, because real people don't have perfect, airtight alibis. On the other hand, most criminals aren't exceptionally clever...

Chapter 19: Styles Of The Creative Process

1. Okay, technically far more: if you assume just one motive high, then three. If you look at all combinations of one, two, or three high, then seven. If you look at combinations of high, medium, and low…

Chapter 25: Recharging Your Motives

1. There are whole books' worth of research papers on this. For those who are interested, the early research by McClelland and others identified links between Achievement Motive and ADH, Affiliation motive and dopamine, and Influence motive and both norepinephrine and epinephrine. Later work (recently often by Oliver Schultheiss) has shown additional links, including testosterone levels, which, inevitably, make it more complex. Nevertheless, it is clear that implicit motives are rooted in deep levels of the brain (the limbic system, to be precise).

Chapter 27: Workshops

1. This "power shared is power multiplied" concept, or empowerment, is an even higher level of Influence motive than Socialized Influence. Researcher Abigail Stewart developed four stages of Influence motive development; Socialized Influence is the higher form of Stage III; Empowerment is Stage IV. As you might expect, the higher level it is, the rarer. Note, however that the difference between Stage III personalized (selfish) and socialized is Activity Inhibition, which allows you to channel, control, and postpone your emotional impulses, and this is one of the characteristics saw in proliferation in writers published at novel-length (which includes all the members of the CSFW I interviewed!).

ABOUT JABBERWOCKY BOOKS AND AUTHORS

FOR NEWS ABOUT JABBERWOCKY BOOKS AND AUTHORS

Sign up for our newsletter*: http://eepurl.com/b84tDz
visit our website: awfulagent.com/ebooks
or follow us on twitter: @awfulagent

THANKS FOR READING!

*We will never sell or give away your email address, nor use it for nefarious purposes. Newsletter sent out quarterly.